Bruce Aidells'

COMPLETE

SAUSAGE

BOOK

Bruce Aidells'
COMPLETE
SAUSAGE
BOOK

Recipes from
America's Premier Sausage Maker

Bruce Aidells & Denis Kelly

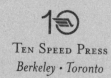

TEN SPEED PRESS
Berkeley • Toronto

Ten Speed Press
Box 7123
Berkeley, California 94707
www.tenspeed.com

Distributed in Australia by Simon & Schuster Australia, in Canada by Ten Speed
Press Canada, in New Zealand by Southern Publishers Group, in South Africa by Real
Books, and in the United Kingdom and Europe by Airlift Book Company.

COVER DESIGN: Jeff Puda
FRONT COVER ILLUSTRATION: Addis, www.addis.com
BOOK DESIGN: Tasha Hall
PHOTOGRAPHY: Beatriz da Costa
FOOD STYLING: Alison Attenborough
PROP STYLING: Eduoard Prulhiere

Library of Congress Cataloging-in-Publication Data
Aidells, Bruce
    [Sausage book]
    Bruce Aidells's complete sausage book : recipes &
techniques from America's premier sausage maker / by
Bruce Aidells & Denis Kelly
        p.   cm.
    ISBN 1-58008-159-2
    I. Cookery (Sausages) 2. Sausages. I. Kelly, Denis, 1939-
II. Title.
TX7490.5.S28 A3724   2000
641.6'-dc21   99-58199

Printed in Canada
FIRST PRINTING, 2000
5 6 7 8 9 10 — 07 06 05 04 03

Acknowledgments

No book is written without a lot of valuable help. We wish to thank our editors, Lorena Jones, Judith Jones, and Jackie Killeen; our photographer Beatriz da Costa, and our food stylist Alison Attenborough.

Martha Casselman, our literary agent, has been by our sides with valuable advice and encouragement for more than 15 years. Thank you.

And many thanks to our friends and colleagues who graciously contributed recipes: Bruce's wife and chef-owner of Boulevard Restaurant, Nancy Oakes; Loni Kuhn; Robyn Cherin; Edy Young; Priscilla Yee; Bette Kroenig; Judy and Gary Wagner; Franco Dunn; and Steve Armbruster.

Contents

Introduction

SAUSAGE—AS SOON AS YOU SAY THE WORD, THE MEMORIES BEGIN: SUNDAY morning, thick patties sizzling in the pan, filling the house with the fragrance of sage, pepper, and succulent pork. Or a late spring Saturday afternoon at the ball game, eating hot juicy franks with mustard and sauerkraut.

Just about everyone in America, from every background and region, has fond and satisfying memories of sausages. Wherever you grew up, from Bayonne to the Bayou Teche, it's likely that sausage of one kind or another was found on your table or sold in the streets of your neighborhood. Whether it's a hot dog or kielbasa, boudin or bratwurst, there's something about sausage that excites the taste buds and stays in the memory.

We grew up eating sausages of every type, taste, and description. Although we're from different regions and ethnic backgrounds, we both pursued a passion for sausages across America, eating them at festivals and greasy spoons, fancy restaurants and waterfront dives, sampling Sheboygan brats, Cajun boudin, Italian cotechino, Oakland hot links, Chicago franks, whenever and wherever we had the chance. And one day, putting away a prodigious platter of Cajun cassoulet at a favorite restaurant, we decided to write a book about sausage in America—its history and traditions, how to make it, how to use it, how it flavors so much of the best of our cooking.

By this time we had both been involved with food and wine professionally for many years—Denis Kelly as a writer and teacher and Bruce Aidells as cookbook author, cooking teacher, and expert sausage maker. Bruce had become so enthusiastic about the savory subject, in fact, that he had become one of the country's premier sausage makers, producing delicious, hand-crafted sausages at his Bay Area–based Aidells Sausage Company. How did Bruce get into the sausage-making business? He tells the story best: "I first started making sausages when I was living in London, working as a cancer researcher, and trying to convince myself that the traditional British banger was made from anything other than sawdust, salt, and grease. I'd been eating sausage all my life—from traditional, garlicky Jewish salami and frankfurters to more exotic types found in my neighborhood in Los Angeles, like chorizo and linguiça. After a few months in cold, gray London subsisting on a diet of pub food and bangers, I was suffering from sausage deprivation and figured I could do better making them myself.

With the help of a cookbook and a small electric grinder I made up tasty batches of chorizo, American pork sausage with sage and pepper, Italian sausage with fennel, and Provençal sausage with garlic and herbs. It took me most of the night to stuff all I'd made, but the next day when I fried them up and sat down to a hearty and delicious meal for the first time in months, I was hooked. From then on I never looked back, making (and eating) sausage at every opportunity.

When I returned to Berkeley, the Gourmet Ghetto near Chez Panisse was in full swing, and I ended up becoming a chef at Poulet, a popular restaurant and charcuterie. I just naturally kept on making sausage and learned what a wonderful flavoring ingredient it can be in soups, stews, pâtés, salads, and other hearty dishes. As the European peasants and regional American cooks had known for years, sausage is a great flavoring for almost any dish, and it doesn't take a lot to create exciting flavors and taste in a variety of dishes.

From then on the sausage phenomenon grew and grew, and finally I found myself making and selling a whole range of sausages—andouille and chaurice, chicken-apple sausage, Italian sausage, chorizo, and kielbasa—to restaurants and chefs. The response from them and from butchers, retailers, and home cooks all over the country testify to the interest in authentic handmade sausages in America today."

Ethnic and Regional Roots

SAUSAGE IS FOUND IN VIRTUALLY EVERY REGION AND ETHNIC TRADITION IN America. From the simple and satisfying pork and sage sausage of the

Midwest, Cajun chaurice and New Bedford Portugese linguiça to Italian sweet fennel sausage and Coney Island franks, sausage in one shape or another has long been an important part of American cooking. Sausages can serve as main dishes or as accompaniments and flavorings with vegetables, pasta, or beans. Whether you make them yourself or buy them ready-made, you can use sausages in dishes that range from traditional specialties like red beans and rice or cotechino with white beans to creative new combinations with vegetables, poultry, pasta, and seafood.

In this book, we take a close look at the regional and ethnic traditions that are at the heart of American cooking, and see how sausages are used to flavor and lend individual accents to these varied cuisines. We'll show you exactly how to make the authentic sausages indigenous to each region: andouille and boudin from the Cajun country, hot and mild sausages from the Italian neighborhoods of northeastern cities, the ubiquitous American breakfast sausage, smoked and fresh kiebasas as Polish-Americans make it in Chicago, Sheboygan's famous bratwurst, Chicago hot dogs, chorizo, linguiça, Oakland hot links, and many more.

But this is more than just a book about sausage making. It is an overview of American cooking, using the sausage to link all the themes together. We'll describe America's regions and neighborhoods, their history, culinary traditions, and festivals. And we'll give you plenty of recipes that use sausage to flavor everything from a traditional gumbo to fashionable composed salads.

A Juicy History

"A cook turns a sausage, big with blood and fat, over a scorching blaze, without a pause to broil it quick." A modern Californian grilling a tasty sausage over mesquite charcoal? Well, it was probably a blood sausage much like our boudin noir, and it might even have been grilled over charcoal, but the time and place was Greece in about 700 B.C. This quote from Homer's *Odyssey* is just one of many ancient references to one of mankind's oldest and most succulent delicacies. Homer, who had a particular affection for sausages, refers to them again and again in his descriptions of food and feasting. References to sausages abound in early Greek and Roman sources, from Athenaeus's marathon banquet described in *Deipnosophistae* (The

Learned Drinkers) to one of the earliest cookbooks extant, Apicus's *De Re Coquinaria*.

The origin of sausages dates back even further in culinary history. The art of salting, curing, and smoking meat goes back to the beginnings of domestication and agriculture in the Near East, and perhaps even earlier. As soon as mankind was able to achieve a regular surplus of meat, we began to look for ways to preserve it. Cutting up scraps of meat, salting them, and sealing them in casings made from the intestines and other organs of animals was one of the first discoveries of early pastoralists. The pig, the main source of most sausages, was domesticated quite early, in about 5000 B.C. in Egypt and China, and pig-raising spread quickly throughout the Near East, Europe, and Asia.

Since then, virtually every society has developed its own version of sausage. The name derives from the Latin word for salted, *salsus*, and salt for preserving meat, fish, and cheese has been an important commodity from Roman times to the present. Sausages are found in virtually every region in Europe, giving flavor and substance to dishes that define the style and flavor of its varied cuisines. Try to think of German, Italian, Polish, and Portuguese cooking, to name a few, without traditional sausages like knockwurst, salami, kielbasa, and linguiça.

In America, the original population of Native Americans found ways to preserve the land's bounty, and they passed their methods on to early settlers. Pemmican, a mixture of buffalo or venison, fat, berries, and herbs, was packed into hide containers and helped many an Indian (and settler) village through winter and hard times.

Settlers from England brought with them a long tradition of sausage making. Colonial cookbooks recorded English recipes published by Hannah Glasse and other early writers. They gave the basic ingredients of American breakfast sausage as it is made even today: ground pork, salt, black pepper, and sage. As settlers arrived from other areas in Europe, Asia, and Africa, they brought with them their culinary traditions, and these almost always included sausages. The French in the South and Louisiana; Italians, Jews, Greeks, and Portuguese in the teeming cities of the Northeast; Germans, Poles, Hungarians, and Swedes in the Midwest; Spanish in the Southwest; and Chinese on the West Coast—all brought with them the sausages that gave character to their cooking.

The history of American food and its sausages is, like America, a history of immigrants. In this book, we'll present this rich array of flavors and see how sausages are used to define many of America's favorite dishes. And we'll show some of the ways that today's creative chefs are inventing new sausages, which are expanding the frontiers of American cooking.

Types of Sausages

THERE ARE AS MANY TYPES OF SAUSAGE AS THERE ARE COOKS AND CULTURES, offering a tremendous variety of flavors, textures, and uses. The most basic way to define sausage is: a combination of chopped meat, fat, salt, and spices. Over the years, sausages have been made from an ever-widening array of ingredients—beef, poultry, game, seafood, even vegetables—but pork has been the constantly recurring favorite. Pigs are easy and economical to raise, and their bland and succulent meat combines well with spices and flavorings. Pork also has a mild-tasting fat that binds well and gives a rich and juicy flavor to the sausage.

The most common and easiest-to-make sausage is the standard American breakfast patty consisting of freshly ground pork seasoned with salt, sage, and black pepper. Virtually every culture has some kind of similar, easy-to-make fresh sausage. Many Italian sausages are simply made of freshly ground pork that is flavored and then stuffed into casings of hog or sheep intestines. Cajun boudin, spicy country sausage, fresh bratwurst, kielbasa, and chorizo are all popular and easily made fresh sausages. Fresh sausage is perishable, however, and will keep in the refrigerator only for a few days, but it freezes well for 2 to 3 months. Fresh sausage, in bulk or in casings, can be one of the most versatile and helpful ingredients in your freezer.

Edna Lewis, a fine interpreter of regional American food, says that having some country ham in your refrigerator is like owning one good black dress. You are always prepared, no matter what the occasion. The same could be said of sausage, fresh or smoked. With a stash of sausage in the freezer, you can always turn the most meager leftovers, dried beans, or pasta into a feast, whatever the circumstances or no matter how many guests drop in unexpectedly.

Many sausages are dried and/or smoked to aid preservation and enhance flavor. In the days before refrigeration, householders discovered that hanging pieces of salted meat, poultry, or fish above the hearth preserved them for future use. Smoked sausages, where the meat is mixed with salt and spices and then hung for a time in smoke, have long been a source of protein through the cold winter months. Air-drying sausages, such as salami or Lebanon bologna, dehydrates the meats, discourages bacterial activity, and helps to preserve them even more. Drying and smoking also concentrate flavors and add a special tang to these sausages, which makes them very popular as seasonings in dishes. Care must be taken when using these techniques, however, to prevent spoilage. In our section on smoking, we describe how to air-dry and smoke sausages safely.

There is another major type of sausage in which the meat is emulsified with the fat and spices to provide a smooth texture and subtle flavors. America's most popular sausage, the hot dog, is the most common emulsified sausage, but knockwurst, bologna, and other smooth sausages are also widely appreciated in the United States. Emulsified sausages are generally tricky to make in the home kitchen. But we have worked out a recipe for a Chicago-style hot dog that produces very good results.

How To Use This Book

AS WE SAID EARLIER, YOU DON'T HAVE TO MAKE YOUR OWN SAUSAGE TO COOK most of the recipes in this book. Fine, high-quality sausages are increasingly available in American markets, and many can be purchased by mail order. These and similar commercial sausages can be used in almost all of the recipes. A section on Mail-Order Sources (page 307) offers a guide to ordering sausages as well as sausage-making ingredients and equipment, and other products.

Most of our recipes are about how to use sausage. Making your own sausage is a lot of fun, though, and not very difficult, so we hope you'll try a few recipes in Part I. But if you prefer to skip the sausage-making recipes, you can use store-bought sausage in the second half of the book, "Cooking with Sausage."

Although all of the recipes have been carefully tested, and the amounts are exact, no recipe is written in stone, so feel free to experiment and improvise. We often list alternative ingredients or suggestions for changes in the recipes, which should serve as guidelines.

Cooking is fun, and cooking with spicy and flavorful sausages can be even more so. Let your taste buds be your guide, try new ingredients when the spirit moves, and enjoy yourself.

Our portion sizes tend to be on the generous side. We don't like to run out of food and would rather err on the side of too much than too little. Many of the dishes are even better rewarmed. Some dishes can be served either as hors d'oeuvres or as a main course, and we try to indicate probable servings for each.

Part I

The Spice in the Melting Pot

Wherever you go in America you'll find sausages. Whether it's a Coney Island frankfurter or a Sheboygan brat, potato sausage in Minnesota or kielbasa on Chicago's North Side, chorizo in the Southwest or sage and pepper farmer's sausage in the Heartland, there's always some kind of delicious sausage to sink your teeth into.

These tasty sausages are linked to America's ethnic traditions. When we came to this country we brought our sausage traditions along. American sausages are as different as our origins, and they are truly a variable feast. A bit of sausage can make a recipe Italian or German or Polish in flavor. Sausages are the spice in the melting pot, the bits of our heritage that make life (and food) in America interesting and endlessly creative.

One characteristic of American cooking today is an emphasis on lightness and flavor. Sausage has long been used as an accent in dishes and, contrary to popular myth, can provide protein and spiciness without adding excessive amounts of calories and cholesterol. Chicken or turkey sausages are even lighter and just as flavorful. As you'll see in our section on making sausages, the fat content of homemade or small-production sausages is much lower than that of the commercial products—most often on a par with lean hamburger. When used as a flavoring, sausage can provide excitement to a great range of foods. One of the reasons sausage has been such a popular part of cooking throughout history is its ability, at little extra cost, to enhance even the most humble ingredients.

Even though we've designed this book to let you cook many of our recipes without making your own sausages, there are plenty of easy-to-make sausages that should tempt you to try your hand. We think you'll be surprised at how easy it all is and how tasty and delightful homemade sausages can be.

When you do make sausage, invite some friends over to pitch in and help. Sausage making has always been a communal activity, and making sausages together, frying up samples, and tasting, can double the fun and halve the work. Tasting can get out of hand though. Be sure to save enough sausage meat to fill a respectable amount of casing.

Chapter 1

THE JOY OF HOMEMADE SAUSAGE

Tips & Techniques

MAKING SAUSAGE AT HOME IS NOT DIFFICULT OR OVERLY COMPLICATED, AND it can be a lot of fun. There's something about chopping the meat and mixing in the spices, stuffing the sausage into casings, and tying off the plump links that is, in a word, satisfying. When you panfry your own linguiça or andouille, chorizo or boudin, and the rich aromas drift through the house, the effort seems like nothing. You join those uncounted generations of sausage makers who have made the world, and its food, a bit more lively and interesting.

Homemade sausages have real advantages over most commercial products. There are no additives, extenders, or other ingredients to cause worry or concern. If you choose to cold smoke or air-dry your homemade sausages, you need to add curing salts for safety's sake (see page 21, "Note on Nitrites"), but the amount of curing salts required will be at the absolute minimum to retard bacterial growth if you follow our directions. And you certainly don't have to cold smoke or air-dry sausages; you can hot smoke them or leave them fresh.

An added plus is the lesser amount of fat used in sausages made in the home kitchen. Some fat is necessary for flavor and juiciness in all sausages, but you can keep it to a minimum, and well below most store-bought sausage. Amounts vary for each type, but in general the fat content of homemade sausages is significantly lower than most commercial products.

Equipment

NO SPECIAL EQUIPMENT IS NECESSARY—A SHARP KNIFE OR A FOOD PROCESSOR will do—although if you really get into sausage making you might want

3

to acquire some specialized tools of the trade, such as a meat grinder or sausage stuffer. For a simple sausage, all you have to do is mince the meat and fat to the desired texture, mix in the spices, form the meat into patties, and fry—as easy as making hamburgers. Or you can go a step further and use a long funnel to stuff the sausage meat into casings and tie off links. You just slip the casing over the end of the funnel and push the chopped meat in by hand or with the end of a wooden spoon. It can be a bit slow for large quantities, but you'll be making sausage the same way Italian or Polish grandmothers have over the centuries, and they get very few complaints.

A meat grinder, however, will make your sausage making a lot easier, if you want to make up any quantity. If you add a sausage horn attachment for the grinder and a small kitchen scale, you'll be well on your way to becoming a bona fide sausage maker.

We prefer to use a meat grinder, hand-operated or electric, equipped with plates of differing hole sizes (⅛ inch, ¼ inch, and ⅜ inch) to allow for varied textures, along with a sausage stuffing attachment, or horn. With the various-sized plates, you can grind the meat as fine or as coarse as you like. Then, after the meat is mixed and seasoned, just attach the horn to the grinder, slip the sausage casing over the tip, and use the grinder to feed the meat into the casing simply by turning the handle. Hand grinders and some electric models are relatively inexpensive; an electric grinder makes sense if you are going to put up large batches of sausage. Keep the blade and plates clean and dry, and lubricate the moving parts of the grinder with vegetable oil each time you use it. The meat grinder attachment and sausage horn available for the KitchenAid mixer work well and are easy to use. Incidentally, food processors are all right to use for grinding meat occasionally, but they don't produce pieces of consistent size and texture.

If you make sausage on a regular basis or in large lots, you might want to get a sausage stuffer—a long cylinder with a piston that pushes the ground meat into the casings. For sausage-making equipment, visit a hardware store or butcher-supply house in an Italian, German, or Polish neighborhood, or consult our listing of mail order sources (page 307).

Any good kitchen scale should work fine for measuring ingredients. If you don't have a scale, remember that 2 cups of ground meat weighs about 1 pound. If you are fortunate enough to have a friendly butcher, you might be able to buy the meat and fat and have him grind it for you. Tell the butcher to use the "chili" blade, so the meat is not too finely ground. Be sure to have the meat ground fresh and use it the same day you buy it.

Ingredients

℮ Meat

MEAT FOR SAUSAGE MAKING SHOULD BE AS FRESH AS POSSIBLE AND KEPT refrigerated right up to the time you use it. It is all right to use the tougher and cheaper cuts because the meat is going to be ground or chopped. Shoulder cuts are best, as they are cheap, flavorful, and easy to bone. Pork is preferred for most types of sausage, and the shoulder, sometimes called Boston butt, provides juicy, tasty meat. Beef chuck and lamb shoulder are also popular. If you are using venison or other large game, the shoulder is the best for sausage, although loin or leg can be used. For poultry sausage, we prefer chicken or turkey thigh meat.

When boning and cutting up meat for sausage making, be sure to remove and discard any gristle or connective tissue. Meat trimmings are sometimes used to make sausage, but sufficient amounts of trimming are usually available only in a butcher shop or large restaurant kitchen.

℮ Fat

SAUSAGE NEEDS FAT FOR JUICINESS AND FLAVOR. COMMERCIAL PRODUCTS CAN contain from 30 to 50 percent fat, while sausages made in the home from our recipes and by artisan producers use between 15 and 25 percent. (For comparison, lean hamburger contains 15 to 22 percent fat, regular up to 30 percent.) The amount of fat you consume will be significantly less if you follow our usual practice and drain off the excess after browning the sausages.

Pork fat is preferred for its mild flavor and high melting point. Lamb fat has too strong a flavor, while poultry fats are too soft and melt too easily. Beef is acceptable, although a bit too grainy for some sausages. Pork back fat with the skin removed has the best texture and is favored for most sausages. Belly or bacon fat is too soft, and kidney fat too hard. Most butchers will be more than willing to sell or give you the type of fat you need for virtually any sausage.

If the meat is coarsely ground on a ⅜-inch plate and the fat on a finer plate, ⅛-inch or ¼-inch, much less fat can be used. Our recipes generally follow this procedure. Finer-ground sausages tend to need more fat because they have a mealier texture, while chunky meat stays juicier with less fat added.

Since you will be using less fat than commercial sausages, you should be careful not to overcook the sausages. An internal temperature of 155° to 160° when you insert an instant-read thermometer into the end of the sausage is more than adequate to produce a safe and juicy result. Commercial sausage makers are required to cook pork sausage to an internal temperature of only 144°, so you will be well beyond the minimum.

℮ Seasonings

THE SPICE BLEND IS WHAT GIVES EACH SAUSAGE ITS UNIQUE FLAVOR, AND fresh spices are essential to fine sausage making. Throw out spices that are on the shelf for more than 3 months, and buy fresh ones. We prefer to grind our own black pepper, usually coarsely, although we do call for a fine grind in some smoother sausages. In general, it is best to grind most other spices, such as nutmeg, coriander, cloves, etc., just before using—it makes a difference you can taste.

Fresh herbs can be used in place of dried (in the proportion of two parts fresh to one part dried), and amounts of cayenne and other hot peppers depend on the heat levels you prefer. Herbs and spices vary widely in flavor and potency, so you should always fry up a small portion of the sausage meat and taste it, then let your taste buds be your guide.

Salt is an important element for preservation and flavor. It discourages the growth of unwanted bacteria and other organisms and enhances the impact of the other spices. We use less salt in our recipes than most commercial sausage makers, and prefer kosher salt for its purity and milder flavor. If you don't have kosher salt, use a little less pure table salt (2½ teaspoons instead of 1 tablespoon) than the recipe calls for. To test salt for additives, dissolve a couple of teaspoons in a glass of water. If the solution remains cloudy after stirring, the salt has too many impurities and should not be used.

℮ Other Ingredients

THE AVERAGE COMMERCIAL SAUSAGE IS OFTEN LOADED WITH EXTENDERS, MSG, binders, preservatives, sugar, and water. We think they provide a pretty good argument for making your own sausages or for seeking out the small artisan producers of authentic sausages. We will occasionally add a little bit of sweet wine or sugar if a recipe calls for it, and we use small amounts of water or wine to moisten the meat and help blend together the ingredients. In our recipes, we do recommend adding curing salts if you are going to cold smoke or air-dry sausages, for safety's sake. They are not necessary for fresh sausage or if you choose to hot smoke sausage (see page 13, "Smoking Sausages").

Casings

CASINGS ARE NOT NECESSARY FOR HOME SAUSAGE MAKING (UNLESS THEY ARE to be smoked), and most of our sausages are delicious if the mixture is just formed into patties and fried. Many of our recipes call for bulk sausage, and you can wrap and freeze meal-sized portions of any sausage for future use.

But a juicy link hot from the grill is so toothsome and delicious that you'll most likely want to stuff at least some of your homemade sausages into casings. Most authentic sausages are stuffed into natural casings of hog, lamb, or beef intestines, thoroughly cleaned with the soft tissues removed. These thin membranes are dried and packed in salt for storage. Many commercial sausages use artificial casings made of collagen or are sold "skinless."

Casings are usually sold in bundles called "hanks." Depending on the type and size of the casing, a hank will take care of 50 to 150 pounds of meat, but don't worry if that sounds like a lot. Packed in salt, casings can last several years in the refrigerator. They can be purchased from custom butchers, butcher-supply houses, or by mail order (page 307).

Hog casings are the most versatile and popular, and range in size from 1¼ to 2½ inches in diameter. They are relatively tender, not very expensive, and easy to work with. If you were to pick one casing to buy, we would recommend a medium hog casing (32 to 35 mm or 1¼ inches). This is the size, for example, of the standard Italian sausage, and most of our sausage recipes can be made using this size casing. One hank will hold 100 to 125 pounds of sausage meat.

Lamb or sheep casings are the narrowest and most delicate; they are also the most expensive. Typically used in breakfast links and old-fashioned hot dogs, they range from ½ inch (lamb) to a little over 1 inch (sheep) in diameter. One hank should hold about 50 to 60 pounds of sausage meat.

There are two popular types of beef casings: beef middles and beef rounds. The rounds, which are used for sausages such as ring bologna or ring kielbasa, range in diameter from 2 to 3 inches and will hold between 75 and 100 pounds of product per hank. Beef middles are often sold sewn and are used to make large, semidry sausages such as summer sausage, as well as liverwurst and braunschweiger. An individual sewed middle will range in diameter from 2 to 4½ inches and will hold 2 to 3 pounds of meat. Beef casings can be tough and are most often peeled away before the sausage is eaten.

Caul fat is a membranous fat that can be used to wrap patties of meat called crépinettes. This membrane helps to keep the juices in and gives the patty a nice appearance. Caul fat can be stored frozen, and unused caul fat can be refrozen. It can be difficult to find, although specialty butchers and wholesale meat distributors often carry it.

Handling and Storage

WE CANNOT STRESS ENOUGH HOW IMPORTANT FRESH MEAT AND PROPER STORAGE and handling are to quality sausage making. Meat should be purchased from a reputable butcher and used the same day. You can use frozen meat, but it should be frozen at its peak of freshness. For best results, meat should be thawed as slowly as possible, for 1 or 2 days in the refrigerator, depending on how big the pieces are. Frozen meat should not be kept for more than 3 months; otherwise it can develop a rancid flavor. You may use frozen fat, as this is often the only way to find it. As long as you don't let the fat warm up to above 45°, you can refreeze it.

Ground meat will spoil sooner than whole cuts, so keep sausage meat cold and use it as quickly as possible. We suggest you cut the meat into pieces and put it into the freezer for 30 minutes before grinding. After you've ground the meat and fat, put the mixture back into the refrigerator until you are ready to stuff the casings. If you are making more than one type of sausage at one time, grind and season all the mixtures, refrigerate, and then stuff them into the casings all at once. When making sausage, the temperature of the meat should not get above 50° for any extended period of time.

Sanitation

JUST AS IMPORTANT AS THE USE OF IMPECCABLY FRESH INGREDIENTS IS THE need to practice good sanitation when making sausage.

- After washing the grinder and stuffer with hot water, cool them in the refrigerator or freezer before use. Have all your cutting boards, tables, equipment, and knives scrupulously clean. Periodically sterilize wooden cutting boards with a solution of ¾ cup bleach and 1 gallon warm water. Let stand for 5 minutes and rinse with clean water. Wash hands frequently with plenty of soap and hot water during sausage making.

- When making several varieties of sausage, preweigh the meats and fat, and store them in labeled bowls in the refrigerator until you are ready to grind them. Work on only one batch at a time, and keep the other batches refrigerated. After the meat has been ground and the spices mixed in, store it in the refrigerator until ready to stuff into the casings.

- Make your sausages during the cooler times of the day, morning or evening. If possible, the room temperature should not be above 70°.

- Have all the ingredients ready to go and the spice mix made in advance.

- Don't let the grinder or stuffer sit with meat in it. If you are going to take a break or move on to something else, take the grinder apart, and remove and discard any residual meat or fat. Wash and dry the grinder and reassemble it when you are ready to use it again. Meat should not sit in a grinder or stuffer for more than 15 to 20 minutes at 70° room temperature, less time if the room is hotter.

- When smoking or air-drying sausage, do not dry them in too warm a place. Always hang sausage on clean sticks.

Step-by-Step Method for Making Sausage at Home

ℭ Grinding

1. **If you have a meat grinder,** hand-operated or electric, attach the size plate (with holes of ⅛ inch, ¼ inch, or ⅜ inch) that the recipe calls for. Cut the meat and fats into ¾- by ¾-inch-wide strips (no larger than the mouth of the grinder), 1 to 6 inches long. While cutting up the meat, take care to remove any gristle and connective tissue. Grind the meat and the fat together into a large bowl. The mixture should come off the grinder plate in "worms." If the meat looks mushy, it means the grinder knife is not making good contact with the plate or the knife is dull. Remove the plate and knife, clean away any gristle, and reassemble, making sure the plate is reasonably tight against the knife. If you continue to have this problem, you might have to buy a new knife.

   If you are using a food processor, cut the meat and fat into ¾-inch cubes to get reasonably consistent chopping. Process in very small batches of 1 pound or less by using the pulse switch or turning on and off until the desired consistency is reached. Do not overprocess the meat. For 3 to 4 pounds of sausage you will probably need to process 3 or 4 batches, depending on the size of your food processor. Mini food processors or blenders should not be used to make sausage.

2. Add salt and spices, and mix in any water or liquid and optional curing salts (cold water from the tap is fine). Knead the sausage meat with your hands, squeezing and turning the mixture. Do not overmix, as this could cause the fat to melt and might give the sausage a white, fatty appearance.

3. Make a small patty of the sausage meat and fry it. Taste and adjust the salt or other seasonings. Cover and refrigerate the meat until you are ready to stuff it into the casings or use in a recipe. You should try to stuff the sausage meat into the casings on the same

day it was ground, since it gets quite stiff and difficult to handle if refrigerated too long.

℮ Preparing and Stuffing the Casings

4. You will need about 2 feet of medium hog casings or 4 feet of sheep casings for each pound of sausage mixture. **If you are using salt-packed casings,** remove a length of casing from the salt and place it in a bowl of warm water. Put the bowl in the sink and attach one end of the casing to the kitchen faucet. Gently run warm water through the casing to wash out the salt. Continue to soak the casing in warm water for 1 to 2 hours, or until it is soft and pliable. **If you are using preflushed, liquid-packed casings,** you have to soak them in clean warm water for only 15 to 30 minutes, and flush them briefly as above.

5. Attach a sausage-stuffing horn to the front of the grinder or stuffer. Don't forget to remove the plate and knife. Spread open one end of the casing and shake a drop of water onto it. The water will help lubricate the casing as you gently pull it over the end of the horn. Carefully push the whole casing onto the horn, leaving 3 or 4 inches dangling.

6. Fill the grinder or stuffer with the sausage meat and feed it through the grinder until it begins to enter the casing. Tie the end of the casing into a knot. With a skewer or hat pin, prick any air bubbles that appear as the casing fills up. A second pair of hands is very helpful when stuffing sausage. Continue to stuff the casing, using your thumb against the tip of the horn to control the rate and tightness of the filling. Do not fill the casings too full, or the sausage might burst during linking or cooking, but do pack them firmly.

7. When you have filled all but 3 to 4 inches of casing (still attached to the horn), remove the horn from the grinder and push any remaining sausage meat through the horn into the casing with the handle of a wooden spoon. Slip the casing off the horn.

8. Drain any leftover casings, salt with kosher salt, and refrigerate for later use.

☙ Linking

9. Depending on the type of sausages, links should be 5 to 8 inches in length. Starting from the knotted end of the casing on your right, measure the desired length and pinch the casing between your right thumb and forefinger. Move the same number of inches down the casing and pinch again to form a second link. Holding the second link in both hands, twirl it clockwise so that it twists the casing at both ends and seals both links. Measure to the left the same length again and pinch the casing, then measure and pinch off again to form link number four. Twist the fourth link to seal it and link number three. Continue to twist alternate links until you reach the end of the casing. Knot the end to seal the last link. There should be approximately ¼ to ½ inch of twisted casing between each link. Cut through the middle of the twisted casing to separate each sausage and seal the ends.

   If the sausage bursts while linking—and this happens to even the most experienced sausage makers—cut through the casing at the break and tie off or knot both ends and continue linking. You can either restuff the leftover meat or make patties out of it.

☙ Maturing and Storing Sausages

10. The meats, spice, and other flavorings need time to mature in the sausage mixture. This maturation will contribute to a mellow flavor and better texture. Place the sausages, uncovered, on a rack in the refrigerator overnight or suspend them by a hook from a rack in the refrigerator. If the sausages do not contain curing salts, we don't recommend maturing them unrefrigerated unless you have a very cold garage or basement that does not get above 40°. Use a thermometer to be sure, since fresh sausages are basically raw ground meat and can spoil easily. Unsmoked raw sausages should be kept for no more than 3 days in the refrigerator. If you want to keep fresh sausages longer, wrap them well in freezer paper or foil, and freeze them for up to 2 months. Smoked sausage will keep refrigerated for a week; frozen, it will keep for 2 months.

Cooking Sausage

WE LIKE TO **panfry** RAW SAUSAGE IN A DRY HEAVY SKILLET OVER MEDIUM heat. Put the sausages into a cold pan and cook them in their own juices, turning them until they are browned on all sides. This should take 10 to 15 minutes, depending on the thickness of the sausages. When panfrying smoked sausages, add about ¼ inch of water to the skillet to help soften the casings. Cover and cook until the liquid evaporates. Continue to cook until the sausages are evenly browned, about 10 minutes.

Grilling is a wonderful way to cook sausages. You can grill them raw or precook them by poaching in hot (180°) water for 15 to 20 minutes for sausages in medium hog casings. If you intend to grill sausages directly over a charcoal fire, it's a good idea to prepoach them to reduce the amount of fat that will drip onto the fire and flare up. We prefer to cook poached sausages in a covered kettle-style barbecue, turning them frequently until they are evenly browned, which takes 7 to 12 minutes, depending on the diameter of the sausages and how hot your coals are. The internal temperature of the sausages should reach 155° to 160° when measured by inserting an instant-read thermometer 2 to 3 inches into the end of a sausage. Don't use extremely hot coals, which can cause excessive flaming and will burn the outside of the sausages before the insides have cooked.

The trick to **poaching** sausages is to cook them very gradually so that the moisture stays in the sausage and they don't become too dry. (This is why we don't suggest you prick sausages beforehand.) To poach 3 pounds of sausage stuffed into medium hog casings, bring 2 to 3 gallons of lightly salted water to a temperature of 180° to 200°. An accurate instant-read thermometer is useful here. The water should not be boiling. Put the sausages in the hot water and poach them over very low heat. The water should stay between 160° and 180°. Depending on the thickness of the sausages, they will take 15 to 40 minutes to cook to an internal temperature of 155° to 160°. Sausages stuffed in medium hog casings should take about 20 minutes; thicker or thinner sausages will take more or less time. Remove the sausages and eat at once, or cool in a colander under cold running water and refrigerate or freeze. Reheat them later by panfrying, grilling, or poaching.

Smoking Sausages

COUNTRY PEOPLE HAVE LONG KNOWN THAT MEAT HUNG IN THE SMOKE OF hearths and chimneys lasts longer and often tastes better than fresh meat. Smoking, drying, and salting were the main means of preserving meats in the days before refrigeration.

In early America, salted and smoked meat and fish were the mainstays of rural householders. Farmhouses and plantations, from the poorest prairie sod huts to the rich estates of the Tidewater, all had their smokehouses to preserve the summer's harvest of flesh through the cold, hard winter. Virginia ham or smoked hog jowl, Nova Scotia lox or kippered herring, andouille or kielbasa—the products of the smokehouse became an integral part of the flavor of American cooking.

Today, with modern refrigeration, we are not so concerned with smoking as a means of preserving meat, poultry, and fish. We don't need to hang hams or sausages for days or even weeks to keep them from spoiling over the winter. Rather, we are looking for the fragrant smoky flavors of hickory or oak, applewood or mesquite.

With very little equipment or effort, the home cook and sausage maker can achieve the taste and aroma of traditionally smoked foods. Whether it's done in a kettle-style barbecue, a water smoker, a semiprofessional commercial smoker, or a converted old refrigerator, home smoking can give a flavor of the past and that special tang of hearth or campfire that brings back a hint of an ancient, savory feast.

℃ Cold Smoking

THE TYPE OF SMOKING MOST COMMON ON PLANTATIONS AND FARMS IN America over the last two centuries is called cold smoking. The term "cold," however, is misleading since it's not very cool in country smokehouses. In general, cold smoking takes place at temperatures that range between 90° and 120°, not enough to cook most foods, whereas hot smoking uses higher temperatures to cook the food as it smokes. Cold smoking is used to produce country or Virginia hams, most commercial smoked sausages, and bacon, all of which are then cooked before eating. Since uncooked food absorbs flavor more quickly, cold-smoked sausages are generally smokier in flavor than hot-smoked. Cold smoking can be done successfully at home using a homemade smoker, water smoker, or small electric smoker. Cold-smoked sausages must include sodium nitrite curing salts for safety.

℮ Hot Smoking

IF YOU HAVE EVER EATEN TEXAS-STYLE BARBECUED MEAT, THEN YOU'VE EATEN food that has been hot smoked. This type of smoking is done at temperatures high enough to cook the food while imparting a mild and pleasantly smoky flavor. Hot smoking is really a type of smoke-cooking. Again, as with cold smoking, the world "hot" is a relative term. Usually hot smoking takes place at temperatures that range between 170° and 250°, the aim being to slowly roast the meat or sausage while it absorbs a smoky flavor. Because it is cooked slowly and evenly, the meat or sausage comes out tender and juicy. With the advent of the covered kettle barbecue and the water smoker, hot smoking has become quite popular with home cooks, and most sausage recipes in this book can be hot smoked that way. Hot-smoked sausages do not require the addition of sodium nitrite or curing salts, as at the hotter temperatures the food cooks before unwanted bacteria and other organisms can multiply. Hot-smoked food has the same perishability as any roasted meat. It will keep for about 5 to 7 days in the refrigerator.

℮ Smoking: Art or Science?

SMOKING IS NOT AN EXACT SCIENCE, AND NO RECIPE CAN BE ABSOLUTELY PRECISE. The many variables make exact instructions impossible. The temperature, density, and thickness of the meat or sausage, the outside air temperature and humidity, the type of smoke, the amount of food in the smoker, and the smoking temperature all make a difference. Don't worry, though; you will get good results if you pay attention to temperatures by using an instant-read thermometer to monitor the food as it is smoked. To use an instant-read thermometer, insert it into the meat or sausage from time to time to determine when the proper temperature is reached—for hot smoking, 155° to 160°. For cold-smoked meats, follow the directions on page 17. If your model does not have a built-in thermometer, a second instant-read thermometer can be set into the top vent of a smoker to keep track of the smoking temperatures. Do not use a traditional meat thermometer that is left in the meat while cooking, as they are often unreliable.

Some home-smoking enthusiasts keep a smoking journal to record information like temperature, type of wood, length of smoke, etc., for future reference.

℮ Woods

HARDWOODS ARE BEST FOR SMOKING. SOFTWOODS, SUCH AS PINE, FIR, CEDAR, and spruce, are not suitable because they produce smoke so full of pitch and resin that it gives food a turpentine flavor and coats everything with a black, sticky film. If you can't positively identify the wood, don't use it for smoking. Never use backyard clippings, which may contain noxious insecticides or poisonous plants, such as oleander or poison oak. The most popular woods for smoking sausages are hickory, alder, mesquite, oak, and fruitwoods, such as apple or cherry. Dried corn-cobs also make a good smoking fuel. Different woods impart different flavors; some work better with fish or poultry, while others are more compatible with beef or pork. Try experimenting with your own combinations of wood and sausage to see what suits your taste. For hot smoking, you should use chunks of wood, soaked first so that they'll smolder and not burn. You can use wood chips, but you'll have to replenish them more often. For cold smoking, use hardwood sawdust or wood chips.

℮ Equipment

Gas or electric smokers. These are small versions of commercial smokers, usually consisting of a metal box with a gas or electric heating element on the bottom. Wood chips or hardwood sawdust are placed in a pan over the heat. Sausages or meat are put on a rack or suspended on hooks over the fragrant smoke. If you pay careful attention to the temperature and heat source, these smokers can be used successfully for both cold and hot smoking. They can be purchased from camping, hardware, or sporting goods stores and are also available by mail order (see page 307).

Homemade smokers. These may be as simple as a converted 55-gallon drum, a metal garbage can, or an old refrigerator, or as elaborate as a custom-built brick smokehouse. Designs abound in do-it-yourself journals and books on country living. Like commercial smokers, they usually consist of a heat source such as a hot plate, a pan to hold the wood chips or sawdust, and racks or poles to hold the meat or sausages. Depending on the design, they tend to work well for cold smoking, but are often inadequate for hot smoking because consistent high temperatures are hard to maintain. Generally, with most homemade smokers, it's a good idea to smoke the food first, and then finish it by cooking in a slow oven at 200° to 250°. We built our own smoker out of an old refrigerator and have used it successfully over the years to smoke sausages and other meats. We followed the basic design set forth in Jacques Pépin's *The Art of Cooking*, Volume II (Knopf, 1988).

Water smokers and kettle barbecues. In recent years, these versatile barbecue-smokers have become quite popular and are now widely available. Most use charcoal as the heat source, but there are also gas or electric models. Most water smokers have a domed top and look like an elongated kettle barbecue. At the bottom, there is a fire pan for charcoal and aromatic wood. Above the heat source is a water pan and one or two grills to hold the food. Water smokers are quite versatile and can serve as a covered barbecue, steamer, open braiser, dry roaster, and hot or cold smoker. Kettle barbecues can also be used to grill, roast, or smoke-cook meats, poultry, and fish.

Step-by-Step Method for Air-Drying and Cold Smoking
(for sausages with curing salts only)

1. When the sausages have been filled, hang them from a stick in a cool place (under 70°). Have a fan going on slow speed about 5 feet away. Air-dry overnight to create a dry surface, which will help the sausage absorb smoke better.

2. Set up your smoker *outside*. Place 6 cups hardwood sawdust in a pan or cast-iron pot on the bottom of the smoker or on the heat source.

3. Put 1 cup hardwood sawdust in a 6- to 8-inch frying pan over high heat on a portable hot plate or burner set up outside. This *must* be done *outside; never indoors*. After a minute, the sawdust will begin to smolder and smoke.

4. When all the sawdust in the pan has turned black, with tiny glowing embers and areas of gray ash, remove the pan from the heat

and dump the burning sawdust on top of the sawdust inside the smoker.

5. Arrange the sausages in a single layer on a rack or suspend the sausages from a smoke stick.

6. Partially open the vents of the smoker and insert an instant-read thermometer into one vent. The temperature should stay between 90° and 120° throughout the smoking process.

7. About every 3 to 4 hours, gently stir the sawdust in the pan. Be sure that smoke is gently rising out of the vents of the smoker. Throughout the smoking period, add more sawdust as necessary, making sure to stir the old ashes over the new sawdust.

8. Consult the individual recipe to see how long to smoke the sausage. Most recipes recommend smoking overnight. You don't have to get up in the middle of the night to add more sawdust, though. Make sure the pan is full of sawdust and just give the sawdust in the smoker a good stir before you go to bed, and another as soon as you wake up. If the fire has burned out, restart as described above.

9. As long as the temperature inside the smoker does not exceed 130°, it won't be necessary to check the internal temperature of the sausage. Cold-smoked sausage will require further cooking before eating, however.

Step-by-Step Method for Hot Smoking or Smoke-Cooking in a Water Smoker

1. At least 1 hour before you plan to start smoking, soak at least three or four 2- by 3-inch chunks of wood in water.

2. Set up the smoker outside. Put a layer of charcoal briquettes in the bottom of the smoker. Remove the top and center rings. Open all vents. Start the fire with a fire chimney or electric starter. Don't use liquid charcoal starters, which can impart an unpleasant taste to the smoke. The coals are ready when they are coated with a light gray ash, usually after about 30 minutes.

3. Spread the coals evenly and set up the smoker. Put the water pan in position and fill with hot water or other liquid. Carefully put the middle ring in place on top of the bottom section. Set the cooking racks in place and arrange the sausages on them in a single layer. Leave an inch or two between sausages so the smoke can circulate. Open the side door of the smoker. Add 3 or 4 chunks of soaked wood. Shake off any excess water before placing them on top of the coals, using tongs to keep from burning your hands. Using mittens or hot pads, partially close all the vents while hot smoking. Insert an instant-read thermometer in the top vent.

4. After 30 minutes, check the temperature inside the smoker. The thermometer should read at least 170°; the ideal range for hot smoking is between 170° and 250°. If the smoker is not maintaining sufficient heat (more than 170°), open the vents. If the fire is dying out, open the side door, and the additional oxygen will get the fire going again. If the smoker is still not hot, add more charcoal. If the temperature gets too hot (above 250°), try closing the vents. If this doesn't work, add some cold water to the water pan, or remove some of the briquettes.

5. The water smoker functions best when not opened frequently. Add a dozen or so charcoal briquettes every 1½ hours. You may need to add more hot water to the water pan, which should always be at least half full of liquid. For long periods of smoking you'll have to add more charcoal, and possibly more wood.

6. It should take roughly from 1½ to 4 hours to hot smoke sausages, depending on the diameter and type of sausage. Remember to rely on your instant-read thermometer—155° to 160° is the desired internal temperature. Insert the thermometer 2 to 3 inches into the end of a sausage. Hot-smoked meat is often bright pink just below the surface, so don't rely on the appearance in determining whether sausages are done or not.

Step-by-Step Method for Hot Smoking or Smoke-Cooking in a Kettle Barbecue

1. Soak 3 to 4 cups of hickory chips or 4 to 6 chunks of hardwood in water for at least 30 minutes.

2. Mound 10 to 15 charcoal briquettes to one side of a covered barbecue. Once the coals are hot, allow them to burn down to medium-low. This takes about 30 minutes, and they should be covered with gray ash.

3. Spread the coals in a single layer on one side of the barbecue. Sprinkle 2 cups of soaked hickory chips or 2 to 3 chunks of soaked hardwood over the coals. Place a drip pan with a little water in it on the opposite side from the charcoal. Replace the grill and spread the sausages on it over the pan. Cover the barbecue, making sure the vent in the lid is directly above the sausages. Open the top and bottom vents about ¼ inch.

4. Smoke the sausages at 170° to 250°. You can measure the temperature by inserting an instant-read thermometer into the partially opened top vent. Add more chips and charcoal as needed.

5. After 30 minutes, turn the sausages over and continue to smoke for another 30 or more minutes, until an instant-read thermometer inserted through the end of a sausage measures 155° to 160°. Sausages in medium hog casings will take about 1½ hours to smoke-cook; in wide beef casings they may take as long as 4 hours. You should turn the sausages occasionally as they cook.

Safety Tips and Helpful Hints

- **Smoking should be done outside only. Never smoke anything indoors as the fumes produced can be *lethal*. Do not use gasoline, alcohol, or any other highly flammable liquid to ignite charcoal. Read all manufacturer's instructions provided with your smoker for any safety information.**

- Don't use commercial fire starters.

- Never pour water directly onto hot coals. Dust and soot could coat the food.

- Because of the variables in smoking, always allow extra cooking time. Use an instant-read thermometer to test for doneness.

- The smoker can become very hot during use, so set it up away from the house and out of the way of general traffic.

- Always smoke with the cover on.

- Use mittens or hot pads when handling the hot smoker.

- Turn food with tongs to prevent piercing the sausages and losing juices.

- Look at the food only when absolutely necessary. Every time you lift the lid, you add 15 minutes to the cooking time.

- Close all vents when finished to allow the fire to burn out. Do not use water to extinguish the coals, because it can damage the finish of the smoker.

Note on Nitrites: Curing Salts

SODIUM NITRITE, LONG USED IN CURING MEATS AND SAUSAGES, BECAME A BAD word in the 1970s because it was thought to produce cancer-causing compounds called nitrosamines. The National Science Foundation investigated and found that nitrites did not cause problems in most cured meats and sausages (bacon was the exception). Current scientific opinion holds that the use of sodium nitrite within legal limits causes no significant health problems and prevents the growth of botulinums and other noxious organisms.

On the other hand, we'd just as soon not use sodium nitrite or any other additive unless we need to. Raw sausages and hot-smoked sausages do not require the addition of curing salts, because they are kept refrigerated or frozen and are cooked at high enough temperatures to arrest bacterial activity. If you decide to air-dry or cold smoke sausage, however, curing salts must be used to prevent any possibility of botulism. During cold smoking and air-drying, the temperatures are ideal for the growth of bacteria, so the protection offered by curing salts is necessary for safety.

The United States Department of Agriculture (USDA) requires 6.1 grams of sodium nitrite to cure 100 pounds of meat. Since these are very small quantities to measure accurately, home sausage makers rely on professionally mixed curing salts that contain nitrite mixed with other substances, such as salt or sugar. Instead of 6.1 grams, 4 ounces by weight of one of these premixed curing salts is used for 100 pounds of meat. Purchase brand-name curing salts such as Prague

Powder, Ham Cure, or Morton Quick Cure from butcher-supply houses or by mail order (page 307). Follow manufacturers' directions.

In our recipes we specify amounts for the commercial curing salts and not for pure sodium nitrate. Do not use saltpeter (potassium nitrite) as a curing salt, since it is no longer recommended by the USDA.

Chapter 2

TRADITIONAL AMERICAN SAUSAGE

AMERICAN MEMORIES: SAUSAGE SPUTTERING ON THE STOVE, WAFFLES BAKING in an old-fashioned waffle iron, applesauce and maple syrup on the table, coffee steaming in a white enamel pot.

Country sausage has always been a mainstay in American cooking. It is part of the quintessential American breakfast, of course, but it has also been used as a flavoring by creative cooks from colonial times to the present. In New England, the Midwest, and the South, this savory mixture of pork, sage, black pepper, and spices is featured in a wide variety of dishes from soups to stews to casseroles of every type imaginable. Country sausage is also a wonderful flavoring for greens and other vegetables, providing an extra dimension of flavor and a hint of spice to otherwise bland ingredients.

When we reminisce about thick patties of sausage frying in black skillets, it's country sausage we're dreaming of. Just about every farm family had its own variation for sausage made fresh at the fall hog-killing time. Most recipes share the basic mixture of fresh pork and pork fat with seasonings that usually include salt, sage, and red and black pepper. After this, variations abound. Spices such allspice, nutmeg, cloves, and ginger are often added, along with aromatics like lemon peel or garlic. Fresh or dried herbs that range from mild hints of parsley to the more powerful flavors of thyme, rosemary, marjoram, or savory add color and complexity. Amounts of pepper, red and black, vary considerably, depending on the heat tolerance of local palates.

American Farmhouse Sausage

AMERICAN FARMHOUSE SAUSAGE HAS ITS ORIGINS IN THE ENGLISH CULINARY traditions that were maintained in farm kitchens. The basic mix of ground fresh pork, sage, and black pepper can be found in Hannah Glasse's *Art of Cookery*, published in the mid–eighteenth century in Dublin and widely circulated throughout England and America. Mary Randolph, whose *The Virginia Housewife* (1824) was perhaps the most influential cookbook in nineteenth-century America, reproduces Glasse's sausage recipe virtually intact.

Later cooks added cayenne and other spices that reflected the fiery flavors of African, Spanish, and Creole cooking to create many lively variations on this basic country sausage.

An American Staple
"Take the tender pieces of fresh pork, chop them exceedingly fine, chop some of the leaf fat, and put them together in the proportion of three pounds of pork to one of fat, season it very high with pepper and salt, add a small quantity of dried sage rubbed to a powder, have the skins nicely prepared, fill them and hang them in a dry place. Sausages are excellent made into cakes and fried, but will not keep so well as in skins." (*The Virginia Housewife*, 1824).

THIS RECIPE GIVES THE BASICS AND IS OPEN TO WHATEVER VARIATIONS YOU'D like to add. You might want to follow it exactly the first time, taste the results with family and friends, and then start experimenting. Another possibility is to purchase good-quality bulk sausage meat, and add your own spices, peppers, and herbs. You can mix in one or more herbs, including marjoram, summer savory, or dried rosemary, along with a spice, such as nutmeg, cloves, allspice, or ginger. Amounts will depend on your preferences, but a good rule of thumb is to start by adding ½ teaspoon of a dried herb and/or a pinch of spice to the basic recipe or to about 4 pounds of store-bought bulk sausage. Two teaspoons of minced garlic can also be added. Fry up a small patty to test and taste, and mix in more flavors as you go. Southern farm wives used to stuff bulk sausage into small muslin bags or pokes, or fry patties and layer them in their own fat for preservation over the winter. The modern alternative is, of course, freezing.

3 pounds pork butt
¾ to 1 pound pork back fat
1 tablespoon red pepper flakes
4 teaspoons kosher salt
2 teaspoons sugar
2 teaspoons coarsely ground
   black pepper

2 teaspoons dried sage
1 teaspoon dried thyme
1 teaspoon ground cayenne pepper
½ cup water
Medium hog casings (optional)

FOR DETAILS ON MAKING SAUSAGE, SEE PAGE 10.

Put the pork meat and fat through the meat grinder, using the ¼-inch plate. In a large bowl, mix the ground pork, fat, red pepper, salt, sugar, black pepper, sage, thyme, cayenne, and water, kneading and squeezing the meat until everything is nicely blended.

If you are making the sausage for patties, simply wrap it in bulk and refrigerate until you are ready to use it. Or stuff the seasoned meat into medium hog casings and tie into 4-inch links.

Fresh sausage will keep for 3 days in the refrigerator, or for up to 2 months in the freezer.

Kentucky-Style Pork Sausage

Makes 3½ pounds

THIS SAUSAGE IS USUALLY USED IN BULK, ALTHOUGH YOU CAN STUFF THE meat into hog casings if you prefer links. To serve for breakfast, traditional style, slice the sausage into ½-inch-thick patties and fry them in a skillet until brown.

2 pounds pork butt	*1 teaspoon ground cayenne pepper*
1 pound pork back fat	*1 teaspoon ground coriander*
1 tablespoon kosher salt	*½ teaspoon freshly grated*
2 teaspoons freshly ground black	*nutmeg*
pepper	*½ cup water*
2 teaspoons ground sage	*Medium hog casings (optional)*

FOR DETAILS ON MAKING SAUSAGE, SEE PAGE 10.

Grind the pork and fat through a ¼-inch plate. In a large bowl, mix the meat, fat, salt, black pepper, sage, cayenne, coriander, nutmeg, and water, kneading and squeezing until all the ingredients are well blended. If you are making the sausage for patties, shape the meat into one large roll, 2 inches in diameter, wrap in waxed paper, and refrigerate until you are ready to use it.

For links, stuff the sausage into medium hog casings and tie at 5-inch intervals. Like most fresh sausage, if wrapped tightly, this will keep in the refrigerator for 3 days, or in the freezer for 2 months.

Iowa Farm Sausage

Makes about 3 pounds

MADE THROUGHOUT THE AMERICAN MIDWEST ON FARMS AND IN SMALL butcher shops, this is the quintessential American breakfast sausage patty. Leave in bulk form, and freeze in packets large enough to feed your family.

2¼ pounds pork butt	*1 teaspoon dried basil*
¾ pound pork back fat	*1 teaspoon red pepper flakes*
¼ cup finely chopped fresh parsley	*1 teaspoon coarsely ground*
¼ cup finely chopped onion	*black pepper*
1 tablespoon kosher salt	*1 teaspoon ground ginger*
2 teaspoons ground sage	*½ teaspoon minced garlic*
1 teaspoon dried thyme	*¼ cup water*

FOR DETAILS ON SAUSAGE MAKING, SEE PAGE 10.

Grind the meat and fat together through a ⅛- or ¼-inch plate. In a large bowl, mix the ground meat and fat with the parsley, onion, salt, sage, thyme, basil, red pepper, black pepper, ginger, garlic, and water. Knead and squeeze the mixture until everything is well blended.

Package the bulk sausage in plastic wrap. This fresh sausage will keep in the refrigerator for 3 days, or in the freezer for 2 months.

•▾•

Yankee Sage Sausage

Makes about 4 pounds

Nᴇᴡ Eɴɢʟᴀɴᴅ ᴄᴏᴜɴᴛʀʏ ᴄᴏᴏᴋs ʜᴀᴠᴇ ʟᴏɴɢ ᴍᴀᴅᴇ ᴀ ꜰʟᴀᴠᴏʀꜰᴜʟ sᴀᴜsᴀɢᴇ from the traditional English mix of ground pork, sage, and black pepper, but they've added a few ingredients of their own. These often include exotic spices brought home by their seafaring ancestors. This recipe, adapted from Judith and Evan Jones's *The L. L. Bean Book of New New England Cookery*, is another regional variation of the basic American sage-flavored sausage. Ginger and cloves give the sausage a bit more spice than usual, and the mix of herbs contributes a lovely aroma. Use it in any recipe calling for fresh country-style sausage.

3 pounds pork butt
½ to ¾ pound pork back fat
3 tablespoons finely chopped or
   dried and crumbled fresh sage,
   or 2 to 3 teaspoons ground sage
3½ teaspoons kosher salt
1 tablespoon coarsely ground
   black pepper
¼ teaspoon ground cayenne pepper

¼ teaspoon dried summer savory
¼ teaspoon dried marjoram
¼ teaspoon dried thyme
⅛ teaspoon ground ginger
Pinch of ground cloves
¼ cup water
Sheep or medium hog casings
   (optional)

Fᴏʀ ᴅᴇᴛᴀɪʟs ᴏɴ ᴍᴀᴋɪɴɢ sᴀᴜsᴀɢᴇ, sᴇᴇ ᴘᴀɢᴇ 10.

Grind the meat and fat through a ¼-inch plate. In a large bowl, mix the meat, fat, salt, sage, black pepper, cayenne, summer savory, marjoram, thyme, ginger, and cloves with the cold water. Knead and squeeze the mixture until thoroughly blended.

You can stuff the meat into sheep or medium hog casings and tie into 5-inch links, but it is quite good as bulk sausage. Simply form the meat into thick ½-pound rolls, wrap, and refrigerate or freeze. The sausage keeps for 3 days in the refrigerator, or for 2 months in the freezer.

Drying Fresh Sage
To dry fresh sage: spread the leaves on a cookie sheet and bake at 350° for a few minutes, until the leaves are dry and you can crumble them in your hands.

Country Ham and Pork Sausage

Makes about 4 pounds

Most commercial hams pale in comparison to country hams. Some of the more heavily smoked versions, like Black Forest ham, can be substituted if you can't find the real thing. In the South and Midwest, and in specialty meat shops elsewhere, you can often find good-quality country ham vacuum-wrapped by the slice. If you're lucky enough to have a whole country ham, this recipe gives you a good way to use the trimmed fat and any leftover meat. Another good source for ham is a Chinese pork butcher. Smoked ham is an integral part of many Hunan dishes, and Chinese cooks value the flavor and quality of the Smithfield variety.

We had no trouble finding excellent Smithfield ham in San Francisco's Chinatown. An added advantage is that you can buy the ham in Chinatown by the piece, so you don't have to get a whole ham just to make this sausage.

The sausage can be substituted in any recipe that calls for country ham, and we've used it in place of ham in some traditional dishes. It works particularly well in recipes that depend on long, slow braising and where you want a smoky ham flavor. Be sure not to add salt to this recipe because country ham is usually quite salty and should season the mixture very nicely just by itself. Start with ½ pound ham, then fry and taste a small patty of the sausage. You can add more ham if you want a saltier and more intense ham flavor.

½ to ¾ pound leftover boiled or baked country ham or ¾ pound raw country ham	1 teaspoon freshly ground black pepper
2 pounds pork butt	1 teaspoon red pepper flakes
½ pound fat trimmed from ham	1 teaspoon ground ginger
½ pound fresh pork back fat	½ teaspoon ground sage
2 ounces skin from ham (optional)	¼ teaspoon ground cloves
1 teaspoon sugar	¾ to 1 cup water
	Medium hog casings (optional)

FOR DETAILS ON MAKING SAUSAGE SEE PAGE 10.

If you are starting out with raw country ham, simmer a ¾-pound piece for about 2 hours, and then cool before grinding. The ham stock can be used for pea or bean soup (see pages 164–165). Taste to make sure it's not too salty, though.

Grind the pork butt through a ⅜-inch plate. Grind the ham, ham fat, pork fat, and skin through a ⅛-inch plate. Thoroughly mix together the ground meats, fat, and skin with the sugar, black pepper, red pepper, ginger, sage, cloves, and water by kneading and squeezing.

For links, stuff into medium hog casings, and tie into 5-inch links. Refrigerate the sausages for up to 5 days or freeze for 2 months.

Country Ham

Country ham is one of the delights of American cooking. The hams from Smithfield County in Virginia have the greatest reputation and are widely available. With their smoky and pungent aroma and a special flavor that is reputed to come from the peanuts the hogs feed on, Smithfield hams are on a par with the great hams of Westphalia, York, Parma, Bayonne, the Dalmatian coast, and the mountains of Auvergne, all with their own regional styles and special flavors. Country hams from other regions have special characteristics derived from the feed of the pigs (peaches, corn mash, peanuts, etc.), the type of cure (dry salt, brine, honey, sugar), and the smoking medium (hickory, oak, corncobs). Hams from Georgia, Kentucky, Tennessee, and Vermont are especially prized. Country hams are usually quite salty and require soaking and simmering before eating.

•▪•

Smoked sausage is usually seasoned with the same spices used to make fresh sausage. As always, there are regional variations, but most smoked country sausage contains the basic mix of pork and sage, with red and black pepper for emphasis. Often, smoked sausage is not tied into individual links. Instead, a continuous rope of sausage is coiled around a stick in large, one-foot loops. Customers simply say to the butcher, "I'll take a foot or two of that there smoked sausage," and it is sliced off and wrapped. Hickory is the most common wood used for smoking sausage, bacon, and ham; but depending on the area, maple, apple, cherry, oak, or pecan can also be used.

2¼ pounds pork butt
¾ pound pork back fat
1 tablespoon brown sugar
1 tablespoon kosher salt
1 tablespoon sweet Hungarian
  paprika
2 teaspoons red pepper flakes

1 teaspoon ground sage
1 teaspoon dried thyme
Pinch of ground allspice
¾ teaspoon curing salts (page 21)
  (optional)
½ cup water
Medium hog casings

For details on making sausage, see page 10.

Grind the pork butt through a ⅜-inch plate. Grind the fat through a ¼-inch plate. In a large bowl, mix together the pork and fat by kneading and squeezing with the brown sugar, salt, paprika, red pepper, sage, thyme, and allspice. To cold smoke the sausage for later use, dissolve the curing salts in the water and add to the mixture. To hot smoke and eat the sausage directly after making it, you won't need any curing salts. Just add the water to the meat and spices, and knead and squeeze everything together thoroughly.

Stuff into medium hog casings, coiling the sausage as you go.

To cold smoke, loop 1-foot lengths of sausage over a 3- to 4-foot smoke stick made of ½-inch doweling. Air-dry in a cool place in front of a fan overnight until the surface is dry to the touch. Cold smoke for 8 to 10 hours, following the techniques described on page 17. Or hot smoke according to the directions on page 18.

Store cold-smoked sausage for 10 to 12 days in the refrigerator or for up to 2 months in the freezer. If you hot smoke the sausage, it will keep fresh for 1 week in the refrigerator or for 2 months in the freezer.

Sausages Add Lots of Flavor

Sausages have an uncanny ability to flavor even the blandest ingredients. All over the world, sausage is used to add spice and excitement to virtually every kind of starch, staple, and vegetable. Rice, potatoes, beans, pasta, and vegetables of all types gain new dimensions with the addition of sausage. And just about every cuisine has its own sausage, its own flavor signature. From the lamb- and garlic-infused *merguez* of North Africa and the peppery Sicilian *salsicce* to the mild and aromatic American breakfast sausage and the sweet and savory *lop chong*, sausages are used in every way imaginable in soups, stews, and salads, as snacks and pick-me-ups, as flavorings, and often as main courses in themselves. Chicken and turkey sausages can also deliver all the flavor of these traditional sausages, but without the high fat and salt content of many commercial varieties.

Sausage has the added advantages of being quick and easy to use and is an inexpensive source of protein. Peasant cooks from northern Europe to Peking have always known that a bit of sausage can be fried up quickly to flavor large quantities of the everyday staple. Sausage often contains all the spice you need for rice or pasta, for example, and you don't have to spend a lot of time preparing and cooking other ingredients. And a little bit of sausage goes a very long way. Many of our recipes call for as little as one-half to one pound of spicy sausage to flavor a dish intended for four to six people.

Cutting Fat

Recipes with poultry keep fat to a minimum needed for flavor, and most recipes using our low-fat poultry sausage suggest that it be browned in a little oil before adding to the dish. If you really want the fat levels low, you can brown the sausage in a nonstick pan without adding oil, and then drain off and discard any fat remaining. You'll lose some flavor, but if you are a fanatic about cutting the calories, that's the way to do it. For salads and pastas where the oil is part of the dressing or sauce, you should use at least half the oil and not drain off the pan juices. A good way to remove fat from soups, sauces, and stews is to blot it up by laying a paper towel briefly on top and then removing the towel with the fat it has soaked up. Use as many pieces of paper towel as you need until all the fat is gone.

Chicken and Apple Sausage

Makes about 4 pounds

We've taken the traditional country sausage recipe and lightened it up a bit by using chicken in place of pork, and by adding dried apples, cider, and sweet hints of cinnamon and ginger. The essential flavors are still there, but without the excess fat and cholesterol of earlier versions. You can use this mild and aromatic sausage wherever you want the characteristic flavors of American country sausage.

You can serve this sausage as a main course with a spicy sauce or relish, or use it as a flavoring agent for vegetables, beans, or rice. We also use the mildly sweet sausage in our Kids' Favorite Chicken and Apple Meat Loaf with Cider Gravy (page 277). We think Chicken and Apple Sausage is delicious as a stuffing for poultry, and even for fish. It is especially good in our Onion, Sausage, and Apple Stuffing (page 299).

Our section on breakfast lists many uses for a lightly spiced sausage including Sausage and Creamy Eggs in Popovers (page 130), and stuffed French toast (page 133), where fried patties are inserted between pieces of French toast and covered with sautéed apples and a syrup made from fresh apple cider.

While we think that all our sausages are delicious when left in bulk and frozen for use as patties or in recipes, our Chicken and Apple Sausage is one that you might also consider stuffing into links. This is not a particularly difficult process and can be the basis for a sausage-making party for family and friends. If you do decide to make links, you should prepare a double or triple recipe to provide enough sausage for many delicious breakfasts to come.

1 cup apple cider
3½ pounds boned chicken thighs
*   with skin (about 4½ pounds*
*   with bones) or 3¼ pounds*
*   ground chicken*
3 ounces dried apples
4 teaspoons kosher salt
2 teaspoons freshly ground
*   black pepper*

2 teaspoons dried sage
¼ teaspoon ground ginger
⅛ teaspoon ground cinnamon
⅛ teaspoon ground nutmeg
1 chicken bouillon cube dissolved
*   in 2 tablespoons boiling water*
Medium sausage casings
*   (optional)*

FOR DETAILS ON MAKING SAUSAGE, SEE PAGE 10.

In a small nonreactive saucepan, boil down the cider almost to a syrup, about 2 to 3 tablespoons. Cool and reserve.

If you are using chicken thighs, coarsely grind with a ⅜-inch plate the boned chicken and skin or chop coarsely in batches in a food processor. Transfer the ground chicken to a large bowl and add the apple cider, apples, salt, black pepper, sage, ginger, cinnamon, nutmeg, and dissolved bouillon. Knead and squeeze the mixture until well blended. Fry a small patty until done and taste for salt, pepper, and other seasonings.

Divide the sausage into 7 or 8 portions (each about ½ pound), wrap tightly in plastic wrap or aluminum foil, and refrigerate or freeze for later use. Or, if desired, stuff the sausage into casings and tie into 5-inch links.

Refrigerated, this sausage will keep for 3 days, or for 2 months in the freezer.

From the South (by Way of Louisiana)

THE SOUTH'S FIRST PIGS WANDERED OFF FROM SPANISH EXPEDITIONS ALONG the Gulf Coast in the 1500s. They thrived in the palmetto groves, rooting in the lush and muddy undergrowth of southern swamps—pig paradise. Others escaped from Jamestown's Hog Island and roamed the tangled forests of the Tidewater. From the beginning, hogs were raised in settlements and plantations up and down Virginia and the Carolinas. These half-wild razorbacks fed on acorns and hickory nuts, wild persimmons and chestnuts, the rich mast of the forest floor. Fattened on table scraps or what it could find in the back streets of frontier towns, fed on corncobs and hot mash, the pig became the South's main source of protein. Fatback, salt back, white bacon, sow-belly or middlin', Virginia ham or country sausage, chitterlings or hog jowl, ham hocks or cracklin'—pork was the meat most often found on southern tables, of rich or poor, of Tidewater planters or leaner folk from up-country.

The pig offered real benefits to frontier settlers. No other animal, domestic or otherwise, gets fat so fast, increasing its body weight 150 times in the first 8 months. Hogs are remarkably self-sufficient, able to feed on the lowliest of foods from farmhouse leavings to whatever they root out from forest or swamp. And the pig thrives on local southern products such as peanuts, peaches, and, especially, corn.

Pork has another advantage over other meats. Because of the subtle unctuousness of its fat and the sweet blandness of its flesh, it usually tastes better preserved (pickled or salted, smoked or seasoned) than fresh. Put up in myriad ways, a constant source of nourishment throughout the year, pork became the South's main meat. It was cooked fresh at butchering time in the fall, but pork was most prominent in southern cooking in its preserved forms—cured and smoked as bacon or ham, laid down in the pork barrel as side meat or fatback, seasoned with herbs and spices as sausage. Its importance is evident from the records of an early plantation on the James River. In just one year, the planter's family, servants, slaves, and guests consumed over 27,000 pounds of different kinds of pork.

Country-style sausage, based on pork, sage, pepper, and other spices, is a staple of southern cooking. There are many regional variations that range from mild to sweet to very spicy. Sausage is served as a breakfast patty or link for Southern breakfasts and is also used to season greens, beans, and rice in many traditional dishes.

Louisiana, however, is where the South's love of sausage reaches its height. The region's cooking makes heavy use of spicy sausages created by Cajun and Creole pork butchers. Louisiana cooking is rooted in French techniques, enriched by native ingredients and cooking methods, and nurtured by cooks from various lands and cultures. Much of the excitement of the cuisine comes from this energetic amalgam of French cuisine with Native American, African, Spanish, and other European traditions and ingredients.

Louisiana was French colony, then Spanish, then French again just before being sold to the United States in 1803. As elsewhere in our burgeoning country, colonists borrowed heavily from local tribes—the Houmas and Opelousas, Choctaw and Natchez—using plants grown in their gardens like corn, squash, and beans, along with native game, fish, and herbs. Choctaw women were long a colorful part of the French market, selling filé powder (ground sassafras), bundles of bay leaves, and other herbs. The abundant game and seafood that is still featured in so many Louisiana gumbos and stews along with filé, bay leaves, and other local ingredients tie these dishes to the Native American tradition.

Black cooks have been a strong influence in Louisiana cookery ever since the introduction of African slaves. Black cooks prepared the food on plantations, adapting traditional European recipes and often using ingredients brought over from Africa, including eggplants, yams, peanuts, sesame, and okra. In fact, the word for the ubiquitous stew of the region, gumbo, derives from the West African word for okra, "ngombo."

In the 1750s and in the years following, French-speaking farmers and fishermen displaced from Acadia (later Nova Scotia) by the English conquest of Quebec drifted up the bayous and rivers west of New Orleans and created a rich and vibrant culture in the swamps and on the prairies. These Acadians, or Cajuns, as they came to be called, incorporated local ingredients into their own Norman and Breton traditions and came up with an earthy, vibrant style of cooking that makes the heart—and the taste buds—sing. Using hot peppers and local spices, the Cajuns cooked just about anything that walked, flew, swam, or crawled in the region, and added energy and a peasant richness to the elegant Creole cuisine of New Orleans. Later,

French-speaking émigrés from the French Revolution and Toussaint' L'Ouverture's slave revolt in Haiti added even more elegance and Gallic spice to Louisiana life and food.

In the nineteenth century, immigrants from other European countries found their way to New Orleans, by then a thriving port for midwestern America and its products. The Irish settled along Irish Channel, Germans occupied the Côte des Allemands upriver from the city, and Italians, Chinese, Greeks, and East European Jews all added to Louisiana's ethnic and culinary richness. Some of New Orleans' most popular dishes, such as muffaletta, po' boys, and ya ca mein, have their origins in the bars and restaurants of neighborhoods like the Third District and the Irish Channel.

Sausages and preserved meats are an integral part of Louisiana cookery and contribute character and flavor to many traditional dishes, from gumbo and jambalaya to chicken étouffée and red beans and rice. Sausage is used as a main ingredient, as a flavoring, and as a spice to add background and color. Cajun and Creole cooks, perhaps more than any others in America, use local sausages to define their style of cooking and to add an extra dimension of flavor.

Many of the region's most popular sausages bear names of traditional French sausages, such as boudin noir and boudin blanc, andouille, and saucisse; others have Spanish roots, such as chaurice, or plain English names like hot or smoked sausage. But all have distinctly Louisiana flavors, and many have little resemblance to the originals. Andouille in France, and in earlier times in New Orleans, contained chopped-up chitterlings, or intestines, stuffed into casings. The modern version is a spicy, chunky pork sausage and is heavily smoked. Chaurice is hot and spicy, similar to Mexican or Spanish chorizo, but the Louisiana sausage is a unique and fiery mix of onions, herbs, and ground pork. Cajun boudin has some vague relation to the delicate French boudin blanc, but its heat level would make the average Parisian's eyes bulge with astonishment.

Sausages are made all over Louisiana, but the Cajuns around Lafayette and New Iberia are the acknowledged masters of andouille and boudin. Signs advertising "Hot Boudin, Cold Beer, and Fais Do-Do This Sunday" testify to the Cajun love of hot food, cold brew, and letting the good times roll with dancing and zydeco music. Spicy smoked pork shoulder, tasso, is another Cajun specialty and is used to "hot up" many favorite dishes like jambalaya and red beans and rice.

Makes about 4 pounds

W E SUGGEST YOU USE THIS SAUSAGE WHEREVER YOU WANT A SLIGHTLY SMOKY, decidedly spicy note. It can dress up beans, pasta, salads, and vegetables by adding lots of flavor without excessive amounts of fat or cholesterol. This poultry-based variation of chaurice is lighter than the pork version but just as fiery.

2 cups sliced onions
1½ pounds boned chicken thighs
    without skin (about 2 pounds
    with bones) or 1½ pounds
    ground chicken
1½ pounds boned turkey thighs
    without skin (about 2 pounds
    with bones) or 1½ pounds
    ground turkey
½ pound bacon, cut into pieces
¼ cup sweet Hungarian paprika
1½ tablespoons chopped garlic
1 tablespoon freshly ground black
    pepper

2 teaspoons yellow mustard seeds
2 teaspoons dried thyme
1 teaspoon English-style dry
    mustard
1 teaspoon sugar
1 teaspoon cayenne pepper
1 teaspoon dried sage
1 teaspoon dried oregano
1 teaspoon red pepper flakes
½ teaspoon ground allspice
Medium hog casings

FOR DETAILS ON MAKING SAUSAGE, SEE PAGE 10.

Simmer the onions in water to cover until translucent, 5 to 7 minutes. Cool under cold running water, and drain. (Make sure the onions are cool. They can be cooked ahead of time and refrigerated for later use.)

With a ⅜-inch plate, coarsely grind the onions with the chicken, turkey, and bacon or chop coarsely in batches in a food processor. If using previously ground chicken or turkey, coarsely grind or chop the onions and bacon and mix thoroughly with the ground poultry. In a large bowl, combine the ground meat mixture with the paprika, garlic, black pepper, mustard seeds, thyme, dry mustard, sugar, cayenne, sage, oregano, red pepper flakes, and allspice. Knead and squeeze thoroughly with your hands. Fry a small patty until done and taste for salt, pepper, and other seasonings.

Stuff into medium hog casings and tie into 5-inch links. Keeps 3 days refrigerated, or 2 months in the freezer.

Hot Boudin

Makes 4 pounds

Cooking Note
Boudin is best heated by steaming. Coil the boudin in a colander or on a plate and place it in a large pot above an inch or so of water. Cover the pot and steam over moderate heat for 15 minutes. Steaming boudin in the casing is the traditional way to heat up the sausage, but we like to form the meat into thin patties and fry it for breakfast or a quick and spicy lunch. It helps to add an egg or two to the mixture to bind it before frying. This is as good as any corned-beef or roast-beef hash you've ever tasted.

EVERY CULTURE HAS A FAVORITE SNACK FOOD, WHETHER IT'S PEANUT BUTTER and jelly or satay, tacos or a bowl of noodles. In the Cajun country of southwest Louisiana, the universal snack seems to be hot boudin. Everywhere you go, on country back roads or the main streets of towns like Lafayette, Opelousas, or Breaux Bridge, you see signs advertising this spicy sausage. The smell of boudin steaming evokes the sounds of Cajun fiddlers and accordion players warming up for their Saturday morning jams. There is always a greasy sack or two of boudin ripped open and spread on newspaper to munch on during the festivities.

Although this spicy mixture of rice, cooked pork, and onions is stuffed into a casing, the casing itself is rarely eaten. The boudin's casing gets a bit tough from steaming, and its stuffing is so soft and juicy that everything seems to gush out when you bite down. The best thing to do is to abandon any hope of elegant dining, and hold the boudin in one hand, put one end into your mouth, and squeeze the savory mixture out of the casing into your mouth as you go along.

4 to 5 cups water	1 cup uncooked long-grain rice
3½ teaspoons kosher salt	2 teaspoons minced garlic
3 pounds pork butt, cut into 2-inch chunks (make sure there is some fat attached to the meat)	2 teaspoons red pepper flakes
	2 teaspoons ground cayenne pepper
	1 teaspoon ground sage
	1 teaspoon ground thyme
4 bay leaves	⅛ teaspoon ground allspice
2 whole fresh chile peppers such as jalapeño	Pinch of ground mace
	½ cup finely chopped fresh parsley (flat-leaf variety preferred)
2 teaspoons freshly ground black pepper	¾ cup finely chopped green onions or scallions
Pinch dried thyme	Medium hog casings (optional)
1 large onion, quartered	

FOR DETAILS ON MAKING SAUSAGE, SEE PAGE 10.

Combine the water and 1 teaspoon of the salt in a saucepan large enough to hold the pork along with any bones or scraps. Bring the liquid to a boil and add the pork, bay leaves, chile peppers, 1 teaspoon of the black pepper, and dried thyme. Return the liquid to a boil, reduce the heat, and simmer, covered, over low heat for 45 to 60 minutes, or until the pork is tender. Add the onion and cook for 5 to 7 minutes, until tender. Strain the mixture. Transfer the meat and onions to a platter to cool and discard the chile peppers and bay leaves. Measure out 1½ cups of the pork stock and combine with the rice in the pot. Cover and simmer over low heat until tender, about 20 minutes.

In a meat grinder fitted with a ¼-inch plate, grind the cooked pork and onions into a large mixing bowl. Add the garlic, red pepper flakes, cayenne, sage, thyme, allspice, mace, parsley, the remaining 1 teaspoon of black pepper, and the remaining 2½ teaspoons of salt, along with the chopped green onions and the cooked rice. Using a wooden spoon, stir the mixture until it is well blended. Taste and correct the salt or other seasonings.

Cool the mixture in the refrigerator for 30 minutes, and then stuff it into medium hog casings or leave it in bulk for further use. It's not necessary to tie boudin into links—just coil it up as you go along. Boudin is quite perishable and should be refrigerated immediately after being made. If it is not going to be used in 2 to 3 days, it should be frozen for up to 2 months.

Hot Boudin and Dixie Beer

The roads outside of Breaux Bridge, Louisiana, run along levees high above the flat countryside, skirting the bayous and swamps of Cajun country. Each little town has its own mom-and-pop grocery story, and just about every one has a hand-lettered sign announcing "Hot Boudin" in the front window. That's what we're here for.

The smell's the first thing you notice when you walk into one of these country stores: pork and onions and pepper from the quintessential Cajun snack—boudin. The sausage is usually right on the counter by the cash register, keeping hot in a slow cooker or baby-bottle warmer. Boudin is not twisted into links in Cajun country. You just show the man how much sausage you want, and he cuts a length from the coil and wraps it in waxed paper. The rest is up to you.

When you walk out into the parking lot, the smell of the boudin becomes well-nigh irresistible. Most people can't wait to get home, or even into the car, before they start eating. Standing in the hot sun with your Dixie beer or Barq's Root Beer in your left hand, you grab one end of the hot boudin in your right hand, put the other end in your mouth, and squeeze. Suddenly you know why it's called *hot* boudin. For a second you're not sure of survival as the incandescent mixture gushes into your mouth. Then as the sweat pops out on your forehead and the flavors begin to sing, you experience the bliss that only Cajun boudin can give.

A long draft of ice-cold Dixie beer prepares the palate for another onslaught, and you squeeze and squeeze again until the casing's limp and empty. Then you toss the beer can, waxed paper, and boudin casing into an old oil drum full of beer cans, waxed paper, and boudin casings, and head for the next town. And the next boudin.

On and on through a long, hot, and spicy day, until at sunset we're standing in yet another parking lot, waiting for the roadhouse that serves great alligator gumbo to open up, snacking on one more boudin, just for comparison, hearing the accordions and fiddles tuning up inside, licking hot grease from tired lips.

French Toast Stuffed with Chicken and Apple Sausage (*page 131*)

Nancy's Asian Dipping Sauce *(page 152)*, Savory Thai Seafood and Sausage Dumplings *(page 154)*, and My Pot Stickers *(page 153)*

Corn and Sausage Chowder *(page 162)*

Makes about 3¹/₂
pounds

Sometimes you can smell them for blocks away when the wind is right, and you speed the car up to get to the barbecue joint just a little quicker. As you get closer, your mouth starts to water, and you know that in just a few minutes you'll be chomping down on one of the great sausages in the world: a barbecued Hot Link. Smoky and spicy, barbecued Hot Links make for good eating on a French roll with lots of tangy barbecue sauce or tucked into a pot of beans or a mess of boiled greens with cornbread.

1½ pounds beef chuck
½ pound pork shoulder
1 pound pork back fat
½ cup water
2 tablespoons finely chopped garlic
1½ tablespoons kosher salt
1 tablespoon sweet Hungarian
  paprika
1 tablespoon coarsely ground
  black pepper

2 teaspoons sugar
1 teaspoon dried marjoram
2 teaspoons ground cayenne pepper
½ teaspoon dried sage
Pinch of ground allspice
Pinch of cardamom
Pinch of cloves
Pinch of coriander
Pinch of cinnamon
Medium hog casings

For details on making sausage, see page 10.

Grind the meats and fat through a ⅜-inch plate. In a large bowl, mix the ground fat and meats with the water, garlic, salt, paprika, black pepper, sugar, marjoram, cayenne, sage, allspice, cardamom, cloves, coriander, and cinnamon. Knead with your hands until everything is well blended.

Stuff into medium hog casings, and tie into 6-inch links. Dry overnight on a rack in the refrigerator.

Hot smoke, following the directions on page 18, until the internal temperature of the sausages reaches 155° to 160°.

Hot Links will keep in the refrigerator for 4 to 5 days, or in the freezer for 2 months.

Serving Hot Links
To reheat these sausages, grill on a covered barbecue for 3 to 5 minutes per side. Serve with plenty of barbecue sauce.

Cajun-Style Andouille

Makes about 5 pounds

This spicy, heavily smoked sausage is a Louisiana favorite, and one of the most versatile and full-flavored sausages in this book. There are so many uses for andouille that we could have written a whole cookbook based on this wonderful sausage alone. In France, andouille and its close relative, andouillette, are made from intestines wrapped in a casing. This sausage was originally made this way in Louisiana (it was called chitterling sausage in *The Picayune's Creole Cook Book*, published in New Orleans in 1901), but these days andouille is made from large chunks of highly seasoned lean pork, stuffed into sausage casings and then cold smoked. It is traditionally used to flavor gumbo and jambalaya, but inventive cooks have found many other uses for its tangy, smoky flavors. Andouille is best cold smoked for at least 12 hours to give it a rich smoky flavor; you'll need to add curing salts if you cold smoke it. If you prefer to leave curing salts out, hot smoking will give enough of the smoky taste that makes andouille so popular.

3 tablespoons sweet Hungarian paprika	½ teaspoon dried thyme
2 tablespoons minced garlic	¼ teaspoon ground mace
2 tablespoons kosher salt	1 teaspoon curing salts (page 21) (optional)
2 tablespoons sugar	5 pounds pork butt, fat and lean separated, cut into 2-inch chunks
1 tablespoon freshly ground black pepper	
2 teaspoons ground cayenne pepper	½ cup water
1 teaspoon red pepper flakes	Wide hog casings

For details on making sausage, see page 10.

Mix the paprika, garlic, salt, sugar, black pepper, cayenne, red pepper, thyme, and mace along with the curing salts in a small bowl. Separate the meat and fat into 2 bowls, and rub each thoroughly with the spice mixture. Cover and refrigerate overnight.

Grind the lean meat using a ⅜-inch plate. Grind the fat in a meat grinder fitted with a ¼-inch plate. Mix the meat and fat together in a large bowl, add the cold water, and knead and squeeze until the water is absorbed and the spices are well blended.

Stuff the mixture into wide hog casings.

If you are hot smoking the sausages, dry for 2 hours in a cool

Chaurice

Makes about 3½ pounds

The name most likely derives from *chorizo*, a Spanish and Mexican pork sausage, and chaurice is part of Louisiana's Latin heritage. It is also one of the hottest sausages in a cuisine known for its fiery flavors. Our recipe is a traditional Louisiana version, but just about every local butcher shop has its own variations. Most chaurice is pure pork, but sometimes beef is included. It is usually fresh, but some sausage makers give it a light smoke.

Most recipes contain onions and parsley, along with chile powder, cayenne, garlic, and aromatic herbs and spices. We like to blanch the onions in boiling water for a minute or so to take away their raw, sometimes metallic, taste. Use only fresh parsley, preferably the flat-leaf Italian variety. Forget about dried parsley—it's like using dried grass clippings.

In Louisiana, chaurice is sometimes fried for breakfast, but it takes an iron stomach to eat such hot food first thing in the morning. It's great used to make a Hot Sausage Po' Boy (see page 178). Because the onions give chaurice such a savory flavor, it goes well with lentils, cabbage, and potatoes. At Aidells Sausage we make a smoked chaurice, which is our favorite sausage with sauerkraut.

Chaurice is often called "Hot Sausage" in Louisiana, but don't get it confused with the "Louisiana Hot Sausage" found in other parts of the country that is generally a poor-quality emulsified German-style pork sausage with a predominant flavor of cayenne. It's not very good, never found in New Orleans, and a poor substitute for chaurice.

1 onion, coarsely chopped
2¼ pounds pork butt
¾ pound pork back fat
3 tablespoons pure New Mexico chile powder
4 teaspoons kosher salt
2 teaspoons minced garlic
2 teaspoons ground cayenne pepper
2 teaspoons red pepper flakes
1 teaspoon sugar
1½ teaspoons dried thyme
1 teaspoon freshly ground black pepper
½ teaspoon ground bay leaf (use blender or spice mill)
½ teaspoon ground allspice
½ cup finely chopped fresh parsley (flat-leaf variety preferred)
Medium hog casings

For details on making sausage, see page 10.

Bring 2 quarts of water to a boil and blanch the chopped onion for 2 minutes. Strain and cool under running water.

Combine the meat, fat, chile powder, salt, garlic, cayenne, red pepper flakes, sugar, thyme, black pepper, bay leaf, allspice, and onions in a large bowl. Marinate the mixture in the refrigerator for at least 30 minutes or up to 4 hours.

Grind the mixture through a ¼-inch plate. Add the parsley and knead and squeeze to mix the meat and flavorings thoroughly.

Stuff the mixture into medium hog casings and tie into 5-inch links.

If you wish, you can hot smoke the chaurice using the method discussed on page 18. Keeps for 3 days refrigerated, or 2 months frozen.

Pickled Pork

Makes 10 to 12 pounds

Вотн ог these versions of preserved pork involve curing chunks of pork shoulder pickled in brine. Pickled pork is ready for use after it is fully cured. It is similar to the French *petit salé*, and, like the French product, pickled pork is usually boiled as a flavoring with legumes or other vegetables. Pickled pork is most often found in the famous Louisiana Monday night dinner, red beans and rice.

Tasso takes pickled pork a step further because it is heavily seasoned and smoked. It is used as a flavoring agent in many Cajun dishes, and adds zest and spice to jambalaya and gumbo. Along with these Louisiana favorites, it also is delicious in any dish where you might use bacon, ham, prosciutto, pancetta, or salt pork for flavor.

While neither tasso nor pickled pork is, strictly speaking, sausage, pickled pork meat is often made into a tasty pickled-pork sausage in New Orleans and the surrounding countryside (see page 50). Tasso is paired with sausages for flavoring in many gumbos and stews. Both preserved meats are an integral part of the spicy cuisines of southern Louisiana and provide much of the flavor in its traditional dishes.

2 boneless pork butts (10 to
    12 pounds total)
18 ounces kosher salt (2 cups)
8 ounces sugar (1 cup)
4 quarts water

4 ounces (½ cup) curing salts
    (page 21)
1 teaspoon red pepper flakes
    (optional)

Cut each pork butt into 5 or 6 large chunks of approximately equal size. In a 2-gallon or larger stainless steel, plastic, crockery, or glass container, dissolve the salt and sugar in the water, stirring continuously until completely dissolved. Add the curing salts and stir until dissolved. Add red pepper flakes and submerge the meat completely in this brine by placing a heavy plate or weight on top. Refrigerate the meat in the brine for 2 days. To see if the pork is completely cured, cut a chunk in half. The pork should be uniformly pink throughout. If it is not, leave the meat in the brine in the refrigerator for another day. Repeat the test. Once the pork is completely pickled, it can be used directly, or serve as a base for Pickled-Pork Sausage or Tasso.

To store pickled pork, wash the cured meat under cold running water, drain, and store it in a covered container for up to 1 week. For longer storage, pickled pork can also be frozen for up to 2 months.

Tasso

Makes 9 to 11 pounds

Tasso is made by rubbing brine-cured pickled pork with a blend of herbs and spices, and then air-drying and cold smoking it using an aromatic wood such as hickory, pecan, or apple. Remember, the tasso is not cooked, so do not eat it as is. It must be cooked thoroughly before eating.

*10 to 12 pounds Pickled Pork
  (page 48)
½ cup sweet Hungarian paprika
½ cup pure New Mexican chile
  powder
¼ cup minced garlic*

*¼ cup freshly ground black pepper
¼ cup ground cayenne pepper
¼ cup red pepper flakes
1 teaspoon ground sage
1 teaspoon dried thyme*

While the pickled pork is draining, mix together the paprika, ground chiles, garlic, black pepper, cayenne, red pepper, sage, and thyme in a large bowl. Roll each chunk of pickled pork in the spice mixture. Shake off the excess. Using meat hooks or string, suspend the meat in a cool place, and let it dry overnight with a fan. The surface should be dry to the touch.

Set up a smoker for cold smoking (see page 17). Smoke the tasso at no greater than 120° for 12 to 24 hours, stirring and adding sawdust if needed. Remove the meat from the smoke when it's done, and cool it to room temperature.

Loosely wrapped and refrigerated, tasso will keep for 2 weeks. It can also be frozen for up to 2 months.

Pickled-Pork Sausage

Makes about 3 pounds

⬤ ⬤

THIS SPICY SAUSAGE USES PICKLED PORK IN PLACE OF FRESH PORK AND IS great in bean dishes or anywhere you want a tangy flavor.

2½ to 3 pounds Pickled Pork
   (page 48)
1 tablespoon coarsely ground
   black pepper
2 teaspoons minced garlic
1 teaspoon red pepper flakes
¼ teaspoon ground cayenne pepper

¼ teaspoon ground sage
¼ teaspoon dried thyme
Pinch of ground allspice
¾ pound fresh pork back fat
¼ cup water
Wide hog casings

FOR DETAILS ON MAKING SAUSAGE, SEE PAGE 10.

Wash the pickled pork under cold running water and drain well. In a small bowl, mix the black pepper, garlic, red pepper flakes, cayenne, sage, thyme, and allspice. Cut the pickled pork and fat into strips small enough to go through the meat grinder. Toss the strips with the spice mixture.

Grind the meat and fat through a ⅜-inch plate. Add the water and knead the meat mixture thoroughly.

Stuff the mixture into large hog casings, and tie into 8- to 10-inch links. Suspend the sausages on a rack over a bowl in a cool place, and dry overnight in front of a fan. The sausages should be dry to the touch.

Set up a smoker for cold smoking (see page 17). Smoke the sausages 10 to 12 hours at no greater then 120°, stirring and adding sawdust as needed. Remove from the smoke and cool to room temperature.

The sausages will keep, loosely wrapped, in the refrigerator for 2 weeks, or for up to 2 months in the freezer. The sausages must be thoroughly cooked before eating.

From the Heartland: German, Dutch, Swedish, East European Traditions

THE MIDWEST IS AMERICA'S HEARTLAND, A VAST, RICH, AND FERTILE REGION that supplies the nation, and much of the world, with its wheat, corn, soybeans, and hogs. The poet Carl Sandburg called Chicago the "Hog Butcher for the World" and that wasn't entirely hyperbole. Down the Midwest's rivers and across its lakes flows an immense treasure of grain and livestock that is processed and shipped from the great midwestern cities and ports. Chicago, first and foremost, but Cincinnati, Cleveland, Milwaukee, Minneapolis/St. Paul, St. Louis, and other cities are all immense food processors that transform and market the agricultural riches of America's great central plain.

This bountiful region with its rich soil has always been an attraction to the land-starved peasants of Europe. From the late eighteenth century, when settlers pushed through the Alleghenies and first looked down on a green sea of forest and plain, pioneers carved out farms and planted crops in the dark virgin soil. The first settlers were Scotch-Irish from the poor uplands of Virginia and Carolina, but they were soon followed by immigrants from northern Europe: Germans seeking freedom of worship, Poles and Bohemians looking for land and a decent life for their families, Hungarians fleeing the aftermath of revolution and political persecution, Scandinavians dreaming of lush pastures.

And they brought their own traditions and food with them. Just as in other regions, immigrants to the Midwest grafted their culinary traditions onto American roots, and adapted native cuisines to what they grew on their new land.

German immigrants formed large communities in the major cities, and the neighborhoods of Chicago, Cleveland, Cincinnati, Milwaukee, and other cities were soon filled with markets, butcher shops, delicatessens, and restaurants that dispensed hearty food, sausages, beer, and *Gemütlichkeit*. German butchers introduced to America the art of fine sausage making that included a staggering array of sausages from every region of Germany. Many of these traditional sausages like braunschweiger, Leberwurst, knockwurst, and the ubiquitous frankfurter joined the mainstream of American cooking and became popular favorites of families from all ethnic backgrounds.

German sausage-making traditions go back a long way—to the beginnings of agriculture and pastoralism in Europe. One of the requirements of the harsh climate in northern Europe is the "Great Killing" that takes place every fall, when all animals that are not essential for breeding new stock are killed off before the onset of winter. It was this lack of fodder during the cold months, as well as the preservative effect of cold weather, that engendered a rich tradition of meat preservation and sausage making in northern Europe, and especially Germany.

The *Schlachtplatte* offered in German restaurants in Milwaukee and Chicago reflects this tradition and hearkens back to the *Schlachtfest*, when all the parts of the slaughtered pig (*schlachten* means "to slaughter or butcher" in German) were offered to families that helped with the butchering. The variety of German sausages seems to be inexhaustible. Usingers of Milwaukee, one of the premium German-style sausage makers in America, offers more than fifty different sausages in its retail store, including gothaer cervelat, summer sausage, mettwurst, teewurst, landjaeger, Thuringer, blood sausage, bierwurst, hessische landleberwurst, hildesheimer liver sausage, jagdwurst, knockwurst, holsteiner, bratwurst, and fritzies, to name but a few.

Sausages are used in a wide variety of German-American dishes and are often paired with cabbage, sauerkraut, and potatoes in traditional recipes.

An important tradition in American cooking is found among the Pennsylvania Dutch, a community that came early to William Penn's Philadelphia colony from Moravia, the Palatinate, and other parts of Germany, seeking religious tolerance. Mennonites, Amish, and the Moravian Brotherhood took root in the rich, deep soil of Pennsylvania, and created a great American cuisine, reflective of a culture that loves and respects good food. Anyone who has ever visited the Lancaster market can testify to the abundance and plenitude of Pennsylvania Dutch farms. Pale pink mounds of sage-flavored farmer's sausage; coils of mahogany-colored smoked sausage; spicy Lebanon bologna; colorful pickles, chowchows, and relishes; heaps of bright green beans; mounds of tomatoes, melons, and squash; pies of every description; pale yellow aged cheeses; pots of white farmer's cheese; and hand-churned butter in tubs and bowls, are all presided over by cheerful, glowing womenfolk and serious men who dress plain but cook tasty.

Eastern Europeans also have a cuisine that uses sausage as an important element in many traditional dishes. Polish sausage or kielbasa has become an American favorite, and versions of this garlicky smoked sausage are found in supermarkets and butcher shops throughout the United States. In the ethnic neighborhoods of the Midwest a wide range of kielbasa can be found—from lightly spiced, fresh versions to coarse-textured smoked sausages with plenty of garlic, spices, and pepper. Other Eastern European nationalities offer their own special sausages such as Hungarian paprika sausage, or debrecini, and Romanian Jewish beef sausage.

Immigrants from Scandinavian countries have enriched American cuisine by their skills with cheese and other dairy products. Wisconsin Cheddar is deservedly world famous, along with other cheeses like brick and Limburger that were developed by the enterprising dairy farmers of the Midwest. Hearty food has always been a part of Scandinavian culture, and Minnesota potato sausage is no exception.

Midwestern farmers raise some of the finest pigs in the world and are proud of their own version of American sage and black pepper sausage (see Iowa Farm Sausage, page 31). Whether in link or bulk form, sausage is found in farm towns and cities throughout the region, on the table for breakfast with hotcakes and biscuits, or in homey dishes like meatloaf or ham loaf.

Smoked Bratwurst

Makes about 3 pounds

ALTHOUGH SIMILAR SPICES ARE USED IN BOTH THE FRESH AND SMOKED versions of bratwurst, the smoked variety has a rich and smoky flavor. Make smoked bratwurst with all pork or a combination of pork and beef. Experiment a bit with different proportions of meat until you find the taste and texture you like. We like about 4 parts pork to 1 part beef, but taste for yourself. This sausage is also excellent unsmoked. If making this variation, leave the curing salts out.

2½ pounds pork butt, or
   2 pounds pork butt and
   ½ pound beef chuck
½ pound pork back fat
1 tablespoon kosher salt
1 tablespoon coarsely ground
   black pepper
1 tablespoon coarsely ground
   mustard seed

2 teaspoons minced garlic
2 teaspoons sugar
1 teaspoon ground mace
1 teaspoon dried sage
½ teaspoon freshly grated nutmeg
½ cup water
¾ teaspoon curing salts
   (optional) (page 21)
Medium hog casings

FOR DETAILS ON SAUSAGE MAKING, SEE PAGE 10.

Mix the meat, fat, salt, black pepper, mustard seeds, garlic, sugar, mace, sage, and nutmeg in a large bowl. Grind the mixture through a ¼-inch plate. Add the water. Add the curing salts, if you intend to cold smoke the sausages. Knead and squeeze the mixture to blend all the ingredients thoroughly.

Stuff into medium hog casings, and tie in 5- to 6-inch links.

If you choose to cold smoke the brats and have mixed in the curing salts, air-dry the sausages in front of a fan overnight. Cold smoke for 12 to 24 hours according to the directions on page 17. Bratwurst can also be hot smoked very successfully. Hot smoke to an internal temperature of 155° to 160° (see page 18).

The smoked sausages will keep for 5 days refrigerated, or for 2 months frozen. Unsmoked sausages will keep for 3 days refrigerated.

Cold Beer, Hot Brats

It's a muggy Wisconsin night in late summer somewhere outside Sheboygan. A red neon sign looms through the darkness, "Cold Beer Hot Brats." We're on our way to the Sheboygan Bratwurst Festival, and our '55 Buick Roadmaster (affectionately termed The Wurstmobile) lurches off the highway into yet another parking lot. We pile into the tavern for a taste test of Sheboygan brats and the inevitable accompaniment, foaming steins of cold Wisconsin lager.

A long, dimly lit bar stretches back into the darkness. Men in shirtsleeves nurse tall seidels of pale golden beer, beads of moisture clinging to the sides of the glasses. Nobody's saying much, staring into the mirrors flanked by naked nymphs and angels, watching the neon beer signs revolve, waiting for a cool breeze off the river.

We pick a spot at the bar and wave the bartender over. "Beer and brats," we say. "Doubles all around, with the works." He nods, smiling.

The beer arrives first, pale and clean, with the bitter tang of hops in the nose, the rich sweetness of malt across the palate. As we sip our beers, we all find ourselves staring into the ornate mirrors, dreaming of bratwurst, of ancient festivals, the works.

A flurry of activity erupts in the quiet bar. Heads turn, suddenly smiling, as the bartender's wife (mother, girlfriend, sister) sweeps up behind us, balancing plates on her plump and lovely arms, blonde hair piled up around her face, red cheeks, pale blue eyes, cheerful and bold and beautiful, saying, "You the boys ordered brats, doubles, works all around?"

She lays the plates down along the bar. Two grilled brats bulge between halves of the hard roll; a slice of pale white onion sticks out underneath; hot brown mustard, coarse-ground with horseradish, opens up the sinuses; long thin slices of sour dill pickles crisscross the brats. This is the best of Sheboygan's wursts: a double brat with the works!

The first question, as with any good sausage sandwich, is the mode of attack. That is to say, how to get all these gustatory wonders into the mouth with a minimum of hassle and a modicum of dignity. At the first bite, however, all hopes of decorum and clean shirts fade. You just open your mouth as wide as you can, and bite down.

And suddenly it all becomes clear. Why everyone seems so peaceful here, so happy. As the spiced juicy meat mingles with the sweet onions, hot mustard, and sour pickles we experience a kind of heavenly harmony, a clear perception of rightness, of how things should be. This might just be the ultimate sausage sandwich. It can't get any better than this.

Sheboygan Brats (Fresh Farm Bratwurst)

Makes about 3 pounds

FOLKS IN THE MIDWEST TAKE THEIR BRATWURST VERY SERIOUSLY, ESPECIALLY in Wisconsin up around Sheboygan, home of the Sheboygan brat. In fact, in Sheboygan they have an annual Bratwurst Festival where thousands of brats are grilled and eaten with onions and mustard on the famous Wisconsin hard rolls. And nobody is shy about washing them down with foaming steins of locally brewed beer.

In Germany and the German communities of Wisconsin, Minnesota, and the rest of the Midwest, this savory sausage is often made on farms and is usually consumed fresh. Many U.S. sausage makers sell bratwurst already cooked, and then it's simply poached or steamed. Steamed brats can be mighty tasty, especially with kraut or onions, hot mustard, and a stein of cold beer, but we think you get more flavor if you grill them over charcoal or under a broiler.

1½ pounds pork butt
1 pound veal shoulder
½ pound pork back fat
1 tablespoon kosher salt
1 teaspoon sugar
1 teaspoon freshly ground
*   black pepper*

1 teaspoon ground mace
1 teaspoon ground caraway seeds
½ teaspoon ground ginger
½ cup milk
Medium hog casings

FOR DETAILS ON SAUSAGE MAKING, SEE PAGE 10.

Mix the meats, fat, salt, sugar, black pepper, mace, caraway, and ginger in a large bowl. Grind the mixture finely through the ⅛-inch plate. Add the milk and knead until the spices are well mixed in with the meat.

Stuff into medium hog casings, and tie into 5-inch links.

You can leave the brats raw or poach them. To poach, bring a large pot of lightly salted water to a boil. Add the sausage and reduce the heat to maintain the poaching water at a temperature between 160° and 180° for 20 minutes. The sausages should reach an internal temperature of 155°. Drain in a colander and cool to room temperature. Do not cool with running water (it causes the sausages to burst).

The sausages will keep refrigerated for 3 days, or in the freezer for 2 months.

Bockwurst

Makes about 4 pounds

THIS MILD-FLAVORED WHITE SAUSAGE IS VERY POPULAR IN GERMAN NEIGH-borhoods throughout the Midwest. It is great tavern food, eaten with some tangy German-style mustard, crusty bread, and a stein of cold lager beer. Bockwurst's rich but delicate flavor is perfect for dishes like our Deep-Dish Chicken and Sausage Pie with Biscuit Crust (see page 234) or Pennsylvania Dutch Schnitz und Knepp (see page 235).

1 tablespoon butter
½ cup finely chopped leeks or

1 teaspoon ground mace
½ teaspoon finely ground white
   or black pepper
inch of ground ginger
cup milk
egg, beaten
cup finely chopped green onions,
   scallions, or chives
cup chopped fresh parsley
edium hog casings

o.

over medium heat. Add the
10 minutes, until the veg-
aside and reserve.
icken, and fat with the salt,
h a ⅛-inch plate into the
g with the milk, egg, green
spoon, beat the mixture

r for at least 30 minutes.
into 6- to 7-inch links.
boil, Add the sausages and
vater at a temperature of
he sausage is firm. Drain
e. Do not cool with run-
The poached sausage will
freezer for 2 months.

Hunter's Sausage

Makes about 3 pounds

THIS HEARTY SAUSAGE HAS AN AMPLE, SMOKY FLAVOR FROM THE BACON AND a nice lift in its aroma and taste from the spices and mustard. Hunter's sausage is excellent grilled and served with a coarse-grained mustard or braised with beer and onions.

2 pounds pork butt
1 pound lean smoked bacon
½ cup water
1 tablespoon whole yellow
    mustard seeds
2 teaspoons minced garlic
2 teaspoons coarsely ground
    black pepper

2 teaspoons sweet Hungarian
    paprika
2 teaspoons dry mustard
1 teaspoon kosher salt
1 teaspoon ground coriander
1 teaspoon freshly grated nutmeg
½ teaspoon ground ginger
Medium hog casings

FOR DETAILS ON SAUSAGE MAKING, SEE PAGE 10.

Grind the pork and bacon through a ¼-inch plate. Mix the ground meat with the water, mustard seeds, garlic, black pepper, paprika, dry mustard, salt, coriander, nutmeg, and ginger. Knead until all the spices are thoroughly blended with the meat. Stuff into medium hog casings, and tie into 6- to 7-inch links. Dry the sausages, uncovered, in the refrigerator for 1 or 2 days.

To poach, bring a large pot of lightly salted water to a boil. Add the sausage and reduce the heat to maintain the poaching liquid at 180°. Poach for 25 minutes. Drain.

Cool and refrigerate. The poached sausages will keep in the refrigerator for 3 to 4 days, or in the freezer for 2 months.

Makes about 4½ pounds

THIS ALL-BEEF SAUSAGE IS LOADED WITH GARLIC AND BLACK PEPPER AND IS a staple at such famous Romanian kosher restaurants as Sammy's in New York. Use it in place of plain beef brisket to perk up flavors and provide a dash of spiciness.

The sausage can be left raw or air-dried and poached before serving. Or it can be cold smoked, and then poached.

3 pounds lean beef chuck
1¼ pounds fatty beef, such as short ribs or plate
¼ pound beef suet or other firm beef fat
½ cup water
2 tablespoons whole yellow mustard seeds
2 tablespoons minced garlic
1 tablespoon coarsely ground black pepper

5 teaspoons kosher salt
2 teaspoons sugar
2 teaspoons ground coriander
1 teaspoon dry mustard
Pinch of ground allspice
Pinch of ground bay leaves
Pinch of ground cloves
1 teaspoon curing salts (page 21) (optional)
Wide lamb or beef round casings

FOR DETAILS ON SAUSAGE MAKING, SEE PAGE 10.

Grind the lean beef through a ⅜-inch plate, the fatty beef and fat through the ¼-inch plate. In a large bowl, mix the ground meats and water with the mustard seeds, garlic, black pepper, salt, sugar, coriander, dry mustard, allspice, bay leaves, and cloves. If you plan to air-dry or cold smoke, add the curing salts.

In you are going to leave the sausage fresh, then stuff into lamb casings, and tie into 5-inch lengths. If you are going to air-dry or cold smoke the sausage, stuff the mixture into the larger beef casings and tie into 6- to 7-inch links.

To cold smoke, air-dry overnight and smoke for 6 to 8 hours according to the directions on page 17. For air-drying only, place in front of a fan with a drip pan underneath to catch any liquid for up to 3 days.

The unsmoked and uncured sausage will keep for 3 days in the refrigerator. Air-dried or smoked sausage will keep for 1 week refrigerated. All types can be kept for 2 months in the freezer.

Cooking Notes
To cook smoked or air-dried Romanian Jewish Beef Sausage, bring a large pot of lightly salted water to a boil. Add the sausages. Maintain a poaching temperature of 180° for 30 minutes. Drain and cool to room temperature.

Garlic, Pork, and Ham Cervelat

Makes about 3 pounds

Cervelat is a large sausage that is often eaten as a cold cut, or it is poached and then used either hot or cold in various dishes. Cervelat used as a cold cut is usually air-dried and then poached. In our recipe, either air-dry the sausage overnight at cool room temperature, in which case you need the curing salts, or dry it uncovered for a few days in the refrigerator and leave the cure out.

Whether you air-dry the cervelat or dry it in the refrigerator, you will need to poach it before eating. Once it is poached, you can eat it hot or cold. Cervelat goes especially well with potatoes. We particularly like it with home fries or in vinaigrette-dressed potato salad, but it also tastes delicious with some cheesy mashed potatoes or German potato pancakes.

1¾ pounds pork butt
1 pound smoked or boiled ham
¼ pound pork back fat
½ cup water or white wine
3 tablespoons minced garlic
2 teaspoons kosher salt
2 teaspoons coarsely cracked
   black pepper
1 teaspoon finely ground
   black pepper

1 teaspoon ground coriander
½ teaspoon dried savory
½ teaspoon ground mace
½ teaspoon ground cumin
Pinch of ground cloves
½ teaspoon curing salts (page 21)
   (optional)
Wide hog casings or beef round
   casings

For details on sausage making, see page 10.

Grind the pork and ham through a ⅜-inch plate and the pork fat through a ¼-inch plate. In a large bowl, mix the ground meats and fat with the water or wine, garlic, salt, coarse and finely ground pepper, coriander, savory, mace, cumin, and cloves. Add the curing salts, if using. Knead until everything is well blended.

Stuff into wide beef or hog casings (beef is preferred since it is easier to peel off before eating the sausage). Tie into 6-inch links. If you intend to air-dry the sausages at room temperature, be sure to include the curing salts. If you dry the sausages in the refrigerator, you can leave them out. Air-dry in a cool room for 12 hours, or in the refrigerator for 3 days.

To poach cervelat, bring a large pot of lightly salted water to a boil. Add the sausages and reduce the heat to the lowest setting.

Maintain the poaching water at a temperature between 160° and 180° for 40 to 50 minutes, depending on how thick the sausages are. They should reach an internal temperature of 155°.

Eat the cervelat as is, or drain and cool. Refrigerate, and eat the cold sausage sliced. To reheat, place the sausages in simmering water and cook for 15 minutes until heated through. The poached sausages will keep for 1 week refrigerated, or for 2 months frozen.

Polish Wedding, Chicago

On a warm Sunday in spring it's pleasant to walk down the sidewalks of Chicago's Northside, beside small neat houses with white picket fences, daffodils and crocuses along the pathways, past groceries with signs in Russian and Polish, butcher shops with "Fresh Kielbasa Here" painted on the windows in whitewash.

We're on our way to the wedding a Polish-American friend invited us to last night. "You want kielbasa, by God," he shouted in the bar of the huge German restaurant in the Loop, "come to my cousin's wedding. You'll eat more kielbasa than you ever thought existed in this world, or the next one too," and toasted us with a foaming stein of dark German draft.

So today we're searching for the wedding party in the parish hall just behind St. Casimir's church. And then we hear, pulsing in the still air from afar like the trumpets of Krakow to wandering pilgrims, the polka! We follow the sounds of accordions, tubas, trumpets, and drums down the street, turn the corner, and suddenly we're there.

The party is outside in the schoolyard next to the church, the band is perched on a makeshift stage hung round with flags and bunting, and the air seems to shake with the music. Everybody's dancing, young and old: women in embroidered dresses, their blond braids whirling; old ladies in black waltzing with men who wear serious mustaches and low-brimmed hats; boys in leather jackets shuffling around the edge of the swirl with girls in short skirts and beehive hairdos; little girls dancing with each other, eyes wide and serious amid the laughter.

All around the schoolyard, tables are piled high with food, and a band of women with kerchiefs and flowered aprons moves back and forth from the parish hall with platters and bowls. Galvanized washtubs full of ice hold kegs of beer, bottles of wine and vodka, root beer and orange soda. Old men with bright cheeks and pale eyes are drinking straw-colored vodka from tiny glasses, beaming at the dancers, nodding their heads to the rhythms.

It's a sausage lover's dream: chunks of grilled smoked kielbasa are laid on heaps of red cabbage; small fresh sausages, brown and crisp, nestle on mounds of sauerkraut; brightly painted bowls are filled with aromatic goulash and bigos—the Polish hunter's stew made with sausage, game, and wild mushrooms; a roast suckling pig glistens, festooned with coils of sausage, surrounded with spiced apples and plums; roast potatoes circle pale pink hams.

We pile our plates high and talk with women in aprons and men with ruddy cheeks about the feast and how the traditional dishes are cooked. Everybody has an opinion and a different ingredient, and we find out about juniper-smoked sausages from the Tatra Mountains; pickled hams and smoked bacon from the plains; kielbasa from Warsaw, from Krakow, and from the butcher just down the block.

The party really gets going after the sun goes down, with tasting and talking, beer and vodka, and polka after polka far into the night. Then suddenly it's quiet, and an old man starts to sing a *tzigane*, a mournful gypsy song. A violin picks up the tune in the darkness. We sip *zubrowka* and dream of mountains and of horses cantering down the passes under a smuggler's moon.

KIELBASA IS THE POLISH WORD FOR SAUSAGE IN GENERAL, AND IN POLAND, a country that loves its sausage and pork products, there are many varieties of kielbasa, both fresh and smoked. When the Poles immigrated to America's heartland, they brought along their love of sausages and their skills in making them. In the neighborhoods of Chicago and other large midwestern cities, kielbasa or "Polish sausage" became popular, and then, as its reputation grew, eventually made its way into American kitchens generally. Now Polish sausage, along with the frankfurter and Italian sausage, has become a classic American sausage and is found in virtually every region and style of American cooking.

Most Polish sausage sold in American supermarkets and delis is a smoked, smooth-textured type, but if you are lucky enough to live near a Polish butcher shop, you should be able to find the fresh variety. In Poland and Polish communities in the United States, fresh kielbasa is often made at home or on the farm during the pig-killing in the fall. Use this sausage in any recipe calling for a fresh mild sausage. Like most farmhouse recipes for country sausage, there are many versions of fresh kielbasa, but almost all contain substantial amounts of garlic, black pepper, and aromatic herbs.

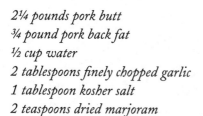
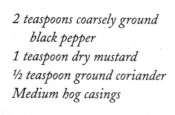

2¼ pounds pork butt	2 teaspoons coarsely ground
¾ pound pork back fat	black pepper
½ cup water	1 teaspoon dry mustard
2 tablespoons finely chopped garlic	½ teaspoon ground coriander
1 tablespoon kosher salt	Medium hog casings
2 teaspoons dried marjoram	

FOR DETAILS ON SAUSAGE MAKING, SEE PAGE 10.

Grind the meat and fat together through a ¼-inch plate. In a large bowl, mix the ground meat with the water, garlic, salt, marjoram, pepper, mustard, and coriander. Knead the mixture until everything is well blended.

Stuff into medium hog casings, and tie into 6-inch links.

The sausage will keep in the refrigerator for 3 days, or in the freezer for up to 2 months.

Smoked Kielbasa

Makes about 3 pounds

THIS RECIPE GETS PRETTY CLOSE TO THE REAL KIELBASA THAT YOU CAN STILL find in small butcher shops in Polish neighborhoods from Chicago to Buffalo. Unlike the ubiquitous "Polish sausage" found in American supermarkets, authentic kielbasa is coarse in texture, quite smoky, and very garlicky, making it a wonderful addition to dishes of all types. It is also delicious grilled and served with coarse-grained mustard, a sweet-and-sour red cabbage coleslaw, and potatoes roasted with garlic and rosemary. We prefer to add curing salts and cold smoking kielbasa, but very good results can be had by leaving the cure out and hot smoking the sausage. Serve smoked kielbasa with a crisp, hoppy lager like Pilsner Urquell, a hearty California Petite Syrah, or a full-bodied Châteauneuf-du-Pape.

1½ pounds pork butt
1 pound beef chuck
½ pound pork back fat
½ cup water
2 tablespoons finely chopped garlic
1 tablespoon kosher salt
1 tablespoon sweet Hungarian
    paprika
2 teaspoons sugar

2 teaspoons coarsely ground black
    pepper
½ teaspoon dried marjoram
½ teaspoon ground coriander
½ teaspoon freshly grated nutmeg
1 teaspoon curing salts (page 21)
    (optional)
Medium hog casings, or wide hog
    or beef round casings

FOR DETAILS ON SAUSAGE MAKING, SEE PAGE 10.

Grind the pork through a ⅜-inch plate, the beef and fat through a ⅛- or ¼-inch plate. In a large bowl, mix the meats and fat with the water, garlic, salt, paprika, sugar, pepper, marjoram, coriander, and nutmeg. Add the curing salts, if you are going to cold smoke the sausage. Curing salts are not necessary for hot smoking. Knead the meat until everything is well blended.

Stuff into medium hog casings, and tie into 8-inch links. Alternatively, stuff into wide hog or beef casings about 24 inches long, and tie the two ends together with a string to form a large ring.

To cold smoke the sausage, first air-dry it front of a fan overnight. Cold smoke for at least 12 hours according to the directions on page 17. Or you can hot smoke the sausage (see page 18).

Smoked kielbasa will keep in the refrigerator for 1 week, in the freezer for 2 months.

HUNGARY, LIKE ITS EASTERN EUROPEAN NEIGHBORS, IS A SAUSAGE-EATING country. Hungarian dry salami is deservedly world famous, and Hungarians enjoy a wide range of sausage, bacon, and smoked meats. What sets Hungarian cooking apart is the liberal use of paprika—the ubiquitous ground red pepper that varies from sweet to hot.

In midwestern ethnic neighborhoods, every butcher has his own variation, but debrecini always has lots of paprika and garlic. Often these sausages are air-dried to intensify the flavors. To air-dry the sausage, hang it in a cool place until it is firm. This usually takes several days, depending on the temperature. If you do air-dry debrecini, don't forget to use curing salts in the recipe. You can then cold smoke or hot smoke the sausage, or leave it fresh.

Makes about 3 pounds

3 tablespoons sweet Hungarian
   paprika
1½ tablespoons finely chopped
   garlic
1 tablespoon kosher salt
2 teaspoons coarsely ground
   black pepper
1 teaspoon sugar
½ teaspoon ground coriander

⅛ teaspoon ground ginger
⅛ teaspoon allspice
1 teaspoon curing salts (optional)
   (page 21)
1¾ pounds pork butt
¾ pound beef chuck
½ pound pork back fat
½ cup water
Medium hog casings

FOR DETAILS ON SAUSAGE MAKING, SEE PAGE 10.

Mix the paprika, garlic, salt, black pepper, sugar, coriander, ginger, and allspice in a small bowl. Add curing salts if you are going to air-dry or cold smoke the sausage. Rub all over the strips of pork, beef, and pork fat. Cover and refrigerate for 2 hours or overnight.

Grind everything through a ¼-inch plate into a large bowl. Add the water and any liquid remaining from the spice marinade. Knead and squeeze the meat until everything is well blended.

Stuff into medium hog casings, and tie into 8-inch links. Air-dry in front of a fan overnight and cold smoke for 8 to 12 hours according to the directions on page 17. Otherwise you can dry the sausages lightly by refrigerating them, unwrapped, overnight. Or you can hot smoke the sausage (page 18). Air-dried or smoked debrecini will keep in the refrigerator for 1 week, the fresh sausage for 3 days. All types will keep in the freezer for 2 months.

Chicago-Style Hot Dogs

Makes about 2 pounds

THERE'S A LOT OF ARGUMENT ABOUT WHERE THE HOT DOG ORIGINATED—some say Frankfurt (frankfurter), others Vienna (wiener), while others relate it to the Czechoslovakian párky or French *saucisse de Strasbourg*. There's even debate as to where it first appeared in America: St. Louis in the 1880s, the Bowery or Coney Island in New York, or even Chicago or Cleveland.

But one thing nobody is willing to argue about is that the hot dog has long been the most popular and famous American sausage. Whether you're munching one of Nathan's Famous Franks with sauerkraut and brown mustard, a Chicago hot dog with the works, an L.A. chili dog, or even a *chien chaud* on the Champs Elysées stuffed into a hollowed-out baguette with Gruyère, you know that you are eating the American sausage.

We do know that a German butcher named Feltman opened up a sausage stand in Coney Island in the 1870s, and that his "hot dachshund sausages" soon became the rage of that popular, and then fashionable, resort. And on an April afternoon at the Polo Grounds in 1901, cartoonist Tad Dorgan christened the sausage in a bun the "hot dog" (he couldn't spell "dachshund"). In 1916, Nathan Handwerker, a former Feltman's employee, opened Nathan's Famous Franks and has sold, literally, millions of his spicy frankfurters over the years. Now we have frankfurters of all types that would make old Mr. Feltman blanch: skinless franks, all-beef franks, old-fashioned franks, corn dogs, bagel dogs, and even chicken hot dogs (ugh!). For juicy texture and plenty of taste, however, we don't think you can beat the original mixture of pork, beef, and spices.

Unlike the other sausages in this book, the hot dog is an emulsified sausage, which means you must achieve a completely homogeneous mixture of meat and fat to make a successful sausage. To do this without the aid of chemicals such as phosphates, extenders like dried milk, and the special mixers found in sausage factories can be a bit tricky. It's easy enough to combine ground meat and spices, but if you don't achieve an emulsion, you don't have a hot dog. When you bite into a juicy hot dog, the sausage should pop when you break the casing. It should be succulent and juicy without being watery. If you don't get the emulsion right, the hot dogs will be dense and grainy, even though the taste may be passable.

So before you set off to whip up your own bunch of juicy hot dogs let us tell you of our experiences.

Try number one looked like the right homogeneous mixture when we stuffed them into the casings. They were nice and plump and about 8 inches long. We poached them and they looked just fine. We drained them and left them to cool in the sink while we went to the store to pick up some buns, beer, and condiments. Thirty minutes later we returned with some friends to taste our efforts. When we looked into the colander, we all had a bit of a shock. Our lovely hot dogs had shrunk to about 3 inches long and half their original diameter. Biting into one was like trying to eat an eraser—grainy, dry, and dense. Back to the drawing board!

Batch number two also was a failure. The meat was overprocessed and became too warm. The fat separated out and the result was a mess when we tried to cook the franks.

Try number three finally brought success because we paid very close attention to temperature and processing times, both of which are critical for achieving a stable emulsion. Once all the meats and fats are ground, you must chill them well in the refrigerator. To emulsify the meat and fat, you will need an instant-read thermometer and a large and powerful food processor. The temperature of the mixture must not rise about 60° at any time during the processing. This is accomplished by adding crushed ice to the mixture and processing in short intervals of 15 seconds. So good luck!

¾ pound pork butt, well chilled
½ pound beef chuck, well chilled
¼ pound pork back fat, well chilled
2 teaspoons sweet Hungarian
    paprika
1½ teaspoons salt
1 teaspoon dry mustard
1 teaspoon minced garlic
½ teaspoon finely ground black
    pepper

½ teaspoon ground coriander
¼ teaspoon ground mace
¼ teaspoon ground cardamom
¼ teaspoon ground cumin or
    ground celery seed
1 tablespoon light corn syrup
1 to 2 cups crushed ice
Sheep casings

FOR DETAILS ON SAUSAGE MAKING, SEE PAGE 10.

To rewarm the hot
dogs, bring a pot of
water to a boil. Put
the hot dogs in,
cover the pot, and
remove from the
heat. Let the
sausages stand for
10 minutes and
enjoy.

Grind the meats and fat through the finest plate of your meat grinder
(⅛ or ¼ inch) into the smallest size possible to help emulsify the
mixture. Chill for 30 minutes in the refrigerator or for 15 minutes
in the freezer.

In a small bowl, mix together the paprika, salt, dry mustard, garlic, black pepper, coriander, mace, cardamom, and cumin. Add half
the meat and fat mixture to the bowl of a large food processor. Put in
half the spice blend, half the corn syrup, and ½ cup of crushed ice.
Process in 15-second spurts for a total of 1 to 1½ minutes. After each
15 seconds of processing, stop the machine, and check the temperature of the meat mixture to make sure it is under 60°. If not, add a
tablespoon or more of crushed ice. The key is to process the mixture
until it has a homogeneous appearance. There should not be any vis-
ible particles of fat, and the mixture should look like a stiff pink
paste. Transfer to a bowl and refrigerate while you process the second
half of the meat, fat, corn syrup, and spices, repeating the same procedure, including the crushed ice. Use a spatula or wooden spoon to
mix together the two batches.

Stuff into sheep casings and tie into 6-inch links. To poach,
bring a large pot of lightly salted water to a boil. Add the hot dogs and
reduce the heat to maintain the poaching liquid at 160° to 180°, for
20 to 25 minutes or until they are firm. Drain and cool to room temperature. The sausage will keep for 3 days in the refrigerator, or 2
months in the freezer.

THE MANY COMMERCIAL VARIETIES OF THIS SWEDISH SAUSAGE SOLD throughout Minnesota and Wisconsin tend toward the bland and boring. When they say potato, potato it is, and not much else. Our version uses a bit more meat and a variety of mild spices. Pork skin adds texture and flavor—the next time you cook a fresh ham or pork shoulder, cut the skin off before cooking and freeze it, or ask your butcher for some. You can also use the rind from slab bacon. Potato sausage is a real favorite for breakfast, since its texture and flavors are similar to hash. It goes beautifully with poached or fried eggs, especially with a few thin pancakes with some lingonberry or red currant jam on the side. And don't forget strong black coffee, flavored with a little cardamom seed.

2 pounds boiling potatoes
⅓ pound pork skin
1½ pounds pork butt
1 pound beef chuck
½ pound pork back fat
2 medium onions
1½ tablespoons kosher salt
2 teaspoons dry mustard

2 teaspoons fresh marjoram or
  1 teaspoon dried
2 teaspoons ground caraway seeds
1½ teaspoons coarsely ground
  black pepper
1 teaspoon ground allspice
Water, as needed
Medium hog casings

FOR DETAILS ON SAUSAGE MAKING, SEE PAGE 10.

Peel the potatoes and cover with water to which you have added a little vitamin C (ascorbic acid) or lemon juice to prevent browning.

Cover the pork skin with water and bring to a boil. Cover the pot and decrease the heat to a simmer. Cook for 30 to 40 minutes until the skin is soft. Drain and set aside to cool.

Grind the meats, fat, raw potatoes, onions, and pork skin through a ¼-inch plate into a large bowl. Add the salt, dry mustard, marjoram, caraway, black pepper, and allspice. Knead until everything is well blended. Moisten with a little water if needed to aid mixing.

Stuff into medium hog casings, and tie into 5- to 6-inch links.

To poach, bring a large pot of lightly salted water to a boil. Add the sausages. Decrease the heat to maintain the poaching liquid at 180° for 40 minutes. Remove, drain, and cool.

The sausages will keep for 3 days in the refrigerator, or for 2 months in the freezer.

Cooking Notes

To cook Minnesota Potato Sausages, place them in a heavy covered skillet in about ¼ inch of water. Cook over medium heat until the water evaporates. Continue to fry the sausages for about 10 more minutes until they are nicely browned, turning them occasionally.

Michigan Dutch Farmer's Sausage

Makes about 3 pounds

Many Dutch immigrants settled in Michigan and became successful dairy farmers. This mild sausage is typical of what you might find in small butcher shops or farms in Dutch communities in and around Grand Rapids. Use it in any recipe calling for a mildly flavored sausage. It is also a good replacement for fresh bratwurst or bockwurst. Once made, the sausage can be left raw or poached. We prefer to poach it, and then grill or brown it in butter.

1 pound pork butt
½ pound pork back fat
¾ pound veal shoulder
¾ pound beef plate or chuck
½ cup water
1 tablespoon kosher salt
2 teaspoons dry mustard
1 teaspoon sugar
1 teaspoon ground coriander
1 teaspoon coarsely ground black pepper
½ teaspoon ground ginger
½ teaspoon ground mace
½ teaspoon dried thyme
½ teaspoon ground cardamom
Medium hog casings

FOR DETAILS ON SAUSAGE MAKING, SEE PAGE 10.

Grind the pork through a ¼-inch plate; grind the pork fat, veal, and beef through a ⅛-inch plate.

In a large bowl, mix the ground meats and fat with the water, salt, mustard, sugar, coriander, black pepper, ginger, mace, thyme, and cardamom. Knead until everything is well blended.

Stuff into medium hog casings, and tie into 5-inch links. To poach, bring a large pot of lightly salted water to a boil. Add the sausage. Maintain a poaching temperature of 180° for 20 minutes, until the sausage reaches an internal temperature of 155°. Drain and cool to room temperature, and refrigerate.

The sausage will keep for 3 days in the refrigerator, or 2 months in the freezer.

From the Southwest

IN THE PAST FEW YEARS, THE FIERY AND COMPLEX COOKING OF AMERICA'S Southwest has been recognized as one of our most exciting regional cuisines. An amalgam of native American, Mexican, and "Anglo" influences has produced an array of delicious and increasingly innovative dishes, from the fashionable restaurants in Dallas, Fort Worth, and Denver to the small cafés of Taos, Tucson, and Santa Fe, and in the kitchens of talented home cooks all cross the southern plains and high plateaus of Texas, New Mexico, Arizona, and Colorado. Using traditional foods such as chiles, beans, corn, chicken, pork, and game, this new generation of southwestern cooks has built upon the past to create a vibrant and exciting style of cooking.

It wasn't always so. A decade or so ago, if you asked for southwestern cooking, you most likely would have received a blank stare at first, followed by a "Mexican" meal of bland chili con carne or a limp enchilada surrounded by some tired refried beans and tasteless "Spanish" rice. Like much of the best modern American cooking, the new southwestern cuisine is grounded in the discovery of our ethnic and regional roots. It is a return to an earlier and more authentic style of cookery that depends on fresh and natural ingredients, carefully and respectfully prepared.

The dishes southwestern cooks are making today differ in many ways from the often frugal and spare foods of a harder, less affluent time, but they share the same basic ingredients: corn—blue, white, or yellow, fresh, parched, or made into hominy; beans of every color and flavor; chiles ranging from mild to scorching; pork, fresh or cured, smoked, or ground into sausage; range-fed beef, lamb, and game; farmyard chickens; squash, tomatoes, and onions from thirsty gardens; herbs like oregano, wild mint, and pungent *epazote* from the high plains.

The often bland flavors of corn and beans are given life and energy by an array of seasonings, led by an astonishing variety of chiles. This family of highly flavored peppers (*Capsicum annuum*) spread north from Mexico to the Southwest in pre-Columbian times. Many types of chiles were used in the sophisticated cuisine of the Aztecs of central and northern Mexico, and over two hundred can be distinguished today in Mexican cookery. Southwestern cooks take advantage of the widely varied levels and gradations of flavor and piquancy of the many types of chiles, and often use these differences as signatures of specific dishes and styles of cooking.

Chiles are used in every stage of their development from green to red ripe to dried. Dried chiles are ground and mixed with herbs like cumin and oregano to make the ubiquitous "chili powder" blend found on supermarket shelves throughout America.

Pork, fresh or cured, has been one of the most important sources of protein in the Southwest since the coming of Europeans in the sixteenth century. Salted, smoked, or made into sausage or chorizo, pork was most often the meat that flavored the dried beans and corn during the winter months. The German influence on sausage making is seen mostly in Texas around the towns of New Braunfels and Castroville.

About Chiles

here are many varieties of fresh or dried chiles used in the Southwest, ranging from mild to very hot. We give suggestions for specific chiles in the recipes, but you should feel free to substitute, depending on what is available in your market, and your tolerance for heat.

Here are some of the main types usually found in Hispanic markets and neighborhoods (in ascending order of hotness):

Anaheim Large, mild green chile, often stuffed. Also called California chile.

New Mexico When green, similar to Anaheim. Dried red chiles are found in *ristras* (long strings of chiles) and used in sauces and for chile powder.

Poblano Large green chile similar to above. Also called pasilla. When dried, called ancho—used widely in sauces and for chile powder.

Mulato Medium-hot green chile similar to poblano. Chocolate brown when dry, with rich flavor. Substitute ancho.

Jalapeño Hot green chile used fresh or pickled (*en escabeche*) in sauces or for garnish. Dried red version is the smoky fiery chipotle, often packed in adobo sauce.

Serrano Small green chile, even hotter than jalapeño. Used in salsas and for dishes with emphatic heat levels.

Handling Chiles

Much of the heat is found in seeds and white inner membranes, so removing these will tone down chiles. Be careful when handling chiles, as they can burn eyes or sensitive skin; wear rubber gloves, and wash your hands afterwards.

Fire-Roasting and Peeling Fresh Chiles or Bell Peppers

To peel green chiles (as well as bell peppers), fire-roast them under the broiler or over an open flame until the skin is charred and put in a plastic or paper bag for 15 minutes to steam. Scrape the skins off under running water. Canned green chiles are good alternatives to fresh, or use fire-roasted and peeled bell peppers and add heat with cayenne, red pepper flakes, or hot sauce.

Using Dried Chiles

Soak dried chiles in hot water until soft and puree in food processor. You can make your own chile powder using dried chiles in a blender (be careful not to inhale dust—it can be irritating) or buy ground New Mexico, California, or ancho chiles from Hispanic markets or mail order (page 307). Most commercial chile powder blends include oregano and cumin; Gebhardt is the best widely available brand.

Chorizo

Makes about 2 pounds

CHORIZO IS THE SPANISH WORD FOR SAUSAGE, SO IT CAN BE A BIT CONFUS-ing when you find the word referring to different types of sausages made in Spain, Mexico, South America, and (with slightly differing spellings) in Portugal (chouriço) and Louisiana (chaurice).

The Mexican version usually contains ground pork mixed with lots of cumin, pure chile powder, and fresh hot peppers, such as serrano or jalapeño. Again, as with many peasant sausages, there are variations depending on the place of origin or family traditions. Some chorizos contain cinnamon; others tequila; some are served fresh and lightly spiced; others are dried, pungent, and decidedly funky. The recipe below is a basic one that you should feel free to vary and embellish with your own personal touch.

Since it's usually used in bulk, chorizo is an easy sausage to make in a food processor. Wrap ½- to 1-pound quantities in foil, label, and freeze until needed. We prefer to use pure ground dried chile powders for heat in this recipe. Pure chile powders are found in most Hispanic markets. If unavailable, use a good-quality commercial chile powder blend. Use chorizo as a filling for enchiladas or tacos, in sauces, or fried with eggs or rice.

1½ pounds pork butt
½ pound pork back fat
1 bunch (4 to 6 ounces) fresh
    cilantro, chopped (1 cup)
    (optional)
1 fresh serrano, jalapeño, or
    other hot chile, seeded and
    finely chopped
¼ cup red wine vinegar
1 tablespoon New Mexico or
    other ground dried chile powder

1 tablespoon sweet Hungarian
    paprika
2 teaspoons kosher salt
1½ teaspoons whole cumin seeds
1 teaspoon ground cumin
½ teaspoon coarsely ground black
    pepper
½ teaspoon ground cayenne pepper
¼ teaspoon ground coriander

FOR DETAILS ON MAKING SAUSAGE, SEE PAGE 10.

Grind the meat and fat through a ¼-inch plate or in batches in a food processor. Transfer the ground meat and fat to a large bowl. Add the cilantro, chile, vinegar, chile powder, paprika, salt, cumin seeds, ground cumin, black pepper, cayenne, and coriander. Mix together with your hands, and chill overnight. Package and place in the freezer or refrigerate and use in 3 days. Chorizo will keep in the refrigerator for 3 days, or in the freezer for 2 months.

El Paso Beef, Pork, and Chile Sausage

Makes about 4 pounds

Dark beer and aromatic spices give this zesty sausage a unique flavor that goes well with lamb or game birds. It is also excellent grilled or used to make empanadas, tamales, or tacos. Leave the sausage in bulk or stuff into casings. The achiote seeds in the recipe are more for color than flavor and can be replaced with deeply colored sweet Hungarian paprika.

1¼ pounds beef chuck
1¼ pounds pork butt
½ pound pork back fat or beef fat
1 cup dark Mexican or German beer
1 tablespoon kosher salt
1 tablespoon chopped garlic
1 tablespoon pure ground New Mexico chile powder
1 tablespoon ground achiote seed or Hungarian paprika

1 tablespoon ground cumin
2 teaspoons sugar
1 teaspoon coarsely ground black pepper
1 teaspoon red pepper flakes
⅛ teaspoon ground cinnamon
⅛ teaspoon ground cloves
Medium hog casings

For details on making sausage, see page 10.

Grind all the meat and fat through a ¼-inch plate. In a large bowl, blend the ground meats and fat with the beer, salt, garlic, chile powder, achiote or paprika, cumin, sugar, black pepper, red pepper, cinnamon, and cloves. Chill for an hour before stuffing, so the beer can be completely absorbed into the meat.

Stuff into medium hog casings, and tie into 5-inch links. Mellow, uncovered, in the refrigerator overnight.

The sausage will keep for 3 days in the refrigerator, or for 2 months in the freezer.

New
Mexico
Chicken,
Pork, and
Roasted
Chile
Sausage

Makes about 5 pounds

SMALL GAME BIRDS THRIVE IN THE PIÑON SCRUB OF THE NEW MEXICAN highlands, and they are often included in the savory dishes of the region. This delicious mixture of fowl, pork, and chiles gives you a taste of the hearty cooking of the high desert, and makes an excellent stuffing for small birds like quail, squab, or game hens, or a filling for chimichangas and empanadas, tacos, and enchiladas.

1 red bell pepper or fresh pimiento
2 green poblano, Anaheim, California, or other mild fresh chiles
1 green jalapeño or other hot fresh chile
1½ pounds chicken breast, boned and skinned
1½ pounds pork butt
1 pound pork back fat
⅓ cup red wine vinegar or lime juice
¼ cup water
1 bunch fresh cilantro, coarsely chopped (1 cup)

2 tablespoons sweet Hungarian paprika
1 tablespoon ground New Mexico chile powder
1 tablespoon ground cumin
4 teaspoons kosher salt
2 teaspoons freshly ground black pepper
1 teaspoon minced garlic
1 teaspoon ground coriander
¼ teaspoon ground cayenne pepper
Medium hog casings

FOR DETAILS ON MAKING SAUSAGE, SEE PAGE 10.

Fire-roast and peel the peppers and chiles (see page 73), and then seed and chop them coarsely. All the peppers combined should yield about 2 cups. Cool them in the refrigerator while you grind the meat.

Grind all the meats and fat through a ⅜-inch plate. In a large bowl, mix the meats and fat with the vinegar or lime juice, water, cilantro, paprika, chile powder, cumin, salt, black pepper, garlic, coriander, and cayenne. Knead the mixture thoroughly until all the ingredients are well blended. Do not overmix. Chill for at least 1 hour or overnight.

Stuff the sausage meat into medium hog casings, and tie into 5-inch links.

The sausage keeps in the refrigerator for 3 days, or in the freezer for 2 months.

Makes about 4 pounds

W<small>E'VE CREATED A LIGHTER CHICKEN AND TURKEY SAUSAGE USING</small> jalapeños and fire-roasted Anaheim chiles blended with garlic, cumin, and cilantro along with some dark beer and an optional belt of tequila. You can use it in place of chorizo or other pork-based southwestern sausage in tacos, burritos, and tamales.

1¾ pounds boned chicken thighs with skin (about 2¼ pounds with bones) or 1¾ pounds ground chicken

1¾ pounds boned turkey thighs with skin (about 2¼ pounds with bones) or 1¾ pounds ground turkey

1 Anaheim chile, fire-roasted (page 73), seeded, deveined, and chopped

1 jalapeño chile, seeded, deveined, and finely chopped (1 to 2 tablespoons)

1 bunch (4 to 6 ounces) cilantro, chopped (about 1 cup)

¼ cup amber beer (such as Dos Equis)

2 tablespoons tequila (optional)

⅓ cup pure New Mexico chile powder

1½ tablespoons kosher salt

2 teaspoons ground cumin

1½ teaspoons freshly ground black pepper

½ teaspoon ground cayenne pepper

Pinch of ground cinnamon

Medium hog casings

F<small>OR DETAILS ON MAKING SAUSAGE, SEE PAGE</small> 10.

If using chicken and turkey thighs, coarsely grind the meat and skin through a meat grinder fitted with a ⅜-inch plate or chop coarsely in batches in a food processor.

In a large bowl, mix the ground chicken and turkey with the chiles, cilantro, beer, tequila, chile powder, salt, cumin, black pepper, cayenne, and cinnamon. Blend thoroughly with your hands. Fry a small patty until done and taste for salt, pepper, and other seasonings.

Stuff the sausages into medium hog casings, and tie into 5-inch links. The sausage keeps in the refrigerator for 3 days, or in the freezer for 2 months.

Texas Smoky Links

Makes about 3 pounds

Sausage making in Texas goes back to the days of the Lone Star Republic, when Germans and Alsatians emigrated to the new country in large numbers, particularly around the towns of Castroville and New Braunfels. What began as food for immigrant communities soon became popular with the rest of the early settlers. Sausages have become one of the staples of a traditional Texas barbecue.

Texas smoked sausages are made with beef and pork; vary the proportions to suit your taste. Hot smoke or cold smoke the sausages, depending on your preference and attitude towards using curing salts.

2 pounds pork butt
½ pound beef chuck
½ pound pork back fat
½ cup water
1 tablespoon coarsely ground
*   black pepper*
4 teaspoons kosher salt
2 teaspoons ground cumin

2 teaspoons chopped garlic
2 teaspoons red pepper flakes
1 teaspoon ground coriander
Pinch of ground allspice
Pinch of cloves
1 teaspoon curing salts (page 21)
*   (optional)*
Wide hog casings

For details on making sausage, see page 10.

Grind the pork through a ⅜-inch plate. Grind the beef and pork fat through a ¼-inch plate. In a large bowl, mix the ground meats and fat with the water, black pepper, salt, cumin, garlic, red pepper, coriander, allspice, and cloves. Add the curing salts if the sausage is to be cold smoked.

Stuff the sausage into wide hog casings, and tie into 8-inch links.

If cold smoking, air-dry overnight in a cool place, and smoke the sausage for at least 12 hours according to the directions on page 17. Otherwise, dry overnight, uncovered, in the refrigerator. Hot smoke the sausages to an internal temperature of 155° according to the directions on page 18.

The sausage will keep for 1 week in the refrigerator, or for 2 months in the freezer.

Chapter 3

MEDITERRANEAN SAUSAGE

SAUSAGES FROM ALL OVER THE MEDITERRANEAN (ITALY, SPAIN, PORTUGAL, Greece, North Africa) came into America through the great ports of the Eastern Seaboard and added life and seasoning to our cooking. Stroll through New York's Little Italy or South Philly's Italian market where you can stop at any lunch counter for a hero sandwich made with Italian sausage, rich with garlic, pepper, and anise, layered with fried peppers and onions. As you walk down the sidewalk, munching the sandwich, savory juice dripping through your fingers and onto your shirt, give thanks to all those nameless immigrant cooks who brought these flavors to American cooking.

Italy, from the Alps to Sicily, is a mosaic of differing flavors. Each village, town, or region seems to have a slightly different accent, in both language and food. The sausages of Italy are as rich and variegated as its culture, and much of the attraction of Italy's sausages, and its people, is found in just this diversity. The standard sweet Italian and hot Italian sausages available in most American cities today offer just a hint of the unbounded variety of Italian sausages.

In America, Italians, like most immigrant groups, tended to form neighborhoods from regions in the old country. *Paisano* means, literally, a person from the same "countryside," and New York's Little Italy could easily be subdivided into Little Sicily, Calabria, or Tuscany, with each region's distinctive sausages sold in the pork stores and restaurants of each neighborhood. We give recipes for some of these individually styled sausages of Italian regions and American neighborhoods. Like most Italians, we'll talk more in "dialect" than "polite Italian," and try to preserve some of the lively diversity of Italy's sausages and sausage dishes as they are found in Italian-American restaurants and home kitchens.

If you've ever sat at a table in a Greek café on New York's 9th Avenue or Chicago's Greek neighborhoods and ordered an ouzo or a glass of retsina, you'll know about the wonderful custom called *mezedes*. These little snacks are considered an indispensable accompaniment to drinks, and usually include olives, some sharp white cheese like feta or Kefalotiri, a bite or two of chewy octopus, and a chunk of grilled loukanika, the flavorful Greek sausage. The spicy sausage can also add flavor to beans, pasta, and salad.

You can sit down to huge platters of linguiça and clams in Portuguese restaurants all over New England, from New Bedford to New Haven. The American descendants of Portuguese fishermen who settled in the region are great lovers of sausage. They use their tangy linguiça, spicy chouriço, and Spanish Basque chorizo with a great range of foods, often mixing the sausages with seafood, chicken, and meat. These sausages are also great for sandwiches or appetizers, and contribute spice to bean and pasta dishes, stews, and casseroles.

In the Eastern and Southern Mediterranean (and in Near Eastern neighborhoods in American cities), you can find garlicky sausages based on lamb, or beef. Merguez from North Africa and shawarma from Lebanon are both redolent of the flavors of the Middle East—garlic and pepper, mint and cumin, lemon and oregano. These tasty mixtures of meat and spices are often used to stuff vegetables, grape leaves, and pastries and add zest to lentils, chickpeas, rice, beans, and pasta.

New York–Style Spicy Hot Italian Sausage

Makes about 4 pounds

THIS SPICY SAUSAGE IS THE ONE YOU'RE MOST LIKELY TO FIND SIZZLING ON a grill at the Feast of San Gennaro or at a lunch counter in New York's Little Italy. Try it grilled, with fried peppers and onions, or poached and sliced on top of homemade pizza.

3 pounds pork butt
¾ pound pork back fat
2 tablespoons anise-flavored liqueur, such as Sambuca (optional)
2 tablespoons anise or fennel seeds
1 tablespoon minced garlic

1 tablespoon red pepper flakes
4 teaspoons kosher salt
2 teaspoons freshly ground black pepper
1 teaspoon ground cayenne pepper
¼ cup water, as needed
Medium hog casings

For details on making sausage, see page 10.

Combine the pork and fat with the liqueur, anise seeds, garlic, red pepper, salt, black pepper, and cayenne in a large bowl. Grind everything through a ⅜-inch plate. Moisten with the water, and squeeze and knead the mixture until everything is well blended.

Stuff into medium hog casings, and tie into 5-inch links.

The sausage will keep for 3 days in the refrigerator, or for 2 to 3 months in the freezer.

Festia di San Gennaro: New York's Little Italy

At the Feast of San Gennaro on Mulberry Street in New York's Little Italy, there's music and laughter, and Italian in every dialect from Sicilian to Toscano, Friulano to Calabrese. Everybody's out on the streets celebrating the saint's day with feasting, talk, and good times. Sausages of virtually every region in Italy are grilled at sidewalk stands, with smells of garlic, peppers, onions, and olive oil everywhere. At one stand there's aromatic Tuscan sausage flavored with sundried tomatoes, basil, and wine; at another, Barese sausage, redolent with anise, Pecorino cheese, garlic, and oregano.

With glasses of rough, homemade Zinfandel in our hands, we order spicy Sicilian sausages from an old man whose dark face is wrinkled and creased from years of smiles and sun. He pricks the skins with a long, thin knife, and lays the sausages carefully on the hot grill over glowing coals. The sausages smoke and jump on the grill, aromas of garlic, pepper, and fennel billowing up. With one deft movement, he flips them over and to the side. He tosses a handful of sliced onions and peppers into a blackened frying pan, and pours in green-gold olive oil from an old wine bottle.

As the peppers and onions sputter in the oil, he splits two rolls and lays them down along the far side of the grill. Suddenly, the old man smiles and nods to us, scoops up the peppers and onions on one side of the roll, the sausage on the other, wraps them together in paper, and hands them to us. He watches us carefully as we bite into the sandwiches. Spicy pork, garlic, hot pepper, fennel, and onions all come together in a rush of flavors and textures. We gulp down big juice glasses full of fiery, slightly sweet Zinfandel, look into his bright and ancient eyes, and smile back.

Tuscan Sausage

Makes about 4 pounds

FOR DETAILS ON MAKING SAUSAGE, SEE PAGE 10.

TUSCANY IS FAMOUS FOR ITS WINES AND OLIVE OILS, AND ALSO FOR ITS delicately flavored sausages. What comes through here is not the heat and spice of the South, but rather the subtle aromas of herbs, tomatoes, and wine. Tuscan sausage accents the flavors of chicken and squab very nicely and can be used in any dish where a mild flavor is desired.

3 pounds pork butt
½ pound pork back fat
½ cup chopped sundried tomatoes
    packed in olive oil
¼ cup Chianti or other dry red
    wine
¼ cup minced fresh basil or
    1 tablespoon dried

4 anchovy fillets, finely chopped
2 tablespoons chopped fresh
    oregano or 2 teaspoons dried
2 teaspoons kosher salt
2 teaspoons coarsely ground
    black pepper
Pinch of allspice
Medium hog casings

Grind the pork meat through a ⅜-inch plate, the fat through a ¼-inch plate. In a large bowl, combine the meat and fat with the tomatoes, Chianti, basil, anchovies, oregano, salt, black pepper, and allspice. Knead together until the mixture is well blended.

Stuff into casings, and tie into 6-inch links.

The sausage will keep for 3 days in the refrigerator, or for 2 months in the freezer.

Italian Sweet Fennel Sausage

Makes about 4 pounds

THIS MILDLY FLAVORED SAUSAGE IS PERFUMED WITH THE SCENTS OF FENNEL, allspice, and oregano. It is the sweet Italian sausage of your neighborhood delicatessen. Use it wherever you want a pleasant fresh sausage with a touch of garlic, spices, and herbs.

3 pounds pork butt
¾ pound pork back fat
½ cup dry red wine
4 garlic cloves, minced
2 tablespoons fennel seeds
1 tablespoon freshly ground
    black pepper

4 teaspoons kosher salt
1 teaspoon dried oregano
⅛ teaspoon ground allspice
Medium hog casings (optional)

For details on making sausage, see page 10.

Grind the pork and fat together through a ⅜-inch plate. In a large bowl, combine the pork and fat with the wine, garlic, fennel, black pepper, salt, oregano, and allspice. Mix well with your hands.

Shape into patties, or stuff into casings and tie into 5-inch links.

The sausage will keep for 3 days in the refrigerator, or for 2 months in the freezer.

Italian Turkey and Sundried Tomato Sausage

Makes about 4 pounds

In this poultry version of an Italian sausage, we've put together a blend of sundried tomatoes, wine, fennel, red pepper, and lots of garlic with turkey as a base. You can vary the recipe a bit for regional character—more garlic and red pepper for a Calabrese touch, for example, or even more garlic along with a couple of tablespoons of grated Romano cheese for a hint of the south. Use this savory sausage wherever you want an Italian accent. It's perfect for pasta, especially when combined with fresh tomatoes, garlic, and basil.

3½ pounds boned turkey thighs with skin (about 4½ pounds with bones) or 3½ pounds ground turkey
⅓ cup chopped sundried tomatoes packed in olive oil
¼ cup white wine
3 tablespoons chopped garlic

2 tablespoons fennel seeds
1 tablespoon freshly ground black pepper
4 teaspoons kosher salt
1 teaspoon red pepper flakes
1 teaspoon sugar
Medium hog casings

For details on making sausage, see page 10.

If using turkey thighs, coarsely grind the boned turkey and skin through a meat grinder fitted with a ⅜-inch plate, or chop coarsely in batches in a food processor. Add the tomatoes, wine, garlic, fennel, black pepper, salt, red pepper, and sugar to the ground turkey in a large bowl and blend thoroughly with your hands. Fry a small patty until done and taste for salt, pepper, and other seasonings.

Stuff into casings and tie into 6-inch links, or leave as bulk.

The sausage will keep for 3 days in the refrigerator, or for 2 months in the freezer.

Barese-Style Sausage

Makes about 4¹/₂ pounds

THIS POPULAR SAUSAGE, MADE IN THE STYLE OF BARI IN SOUTHERN ITALY'S Puglia region, contains Pecorino Romano cheese. The sausage's lively, aggressive flavors make it a favorite in Italian neighborhoods in New Orleans. Don't store this sausage for too long in the refrigerator or freezer, as the cheese can become quite strong with age and overpower the other flavors.

2 pounds lean pork butt
1 pound lean beef chuck
1 pound pork back fat
1 cup (about 4 ounces) cubed
  Pecorino Romano cheese
½ cup dry red wine
¼ cup chopped fresh flat-leaf
  parsley

1 tablespoon freshly ground black
  pepper
1 tablespoon ground fennel seeds
1 tablespoon finely chopped garlic
1 tablespoon kosher salt
1 tablespoon red pepper flakes
Medium hog casings

FOR DETAILS ON MAKING SAUSAGE, SEE PAGE 10.

In a large bowl, toss together the meat, fat, and cheese. Grind through a ⅜-inch plate. In a large bowl, combine the ground meat mixture with the wine, parsley, black pepper, fennel, garlic, salt, and red pepper. Knead the mixture well.

Stuff into casings, and tie into 4-inch links.

The sausage keeps for 2 to 3 days in the refrigerator, or for 1 to 2 months in the freezer.

COTECHINO IS A DELIGHTFULLY AROMATIC, LARGE BOILING SAUSAGE THAT lends flavor to beans, lentils, and soups (see Cotechino with Lentils, page 204). Cooked pork skin is added to give this sausage body and a firm texture. When stuffed into a boned pig's foot, this becomes *zampone*, a specialty of Modena in northern Italy.

Makes about 4 pounds

1 pound pork skin cut from the ham, belly, or back	¼ teaspoon ground sage
3 pounds pork butt	¼ teaspoon dried marjoram or oregano
½ pound pancetta	¼ teaspoon pure vanilla extract
¼ pound pork back fat	Pinch of ground allspice
1 tablespoon coarsely ground black pepper	Pinch of cinnamon
4 teaspoons kosher salt	Pinch of ginger
2 teaspoons sugar	Pinch of freshly grated nutmeg
½ teaspoon dried thyme	1 teaspoons curing salts (page 21) (optional)
½ teaspoon ground bay leaf (use blender or spice mill)	½ cup dry white wine
	Beef round casings

FOR DETAILS ON MAKING SAUSAGE, SEE PAGE 10.

Place the pork skin in a medium saucepan, cover with water, and bring to a boil. Decrease the heat, cover, and simmer for about 45 minutes, until the skin is soft. Drain and cool under running water. The skin must be completely cool or it will clump up when ground. Grind skin, meat, pancetta, and fat through a ¼-inch plate. Mix together with the black pepper, salt, sugar, thyme, bay leaf, sage, marjoram, vanilla, allspice, cinnamon, ginger, and nutmeg. Add the curing salts if you plan to air-dry the sausage. Moisten the mixture with the wine and knead until all the ingredients are well blended.

Stuff into large casings, and tie into large links, 7 to 8 inches long.

Air-dry the sausage on a rack for 2 to 3 days in the refrigerator or, if you are using curing salts, at room temperature according to the directions on page 17. The sausage will keep 5 days in the refrigerator, or for 2 months in the freezer.

Cooking Notes
To poach, bring a large pot of lightly salted water to a boil. Add the sausage. Maintain a poaching temperature of 160° to 180° for 1 to 1½ hours, or until the sausages reach an internal temperature of 155°. Serve immediately, or drain and cool.

Loukanika

Makes about 4 pounds

LOUKANIKA IS NOT ONLY A TASTY SNACK BEFORE DINNER, BUT LIKE MOST fully flavored sausages, it can be a savory addition to many chicken, meat, or pasta dishes. It is sometimes made entirely with pork, sometimes with a mix of pork and lamb, or pork and beef. We use pork and lamb, but you should feel free to experiment. Serve as part of *mezes*, the traditional Greek appetizers, accompanied by ouzo. Loukanika also provides spice and flavor in traditional Greek dishes like Pastitsio (page 198).

¼ cup olive oil
1 cup chopped onions
2 pounds pork butt
1 pound lean lamb shoulder
¾ pound pork back fat
2 tablespoons grated orange zest
1 tablespoon minced garlic
1 tablespoon ground coriander
4 teaspoons kosher salt
1 teaspoon freshly ground black pepper

2 teaspoons dried oregano or
1 tablespoon chopped fresh oregano
1 teaspoon dried thyme or
2 teaspoons chopped fresh thyme
½ cup dry white wine (use retsina, if you like the flavor)
Medium hog casings

FOR DETAILS ON MAKING SAUSAGE, SEE PAGE 10.

Heat the olive oil in a heavy skillet over medium heat. Add the onions, cover, and cook until the onions are translucent, stirring occasionally, about 10 minutes. Spread the onions on a plate and chill them quickly in the freezer for about 15 minutes.

In a large bowl, mix the onions with the pork, lamb, pork fat, orange zest, garlic, coriander, salt, black pepper, oregano, and thyme. Grind the mixture through a ¼-inch plate. In a large bowl, combine the ground mixture with the wine, and knead well until all the ingredients are blended together.

Stuff into medium hog casings, and tie into 6-inch links.

Loukanika will keep for 3 days in the refrigerator, or for 2 months in the freezer.

Linguiça

Makes about 3 pounds

Linguiça is one of a family of smoked sausages that are coarse in texture and usually fairly spicy. Other similar sausages, such as kielbasa, andouille, and smoked country sausage, are the backbone of country cooking all over the world and are found in many dishes and almost every tradition. The Portuguese are particularly passionate about their sausages and use them in a wide variety of dishes. They realize how much flavor and excitement sausages such as linguiça can add to even the simplest dish.

3 pounds pork butt
½ pound pork back fat
3 tablespoons red wine vinegar
3 tablespoons high-quality sweet
    paprika, Hungarian or Spanish
1 tablespoon minced garlic
1 tablespoon freshly ground black
    pepper

4 teaspoons kosher salt
½ teaspoon dried marjoram
½ teaspoon dried oregano
Pinch of ground coriander
1 teaspoon curing salts (page 21)
    (optional)
Wide hog casings

For details on making sausage, see page 10.

Separate all the external fat from the pork and refrigerate it along with the back fat. Cut the lean meat into strips. In a small bowl, combine the vinegar, paprika, garlic, black pepper, kosher salt, marjoram, oregano, and coriander. Add the curing salts if you plan to cold smoke. Liberally coat the meat and fat with this spice rub. Pack the meat and fat into a plastic tub or stainless steel bowl, cover, and refrigerate it overnight to marinate.

The next day, grind the lean pork through a very coarse (⅜- or ½-inch) plate, then grind the fat through a ¼-inch plate. In a large bowl, mix the lean meat and fat along with any liquid and spices still remaining from the marinade. Knead and squeeze the mixture until all the ingredients are thoroughly blended.

Stuff into wide hog casings, and tie into 10-inch links.

Air-dry and cold smoke the sausage for 12 hours according to the directions on page 17. Or hot smoke the sausages according to the directions on page 18, or until the sausages reach an internal temperature of 155°.

The sausage will keep for 1 week in the refrigerator, or for 2 months in the freezer.

Portuguese Chouriço

Makes about 3 pounds

∴∴∴

THIS SAUSAGE IS SIMILAR TO LINGUIÇA, BUT A DIFFERENT SPICE MIXTURE AND a bit of cayenne give it more heat. Use chouriço in recipes where you want plenty of spicy flavor.

3 pounds pork butt
½ pound pork back fat
3 tablespoons red wine vinegar
3 tablespoons high-quality paprika,
   sweet Hungarian or Spanish
1 tablespoon minced garlic
4 teaspoons kosher salt
1 teaspoon ground cayenne pepper

1 teaspoon freshly ground black
   pepper
1 teaspoon ground cumin
½ teaspoon dried marjoram
½ teaspoon ground coriander
1 teaspoon curing salts (page 21)
   (optional)
Wide hog casings

FOR DETAILS ON MAKING SAUSAGE, SEE PAGE 10.

Separate all the external fat from the pork and refrigerate it along with the back fat. Cut the lean meat into strips. In a small bowl, combine the vinegar, paprika, garlic, salt, cayenne, black pepper, cumin, marjoram, and coriander. Add the curing salts if you plan to cold smoke. Liberally coat the meat and fat with this spice rub. Pack the meat and fat into a plastic tub or stainless steel bowl, cover, and refrigerate overnight to marinate.

The next day, grind the lean pork through a very coarse (⅜- or ½-inch) plate, then grind the fat through a ¼-inch plate. In a large bowl, mix the lean meat and fat along with any liquid and spices still remaining from the marinade. Knead and squeeze the mixture until all the ingredients are thoroughly blended.

Air-dry and cold smoke the sausages for 12 hours according to the directions on page 17, or hot smoke (see 18) until the sausages reach an internal temperature of 155°.

The sausages will keep for 1 week in the refrigerator, or for 2 months in the freezer.

Makes about 2¹/₂ pounds

Spanish or Basque chorizo is very different from the more common Mexican variety. The Spanish style is milder, less *picante*, and is often air-dried or smoked to concentrate and intensify the flavors.

If properly air-dried and/or smoked, this sausage doesn't need refrigeration. As a result, dried, smoked chorizo became a staple in the diet of Basque sheepherders who tended their flocks far from civilization and electricity. Since most of us (even sheepherders) have refrigerators these days, you should store the chorizo in the refrigerator even when air-drying and using curing salts.

2½ pounds pork shoulder
½ pound beef plate or fatty chuck
½ cup sweet Spanish or
  Hungarian paprika
¼ cup dried New Mexico chile
  puree (see note below)
¼ cup minced garlic
3 tablespoons dry red wine
4 teaspoons kosher salt

2 teaspoons sugar
2 teaspoons coarsely ground
  black pepper
Pinch of ground cloves
1 teaspoon curing salts dissolved
  in ¼ cup water (page 21)
  (optional)
Medium to wide hog casings

For details on making sausage, see page 10.

Grind the pork and beef through a ⅜-inch plate. In a large bowl, combine the ground meat with the paprika, chile puree, garlic, wine, salt, sugar, black pepper, and cloves. Add the curing salts if you are planning to air-dry the sausages. Mix well, kneading the meats and spices until everything is thoroughly blended.

Stuff into medium to wide hog casings, and tie into 10-inch links.

If you've added the curing salts, air-dry the sausages in a cool place until they are firm. This may take as long as 2 to 3 weeks. Alternatively, you can hot smoke the sausages according to the directions on page 18 until their internal temperature reaches 155°.

After hot smoking, you can store the sausages for up to 1 week in the refrigerator, or for up to 2 months in the freezer. Air-dried chorizo will keep for 1 month in the refrigerator, or for 2 months in the freezer.

New Mexico Chile Puree

To make a small amount, soak two dried New Mexico chiles in boiling water to cover for 10 minutes. Drain, reserving water, and remove stems and seeds, then puree chiles in a food processor, adding a teaspoon of the reserved soaking water.

Spicy Lamb, Pine Nut, and Sundried Tomato Sausage

Makes about 4 pounds

ALL AROUND THE SOUTHERN SHORES OF THE MEDITERRANEAN, WE FIND spicy, GARlicky sausages made from lamb. These tangy sausages are redolent with the flavors of the Middle East (mint, cumin, coriander) and are used to spice up lentils, chickpeas, rice, beans, and pasta. The tasty mixtures are often used to stuff vegetables, grape leaves, and pastries as appetizers. Grilled lamb sausages are especially delicious stuffed into pita bread with a piquant sauce.

2¼ pounds lean lamb from the shoulder or leg
¾ pound pork back fat or beef fat
½ cup chopped fresh cilantro
⅓ cup finely chopped sundried tomatoes packed in oil
¼ cup finely chopped onion
¼ cup finely chopped red bell pepper
¼ cup toasted pine nuts
2 tablespoons olive oil from the sundried tomatoes

1 tablespoon tomato paste
1 tablespoon chopped fresh mint
4 teaspoons kosher salt
2 teaspoons minced garlic
1 teaspoon ground cayenne pepper
1 teaspoon ground cumin
1 teaspoon ground coriander
1 teaspoon coarsely ground black pepper
½ teaspoon ground allspice
1 egg, beaten
Medium hog or lamb casings

FOR DETAILS ON MAKING SAUSAGE, SEE PAGE 10.

Grind the meat and fat through a ¼-inch plate. In a large bowl, mix with the cilantro, tomatoes, onion, bell pepper, pine nuts, olive oil, tomato paste, mint, salt, garlic, cayenne, cumin, coriander, black pepper, allspice, and egg until well blended.

Stuff into medium hog casings or lamb casings, and tie into 5- to 6-inch links.

The sausage will keep for 3 days in the refrigerator, or for 2 months in the freezer.

W̲E'VE LIGHTENED THE SAUSAGE MIX BY USING CHICKEN AND TURKEY instead of lamb or beef, but the zesty flavors of the Mediterranean are still there. We love it with lentils, in pasta salad, or in soup with spinach or other greens.

2 cups sliced onions

1¾ pounds boned chicken thighs
  with skin (about 2¼ pounds
  with bones) or 1¾ pounds
  ground chicken

1¾ pounds boned turkey thighs
  with skin (about 2¼ pounds
  with bones) or 1¾ pounds
  ground turkey

¼ cup chopped fresh parsley

2 tablespoons chopped garlic

2 tablespoons sweet Hungarian
  paprika

2 tablespoons kosher salt

2 tablespoons olive oil

2 tablespoons chopped fresh mint
  or 2 teaspoons dried mint

1 tablespoon tomato paste

1 tablespoon fresh lemon juice

2 teaspoons finely chopped lemon
  zest

2 teaspoons fennel seeds, ground in
  a mortar, spice grinder, or
  food processor

2 teaspoons ground cumin

2 teaspoons ground coriander

2 teaspoons freshly ground black
  pepper

1 teaspoon sugar

1 teaspoon ground turmeric

½ teaspoon ground allspice

½ teaspoon ground cayenne pepper

FOR DETAILS ON MAKING SAUSAGE, SEE PAGE 10.

Simmer the onions in water to cover until translucent, 5 to 7 minutes. Cool under cold running water and drain. Using a ⅜-inch plate, coarsely grind the onions with the chicken, turkey, and skin or chop coarsely in batches in a food processor. If using previously ground chicken or turkey, omit this step. Coarsely grind or chop the onions, and mix them thoroughly with the ground poultry.

In a large bowl, combine the ground poultry mixture with the parsley, garlic, paprika, salt, olive oil, mint, tomato paste, lemon juice, lemon zest, fennel, cumin, coriander, black pepper, sugar, turmeric, allspice, and cayenne. Blend thoroughly with your hands. Fry a small patty until done and taste for salt, pepper, and other seasonings. Stuff into casings, and tie into 6-inch links.

The sausages will keep for 3 days in the refrigerator, or for 2 months in the freezer.

Chapter 4
ASIAN-STYLE SAUSAGE

Chinese, Japanese, Thai, and other Asian cooks have created rich and complex cuisines that have been constant sources of flavor and innovation in American cooking. An obsession with fresh, high-quality ingredients, the ability to balance flavors with skill and imagination, and the subtle use of aromatics and spices are qualities that make Asian cooking so satisfying. A plus is the Asian attitude about meat and fat—most dishes use only enough meat to flavor large amounts of rice, noodles, or vegetables. Meat is seen as a condiment, rather than the main component of the meal.

This is why sausage works so well in Asian-influenced food. Sausages are highly seasoned bits of meats that provide an explosion of flavor in bland ingredients, with a minimum of fat or calories. And if you use our recipes for chicken and turkey sausages, even less fat and cholesterol are added to the dish.

Sausage is especially adaptable to stir-frying, where vegetables, meat, or poultry and flavorings are quickly cooked together and then served with rice or noodles. This quick and healthful method of cooking need not be limited to Asian dishes. It works just as well with a sauce for pasta or a quick sauté of fresh vegetables.

Chinese cooks frequently use the sweet, aromatic sausage *lop chong* in stir-fries and casseroles and stuff wontons and dim sum with highly seasoned mixtures of ground meat and seafood. With the availability of premade wrappers, dim sum, wonton, and even ravioli are easy to make.

Lion's head, a succulent meatball made from pork and aromatic seasonings, is one inspiration for these savory sausages. Another is *lop chong*, the thin, mahogany-red sausages you see hanging in Chinese pork butcher's windows. The fragrant seasonings used in both dishes—five-spice powder, cinnamon, star anise—add a subtle, sweet undertone to the sausage, making it especially good in braises or stir-fries.

We prefer to wrap the sausage meat in the veil-like caul fat of the pig to make crépinettes, but you could just as easily leave it in bulk. If you can't find caul fat, then simply shape into patties.

3 pounds pork shoulder
½ pound pork back fat
2 bunches (8 to 12 ounces) cilantro
    or flat-leaf parsley, coarsely
    chopped (about 2 cups)
4 green onions or scallions, finely
    chopped
¼ cup Chinese rice wine or
    Madeira
4 teaspoons kosher salt

2 teaspoons minced garlic
2 teaspoons Szechuan peppercorns,
    roasted and ground
2 teaspoons Chinese five-spice
    powder or 2 teaspoons ground
    star anise
1 teaspoon freshly ground black
    pepper
Pinch of cinnamon
1 pound caul fat, soaked

For details on making sausage, see page 10.

Grind the meat and fat through a ⅜-inch plate. In a large bowl, mix the meat and fat with the cilantro, green onions, wine, salt, garlic, Szechuan peppercorns, five-spice powder, black pepper, and cinnamon. Knead everything together thoroughly with your hands. Chill the sausage meat for at least an hour or overnight.

To make the crépinettes, spread out sheets of the lacy caul fat and cut into 6-inch squares. Wrap each square around ⅓ cup of the meat mixture. Shape into ovals. For patties, shape about ⅓ cup into ovals. You can freeze any leftover caul fat.

The sausage will keep for 2 to 3 days in the refrigerator, or for 2 months in the freezer.

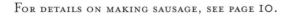

THESE SWEET SAUSAGES SOLD THROUGHOUT CHINATOWN ARE USUALLY steamed or used to flavor other foods. In our recipe, they are slow cooked in an oven rather than air-dried.

Lop Chong (Chinese Sweet Sausage)

2½ pounds pork
¾ pound pork back fat
3 tablespoons light brown sugar
3 tablespoons Scotch whisky
2 tablespoons soy sauce

2 tablespoons water
1 tablespoon sweet sherry
2 teaspoons kosher salt
1 teaspoon five-spice powder
Medium hog casings

FOR DETAILS ON MAKING SAUSAGE, SEE PAGE 10.

Makes 2 to 3 pounds

Grind the meat and fat through a ⅜-inch plate or hand dice the meat and fat into ¼-inch pieces. Place in a large bowl and add the sugar, Scotch, soy sauce, water, sherry, salt, and five-spice powder. Knead until well blended.

Stuff the mixture into hog casings, and tie into 5-inch links. Air-dry the sausage on a shelf in the refrigerator overnight.

The next day, preheat the oven to 200°. Place the sausages on a rack in a roasting pan so they do not touch and bake for about 5 hours. Turn off the oven, and let the sausage cool for 2 hours in the oven.

Discard any fat and store the sausage for 1 week in the refrigerator, or for 2 months in the freezer.

How to Reconstitute Dried Mushrooms

Place dried mushrooms in a heatproof glass bowl or large measuring cup. Cover with boiling water and soak for at least 30 minutes or for up to 3 hours. Remove the mushrooms with a slotted spoon; discard tough stems and reserve the caps. (Decant the soaking water off the gritty sediment to use later in soups and stir-fries or to cook rice.)

Μυch of the flavor excitement in Chinese dishes comes from aromatics, herbs, mushrooms, and spices. Our sausage incorporates smoky dried shiitake mushrooms, fermented black beans, and soy, along with ginger, garlic, and sherry. Five-spice powder—an aromatic blend of star anise, fennel, cloves, cinnamon, and Szechuan pepper—gives an intriguing undertone. Try this sausage in salads such as Cold Chinese Noodles and Sausage with Sesame Dressing (page 156), or appetizers, such as My Pot Stickers (page 153). It is also delicious in Chinese Braised Stuffed Fish (page 224).

1¾ pounds boned chicken thighs with skin (about 2¼ pounds with bone) or 1¾ pounds ground chicken

1¾ pounds boned turkey thighs with skin (about 2¼ pounds with bone) or 1¾ pounds ground turkey

1 ounce (10 to 12) Chinese dried black mushrooms, reconstituted (left)

½ cup finely chopped green onions or scallions, green and white parts

¼ cup Chinese dark soy sauce

2 tablespoons chopped fresh ginger

2 tablespoons sweet sherry

1 tablespoon sesame oil

1 tablespoon chopped garlic

1 tablespoon kosher salt

1 tablespoon freshly ground black pepper

1 teaspoon sugar

1 teaspoon chopped Chinese fermented black beans

1 teaspoon five-spice powder

For details on making sausage, see page 10.

Using a ⅜-inch plate, coarsely grind the chicken, turkey, skin, and soaked mushroom caps or chop coarsely in batches in a food processor. If using previously ground chicken or turkey, chop the mushrooms and mix with ground poultry.

In a large bowl, combine the poultry mixture with the green onions, soy sauce, ginger, sherry, sesame oil, garlic, salt, black pepper, sugar, black beans, and five-spice powder. Knead thoroughly with your hands. Fry a small patty until done and taste for salt, pepper, and other seasonings. Since this sausage is usually used in bulk, it is not necessary to stuff it into casings. Divide the sausage into 7 or 8 portions (about ½ pound each), and wrap tightly in plastic wrap or aluminum foil. The sausage will keep for 3 days in the refrigerator, or for 2 months in the freezer.

Makes about 3 pounds

Pork and shrimp are often mixed as a stuffing for dim sum, the popular steamed dumplings served in the sometimes palatial teahouses of San Francisco's Chinatown. This richly flavored sausage is a great filling for wonton, egg rolls, pot stickers, or any type of meat-filled dumpling—or it can be turned into delicious small meatballs as a garnish for Chinese soup or braised with turnip or mustard greens. This sausage of ours has a bit more flavor and spice than the typical dim sum filling and can be used in a wide variety of dishes. You can grill and eat it by itself, either stuffed in casings or left in bulk and then formed into patties.

2 pounds pork shoulder
½ pound shrimp, peeled and
   deveined
½ pound pork back fat
¼ cup Chinese soy sauce
¼ cup sweet sherry
¼ cup finely chopped green onions
   or scallions, or Chinese garlic
   chives

2 teaspoons finely chopped fresh
   ginger
1 teaspoon minced garlic
½ teaspoon Chinese chili paste
   (available in Chinese groceries
   or specialty shops), or 2 to 3
   dashes of hot sauce, such as
   Tabasco sauce
Medium hog casings (optional)

For details on making sausage, see page 10.

Grind the pork, shrimp, and fat through a ¼-inch plate into a large bowl. Add the soy sauce, sherry, green onions, ginger, garlic, and chili paste. Knead the mixture until everything is well blended together.

Stuff into medium hog casings and tie into 5-inch links, or leave in bulk for patties or meatballs, or to use as a filling.

This sausage will keep for 3 days in the refrigerator, or for 2 months in the freezer.

Thai Chicken and Turkey Sausage

Makes about 4 pounds

WHEN PEOPLE GET THEIR FIRST TASTE OF THAI COOKING, IT'S OFTEN A REV-elation and they are converts for life. It's not exactly a bolt of lightning or a mystical experience, but rather the sudden thought "Why doesn't all food taste like this—fiery and bright and exciting?"

Thai food can become an obsession. It is so addictive that it can make you a little crazy. You stop strangers on the street and tell them about the squid salad you just ate. Breathing garlic, lemongrass, and mint in their terrified faces, you hold them by the lapel as they try to pull away, run after them waving your arms as they bolt through the traffic because you forgot to mention this fantastic green curry in the restaurant down the block.

Green chiles and lots of heat; fresh basil, mint, and cilantro; limes and lemongrass; ginger; green curry; coconut milk; fish sauce—all these flavors make you want to sit up and sing (or at least reach for a Singha beer). Thai green curry paste and Southeast Asian fish sauce are available in Asian groceries or by mail order (see Sources, page 307).

1¾ pounds boned chicken thighs with skin (about 2¼ pounds with bones) or 1¾ pounds ground chicken	3 tablespoons chopped fresh basil
	3 tablespoons chopped fresh mint
	1½ tablespoons chopped garlic
1¾ pounds boned turkey thighs with skin (about 2¼ pounds with bones) or 1¾ pounds ground turkey	1½ tablespoons chopped fresh ginger
	1 to 2 tablespoons Thai green curry paste
	1 tablespoon kosher salt
1 bunch (4 to 6 ounces) fresh cilantro, including stems and roots, cleaned and chopped (about 1 cup)	1 teaspoon red pepper flakes
	1 tablespoon freshly ground black pepper
¼ cup Southeast Asian fish sauce	1 teaspoon ground cayenne pepper
	Medium hog casings

FOR DETAILS ON MAKING SAUSAGE, SEE PAGE 10.

If using chicken and turkey thighs, coarsely grind the meat and skin through a ⅜-inch plate or chop coarsely in batches in a food processor.

In a large bowl, combine the ground poultry with the cilantro, fish sauce, basil, mint, garlic, ginger, curry paste, salt, red pepper flakes, black pepper, and cayenne. Knead thoroughly with your hands. Fry a small patty until done and taste for salt, pepper, and other seasonings.

Stuff the sausage into medium hog casings, and tie into 5-inch links.

The sausage will keep for 3 days in the refrigerator, or for 2 months in the freezer.

Chapter 5

GAME AND SEAFOOD SAUSAGES

SAUSAGES HAVE BEEN MADE FROM GAME IN AMERICA SINCE COLONIAL TIMES. Sausage making is a good way to preserve surplus meat, and when you lugged home a deer or moose or elk, you needed a way to keep all that meat fresh. With refrigeration and freezing, modern hunters don't have to make sausage. But many hunters today make game sausages just because they taste so good.

And you don't have to be a hunter to make game sausages; venison, buffalo, pheasant, and other game animals and birds are farmed these days and are available from specialty butchers. Just ask your butcher or consult our Sources, page 307.

Fish and seafood sausages are popular these days because their subtle and delicious flavors suit the modern taste for lighter dishes. In addition, many diners feel that fish sausages are low in calories, although most recipes do call for goodly amounts of cream. While fish sausages may seem trendy, they are really similar to the quenelles, or fish dumplings, of classic French cuisine. The best are light in texture and subtly seasoned to accent the flavor of the fish and seafood.

The trick to making perfect fish sausages is to have all the ingredients well chilled so that they will stay light and properly absorb the cream. The food processor makes these delicious and delicate sausages easy to produce. They can serve as elegant and unusual first courses or appetizers for a special dinner party.

Pheasant and Wild Mushroom Sausages

Makes about 2 pounds

COLORFUL WILD PHEASANTS ARE STILL PLENTIFUL IN MANY REGIONS IN America, and some of the tastiest birds feed on the grain left behind at the harvest in the Midwest. These days, farm-raised pheasants are widely available for nonhunters from specialty butchers and mail-order houses. The light and elegant flavors of pheasant are popular with American chefs. Home cooks can take a tip from professional chefs and use pheasant in many different types of dishes. If you have several pheasants, you can use the breasts for elegant entrees, the thighs to make tasty sausage, and the wings, back, neck, and legs in a flavorful stock. Consign the pheasant legs to the stockpot. Don't try to make sausage from them. They have tough sinews running from the claw to the joint and very little meat. In general, try to use mature pheasants for sausages; young farm-raised pheasants can be a bit bland. When you dress the pheasant, try to save the fat and skin, both of which add plenty of flavor to the sausage. If you can't find pheasant, you can make this sausage with chicken thighs or with other types of game birds.

Pheasant is delicious with the many varieties of wild mushrooms that are coming into the market these days, particularly morels. If you can't find dried morels in a specialty store, use dried porcini or shiitake mushrooms.

Serve this luscious sausage by itself or sautéed with apples and onions, or dress it up in puff pastry or serve it over flaky biscuits.

⅓ cup (about ½ ounce) dried
    morels, porcini, or shiitake
    mushrooms
1 pound boned pheasant meat
    with skin attached
¼ pound pork back fat
¼ pound pheasant fat, if available
    (if not, use additional pork
    back fat)
2 tablespoons apple brandy,
    Calvados, or other brandy
1 tablespoon chopped fresh herbs,
    such as chervil, chives, or
    parsley (optional)

2 teaspoons chopped shallots
2 teaspoons kosher salt
1 teaspoon chopped fresh thyme
    or ¼ teaspoon dried
1 teaspoon coarsely ground black
    pepper
¼ teaspoon dried sage
Pinch of freshly grated nutmeg
Pinch of ground cloves
Lamb or small hog casings

FOR DETAILS ON MAKING SAUSAGE, SEE PAGE 10.

Cover the mushrooms with hot water and soak for at least 30 minutes. Drain, reserving the soaking liquid for another use. Chop the mushrooms.

Grind the pheasant, pork fat, and pheasant fat through a ¼-inch plate. In a large bowl, knead the ground meat and fat with the mushrooms, apple brandy, herbs, shallots, salt, thyme, black pepper, sage, nutmeg, and cloves until well blended together.

Stuff into lamb casings or small hog casings, and tie into 4- to 5-inch links.

The sausage will keep for 3 days in the refrigerator, or for 2 months in the freezer.

Venison Sausage

Makes about 4 pounds

Venison sausage often suffers from lack of fat, which makes it too dry, and from too many overpowering ingredients, which can mask the rich flavors of the meat. In this recipe we use herbs that complement the flavor of venison, and we allow the meat to marinate and mellow with these herbs overnight. To bring out the earthy flavors of these tangy sausages, grill or panfry them and serve with other wild ingredients, such as wild rice, morels or other wild mushrooms, and steamed wild greens (young dandelions, mâche, fiddleheads).

1½ pounds venison shoulder
1 pound pork butt
¾ pound pork back fat
½ pound slab bacon, rind removed
3 tablespoons dry red wine
2 tablespoons brandy
4 teaspoons kosher salt
2 teaspoons coarsely ground black pepper

2 teaspoons minced juniper berries
1 teaspoon minced garlic
1 teaspoon minced shallots
1 teaspoon fresh rosemary or ½ teaspoon dried
Medium hog casings

For details on making sausage, see page 10.

Cut the meat, fat, and bacon into 2-inch strips. In a large bowl, mix the meat, fat, and bacon with the wine, brandy, salt, black pepper, juniper berries, garlic, shallots, and rosemary. Cover and place in the refrigerator to marinate overnight.

The next day, grind the mixture through a ¼-inch plate. Add any juices remaining in the bowl. Knead to blend all the ingredients thoroughly.

Stuff into hog casings, and tie into 6-inch links. Dry the sausage, uncovered, in the refrigerator overnight.

The sausage will keep for 3 days in the refrigerator, or for 2 months in the freezer.

Hot Sausage Po' Boy (*page 178*)

Rotini with Broccoli Rabe, Sausage, and Balsamic Vinegar *(page 194)*

Braised Sausage with Polenta *(page 206)*

Chinese Braised Stuffed Fish *(page 224)*

Makes about 3½
pounds

Buffalo meat is much leaner than beef, but has the same rich flavors. This versatile meat is delicious grilled, baked, or in a stew. And don't worry about it being an endangered species. Commercial herds of buffalo are now raised in Montana and Wyoming, and the meat is sold in specialty butcher shops. The sausage can be air-dried at room temperature and/or cold smoked, in which case be sure to add the curing salts. Otherwise, eat buffalo sausage fresh or hot smoked. For this hearty sausage, buy the cheaper cuts, such as chuck or stew meat. If buffalo (or beefalo—a new hybrid) is unavailable, beef chuck works just fine. You may also substitute elk or venison for the buffalo.

2 pounds buffalo meat
1 pound pork back fat
½ cup water
¼ cup chopped shelled pistachio
    nuts
3 tablespoons red wine vinegar
1 shallot, finely chopped
1 tablespoon minced garlic
1 tablespoon coarsely ground black
    pepper

4 teaspoons kosher salt
2 teaspoons crushed juniper berries
2 teaspoons Dijon mustard
1 teaspoon dry mustard
½ teaspoon dried thyme
1 teaspoon curing salts (page 21)
    (optional)
Medium hog casings

For details on making sausage, see page 10.

Grind the meat through a ⅜-inch plate, and the pork fat through a ¼-inch plate. In a large bowl, mix the meat and fat together with the water, pistachios, vinegar, shallot, garlic, black pepper, salt, juniper berries, Dijon mustard, dry mustard, and thyme. Add the curing salts if you wish to air-dry or cold smoke the sausage. Knead until everything is well blended.

Stuff into medium hog casings, and tie into 6-inch links. If you choose to air-dry the sausage, hang it overnight at room temperature, and cold smoke for 6 to 8 hours, according to the directions on page 17. Otherwise, mature the sausage, uncovered, in the refrigerator overnight. The next day you can hot smoke the sausage according to the directions on page 18 or use it as is.

Uncured sausage will keep for 3 days in the refrigerator; cured sausage will keep for 7 days. Frozen, all sausages will keep for 2 months.

Game Sausage with Herbs and White Wine

Makes about 3¹/₂ pounds

Use either venison, elk, or moose meat in this sausage. If no game is available, use a mixture of turkey and pork to replace the game. If you can't find fresh herbs, just substitute ½ teaspoon dried tarragon and ½ teaspoon dried basil. Don't bother with dried chervil, though; it has none of the subtle charm of the fresh herb.

1 pound venison, elk, or moose
    meat
1½ pounds pork shoulder
¾ pound pork back fat
½ cup dry white California wine
¼ cup chopped fresh parsley
2 tablespoons chopped fresh herbs,
    such as chervil, tarragon, and
    basil, in any combination
3½ teaspoons kosher salt

2 teaspoons coarsely ground black
    pepper
2 teaspoons minced garlic
1 teaspoon chopped fresh sage or
    ½ teaspoon dried
1 teaspoon chopped fresh thyme or
    ½ teaspoon dried
1 teaspoon chopped fresh marjoram
    or ½ teaspoon dried
Medium hog casings

For details on making sausage, see page 10.

Grind the meat and fat through a ¼-inch plate. In a large bowl, mix the meat and fat with the wine, parsley, fresh herbs, salt, black pepper, garlic, sage, thyme, and marjoram. Knead well to blend everything thoroughly.

Stuff into medium hog casings, and tie into 5-inch links.

The sausages will keep for 3 days in the refrigerator, or for 2 months in the freezer.

Wild Turkey Sausage with Drambuie

Makes about 3 pounds

WILD TURKEYS WERE COMMON IN COLONIAL AMERICA, AND THEY STILL RUN wild in eastern forests and in the Pacific Coast range. If you are fortunate enough to have a wild turkey, then roast or braise the breast, and use the thighs to make this sausage. But don't fret if you don't have the wild bird. Domesticated turkey is delicious, too. It's generally not a good idea to use turkey legs, because their bony sinews make them undesirable for sausage, but if you want to take the time to pull the sinews out, legs will also do.

2¼ pounds turkey thigh meat
    with skin attached
¾ pound pork back fat
¼ cup Drambuie or an orange-
    flavored liqueur such as
    Grand Marnier
¼ cup water
2 teaspoons honey
1 tablespoon kosher salt
2 teaspoons coarsely ground black
    pepper

1 teaspoon dried thyme
1 teaspoon fennel seeds
1 teaspoon sweet Hungarian
    paprika
1 teaspoon minced garlic
½ teaspoon ground sage
⅛ teaspoon ground allspice
Medium hog casings

FOR DETAILS ON MAKING SAUSAGE, SEE PAGE 10.

Grind the meat and fat through a ¼-inch plate. Add the Drambuie, water, honey, salt, pepper, thyme, fennel, paprika, garlic, sage, and allspice. Knead with your hands until all the ingredients are thoroughly combined.

Stuff the mixture into hog casings, and tie off in 6-inch lengths.

The sausage keeps for 3 days in the refrigerator, or for 2 months in the freezer.

Wild Boar Sausage

Makes about 4 pounds

In Northern California, the Russians introduced the European wild boar around Fort Ross in the 1800s, and it mated with feral domestic pigs to create a populous and troublesome game animal. These wild boar are found today all over Mendocino and Sonoma counties and are a real problem for farmers and grape growers. They are even spreading into Marin County just north of San Francisco, and the thought of these tusked and hairy pigs uprooting the rhododendrons next to the hot tub has many a Marinite worried. So no one is particularly outraged when grape growers, farmers, and sportsman hunt this abundant species. As an added plus, the meat is very tasty. If you know someone who hunts in Northern California, you will find boar meat is easier to come by than venison. If not, European wild boar is available from specialty shops, or you can substitute domestic pork in this recipe.

Boar meat is leaner, redder, and gamier than domestic pork and is usually flavored with strong herbs, such as juniper or caraway, that blend well with its pronounced flavor. So if you use domestic pork, you might want to decrease the amounts of these ingredients in the following recipe.

Use meat from the shoulders or legs. Let the sausage mellow for a minimum of one day, preferably two, in the refrigerator before using. We use gin in this recipe since its major flavor is juniper, but you could replace it with a teaspoon or more of crushed dried juniper berries for a gamier character.

3 pounds boar meat or pork butt
1¼ pounds pork back fat
¼ cup gin
¼ cup dry red wine
1 tablespoon minced garlic
1 tablespoon coarsely ground black pepper
4 teaspoons kosher salt
1 teaspoon ground caraway seeds
1 teaspoon chopped fresh marjoram or ½ teaspoon dried
1 teaspoon whole caraway seeds
1 teaspoon chopped fresh sage or ½ teaspoon ground sage
½ teaspoon ground ginger
Pinch of ground allspice
Medium hog casings

For details on making sausage, see page 10.

Grind the meat and fat through a ¼-inch plate. Combine with the gin, wine, garlic, black pepper, salt, ground caraway, marjoram, caraway seeds, sage, ginger, and allspice. Knead until well mixed.

Stuff into medium hog casings, and tie into 5-inch links. Refrigerate the sausages uncovered for a day or two before using.

The sausage will keep for 3 days in the refrigerator, or for 2 months in the freezer.

Duck Sausage

Makes about 2½ pounds

CREATIVE AMERICAN CHEFS HAVE POPULARIZED DUCK SAUSAGE BY PUTTING it on pizza, and serving it with sautéed fruits or grilled radicchio. To make these delicious sausages, use duck legs and thighs, skin and all, along with some boned and skinned lean meat from the breasts. Use the carcass and scraps to make a flavorful duck stock, perfect for cooking lentils or white beans. You can use domestic or wild duck.

1 pound (approximately) meat only from the duck breasts, domestic or wild

1 pound (approximately) meat and skin from 2 deboned duck legs and thighs

¼ pound smoky bacon, chilled in freezer for 30 minutes

¼ cup orange-flavored liqueur, such as Grand Marnier or curaçao

¼ cup water

2 teaspoons kosher salt

2 teaspoons coarsely ground black pepper

1 teaspoon finely chopped garlic

1 teaspoon sweet Hungarian paprika

1 teaspoon sugar

½ teaspoon ground cayenne pepper

½ teaspoon dried thyme

¼ teaspoon ground sage

Pinch of ground allspice

¼ teaspoon dried savory

Medium hog casings

FOR DETAILS ON MAKING SAUSAGE, SEE PAGE 10.

Grind the meat, skin, and bacon through a ¼-inch plate. In a large bowl, mix the chopped meat, skin, bacon, orange liqueur, water, salt, black pepper, garlic, paprika, sugar, cayenne, thyme, sage, allspice, and savory. Blend well with your hands, kneading and squeezing the meat as you mix it.

Stuff into medium hog casings, and tie into 5-inch lengths.

The sausage will keep for 3 days in the refrigerator, or for 2 months in the freezer.

Game Sausage with Rosemary and Mustard

Makes about 4 pounds

Cooking Notes
Brush the sausage
with Dijon mustard,
and bake it in a coil
in a 350° oven for
about ¹/₂ hour, until
the internal tempera-
ture reaches 155°.

Oᴜʀ ꜰᴀᴠᴏʀɪᴛᴇ ᴡᴀʏ ᴛᴏ ʀᴏᴀsᴛ ʟᴇɢ ᴏꜰ ʟᴀᴍʙ ᴄᴏᴍᴇs ꜰʀᴏᴍ Jᴜʟɪᴀ Cʜɪʟᴅ: Tʜᴇ lamb is brushed with a mixture of mustard, fresh rosemary, and garlic. There is never enough of this delicious glaze since it is only on the outside of each lamb slice when you serve. Since game such as venison and elk are also good with mustard, we decided to incorporate this flavoring throughout the meat by using it in a game sausage. Leave the sausage unlinked. We recommend using pork or beef fat in this and other game sausage recipes since game is too lean and its own fat has too strong a flavor.

3 pounds game shoulder, such as	*2 teaspoons kosher salt*
venison or elk	*2 teaspoons soy sauce*
1 pound pork back fat	*1 teaspoon chopped fresh rosemary*
3 tablespoons coarse-grain mustard	*or ½ teaspoon dried*
2 tablespoons fruity olive oil	*Dijon mustard*
1 tablespoon minced garlic	*Medium hog casings*

Fᴏʀ ᴅᴇᴛᴀɪʟs ᴏɴ ᴍᴀᴋɪɴɢ sᴀᴜsᴀɢᴇ, sᴇᴇ ᴘᴀɢᴇ 1O.

Grind the meat and fat through a ³/₈-inch plate. Combine in a large bowl with the coarse-grain mustard, oil, garlic, salt, soy sauce, rosemary, and Dijon. Mix well with your hands, squeezing and kneading the mixture. Do not overmix, or the fat will begin to melt.

Stuff into medium hog casings. Leave as a coil.

The sausage will keep for 3 days in the refrigerator, or for 2 months in the freezer.

Crépinettes are sausage patties wrapped in caul fat (available from butchers). The caul fat holds the moisture in the meat and makes a tight, neat package. If caul fat is unavailable, form the sausage meat into patties and grill or fry. The sausage is delicious grilled and served as is, as part of a mixed grill, or with a salad of bitter greens. Crépinettes are a good way to use up bits and pieces of game; the amount or type doesn't matter much. Simply mix the game (up to 50 percent of the total meat) with the pork. You can use meat or livers from game birds, such as pheasant or quail, or red meat from venison, boar, or other game animals. Use lean lamb if you have no game.

2 pounds spinach, washed, drained, and chopped

2½ pounds meat, at least half pork and the rest from furred or feathered game, including the liver, or lean lamb

½ pound pork back fat, or more fat if the mixture seems too lean

¼ cup port or applejack

2 tablespoons chopped shallots

2 tablespoons chopped fresh herbs, such as basil, tarragon, chervil, thyme, oregano, or marjoram

1 tablespoon kosher salt

2 teaspoons coarsely ground black pepper

1 teaspoon ground fennel seeds or star anise

½ teaspoon dried tarragon

½ teaspoon ground allspice

½ teaspoon ground cayenne pepper

¼ teaspoon dried sage

¼ teaspoon dried thyme

Caul fat

FOR DETAILS ON MAKING SAUSAGE, SEE PAGE 10.

Place wet spinach in a large, heavy pot. Cover and cook over medium heat until the leaves have wilted, about 2 minutes. Remove and cool under cold water. Drain and squeeze spinach to remove as much moisture as possible.

Grind the meat and pork fat through a ⅜-inch plate. Combine in a large bowl along with the spinach, port, shallots, herbs, salt, black pepper, fennel, tarragon, allspice, cayenne, sage, and thyme. Knead until well blended. Shape into ¼-pound oval patties, and wrap in 6-inch squares of caul fat or leave unwrapped. Place on a platter, cover with plastic wrap, and refrigerate.

The crépinettes will keep for up to 3 days refrigerated or for 2 months frozen.

Crawfish Boudin

Makes 2 to 3 pounds

LOUISIANA IS CRAWFISH COUNTRY, AND THE NAME OF THE SUCCULENT freshwater crustacean is pronounced just like that in the bayous, not crayfish or crawdad. You might also hear it called yabbie, mudbug, or creekcrab, but whatever you call it, crawfish is big business around Lafayette and Breaux Bridge. As you drive through the countryside, you can see the ponds and small processing plants that supply this thriving trade. Most crawfish are farmed these days, but the creeks and bayous still supply many a crawfish boil and étouffée.

Breaux Bridge, 120 miles southwest of New Orleans, proclaims itself the Crawfish Capital of the Universe. The town hosts a raucous Crawfish Festival each spring where thousands of hungry Cajuns get together to eat boiled mudbugs, drink lots of Dixie beer, and sample the delicious crawfish boudin made by local producers.

Crawfish boudin is a relatively recent invention of creative Cajun cooks, and it is one of the most convenient and delicious ways to sample this wonderful shellfish. In Louisiana, peeled crawfish tails can be purchased in 1-pound bags along with the orange crawfish fat. This fat is important to Cajun cooks, as it adds flavor and richness. A dedicated Cajun chef will do just about anything to procure this unctuous delight. Crawfish tails and fat are easily frozen and can often be found in specialty stores in large metropolitan areas. They can also be purchased by mail order (see page 307).

4 tablespoons butter
1 cup chopped onion
1 teaspoon chopped shallot
1 clove garlic, minced
1 pound cooked and peeled
    crawfish tails with fat
½ red or yellow bell pepper,
    fire-roasted, peeled, and
    chopped (page 73)
1½ cups cooked rice
¼ cup heavy cream
½ cup finely chopped green onions
    or scallions
¼ cup chopped fresh parsley
1 egg

2 tablespoons sweet sherry
1 tablespoon lemon juice
1 tablespoon tomato paste
2 teaspoons fresh tarragon or ½
    teaspoon dried
2 teaspoons sweet Hungarian
    paprika
1 teaspoon fresh thyme or
    1 teaspoon dried
1 teaspoon red pepper flakes
1 teaspoon grated lemon zest
½ teaspoon ground cayenne pepper
½ teaspoon freshly grated nutmeg
Salt and pepper
Medium hog casings

FOR DETAILS ON MAKING SAUSAGE, SEE PAGE 10.

Over medium heat, melt the butter in a medium frying pan, and add the onion, shallot, and garlic. Cover and cook for 10 minutes, until the vegetables are soft. Set aside.

In a food processor or by hand, coarsely chop the crawfish tails and fat. Be sure not to overprocess. Put the chopped pepper, cooked vegetables, crawfish, rice, and cream in a large bowl. Add the green onions, parsley, egg, sherry, lemon juice, tomato paste, tarragon, paprika, thyme, red pepper, lemon zest, cayenne, nutmeg, and salt and pepper to taste. Mix well. Chill for 30 minutes.

Stuff the crawfish mixture into medium hog casings (do not twist into links), and cook immediately.

Variation: Shrimp Boudin

If crawfish are unavailable, shrimp makes a tasty alternative. Boil 2 pounds unpeeled shrimp in a large quantity of salted water until just done (3 to 5 minutes, just after they turn pink; do not overcook). Peel and cool. Add the shells to a food processor and chop coarsely. Melt ½ stick unsalted butter over low heat. Add the shells and sauté for 5 minutes to extract the shrimp flavor. The shrimp butter will substitute for the crawfish fat. Strain the butter and proceed with the recipe as described above, using the shrimp and butter mixture in place of the crawfish and its fat.

Cooking Note

To cook, coil the boudin in a colander in a stockpot or Dutch oven. Add boiling water to just below the colander, cover, and steam for 20 minutes. After steaming the boudin, you should eat it immediately, or refrigerate it. These seafood sausages are quite perishable. They will keep for a day or two in the refrigerator, but do not freeze well. Crawfish boudin, like traditional Cajun boudin, can be eaten out of hand, stripping the stuffing out of the casing as you go. Or you can sauté boudin with vegetables.

•••

THE INGREDIENTS THAT INSPIRED THESE FISH SAUSAGES ARE PART OF THE bounty of the North Atlantic: cod, clams, scallops, and lobster. Any firm, white-fleshed fish, such as red snapper or Pacific rock cod, can be used here instead of cod, and shrimp can replace the lobster.

1½ pounds cod fillets
2 egg whites
1½ cups heavy cream
2 teaspoons tomato paste
2 teaspoons kosher salt
½ teaspoon finely ground black
   pepper
1 teaspoon chopped fresh thyme or
   ½ teaspoon dried

¼ pound diced cooked clams
¼ pound small bay scallops, cut in
   half, or diced sea scallops
1 cup diced cooked lobster or
   shrimp
3 tablespoons sweet sherry
Sheep casings

FOR DETAILS ON MAKING SAUSAGE, SEE PAGE 10.

Chill the food processor bowl and metal blade in the freezer for at least 30 minutes before starting this recipe. Cut the cod into ¾-inch chunks and freeze for 15 minutes.

In the food processor fitted with the metal blade, process the cod until it is smooth. With the motor running, gradually add the egg whites until they are fully incorporated. Pour in the cream in a steady stream until it is thoroughly blended in. Add the tomato paste, salt, pepper, and thyme and process for 10 seconds.

Transfer the fish mixture to a bowl and fold in the clams, scallops, lobster, and sherry until everything is well mixed. Make a small ball of the mixture, poach in simmering water for 5 minutes, and taste to correct the seasonings if necessary.

Stuff the seafood-fish mixture into sheep casings, and tie into 6-inch links.

Bring a large pot of lightly salted water to a boil. Add the sausages, and adjust the heat to below a simmer, about 180°. Poach the sausages for about 15 minutes, until they are firm. Drain and serve immediately, or cool under running water and refrigerate. This sausage will keep for 3 days in the refrigerator, but does not freeze well.

Cooking Notes

To rewarm the sausages, gently fry them in butter. They are also good eaten cold with a mayonnaise enhanced with cooked minced clams, lemon, and parsley.

Makes 2 to 3 pounds

I‌F YOU'VE EVER BEEN TO SEATTLE'S PIKE PLACE MARKET, YOU WILL HAVE seen the fish mongers tossing salmon to each other. While a colorful stunt for the appreciative tourists, it underscores that salmon is still plentiful enough to literally throw around. Salmon's flavor and texture are ideal for making the fish mousse that gives this sausage its structure. The addition of scallops and shrimp not only makes the sausage visually interesting, but adds their own subtle flavors as well.

1½ pounds fresh salmon, boned and skinned
2 egg whites, well chilled
1⅓ cups heavy cream, well chilled
2 teaspoons kosher salt
1 teaspoon sweet Hungarian paprika
½ teaspoon finely ground white pepper
¼ teaspoon freshly grated nutmeg
½ cup finely chopped fresh parsley
¼ cup chopped fresh mushrooms or ½ ounce dried cèpes or porcini mushrooms, soaked in hot water for 1 hour, coarsely chopped

1 cup scallops, cut into ½-inch chunks
¼ cup fresh shrimp cut into ¼-inch pieces, or ¼ cup lobster meat cut into ¼-inch pieces
5 tablespoons Pernod or other anise-flavored liqueur
3 tablespoons minced green onions, scallions, or chives
2 tablespoons fresh tarragon or chervil, or 2 teaspoons dried tarragon
½ teaspoon ground fennel seeds
Sheep casings (optional)

FOR DETAILS ON MAKING SAUSAGE, SEE PAGE 10.

Chill the food processor and metal blade in the freezer for at least 30 minutes before beginning. Cut about 1 pound of the salmon into ¾-inch chunks, the remainder into ¼-inch pieces. Freeze the large pieces for 15 minutes and refrigerate the others for the same amount of time.

In the food processor fitted with the metal blade, process the partially frozen large chunks of salmon until smooth. With the motor running, gradually add the egg whites until they are incorporated. Then pour in the cream in a steady stream until blended. Add the salt, paprika, pepper, and nutmeg.

Transfer the salmon puree to a bowl and stir in the small salmon chunks along with the parsley, mushrooms, scallops, and the shrimp. Add the Pernod, green onions, tarragon, and fennel seeds. Stir well.

Cooking Notes
The linked sausage can be reheated by poaching for 5 to 7 minutes in 180° water.

Make a small ball of the mixture, and poach in simmering water for 5 minutes. Taste and correct the salt, pepper, and other seasonings.

Stuff the mixture into sheep casings (not hog—they're too coarse), and tie into 5-inch links. Alternatively, spread the fish sausage on lightly oiled plastic wrap and roll into a long cylinder, approximately 1 inch in diameter. Tie the ends with string.

Bring a large pot of lightly salted water to a boil. Add the sausage and adjust the heat to just below a simmer, about 180°. Poach the small links for 15 minutes, the larger plastic-wrapped sausage for 25 minutes. Remove the plastic wrap carefully before slicing. Eat immediately or serve cold. This sausage keeps for 2 to 3 days in the refrigerator, but does not freeze well.

Part II

Cooking with Sausage

ausages of all types have long been used to flavor a wide range of foods. They add zest to starches and vegetables, and sausages are the basis of many classic country dishes from all over the world. Steamed Clams with Linguiça (page 218), Pennsylvania Dutch Schnitz und Knepp (Braised Sausage, Apples, and Dumplings) (page 255), and Bigos (Polish Hunter's Stew, page 263) are all regional favorites that use sausage to provide an added element of spices and flavor.

Sausages are also paired with beans, grains, and other starches, adding life and character to often bland ingredients. Cotechino with Lentils (page 204) and Braised Sausage with Polenta (page 206) are traditional combinations from northern Italy. Moroccan Game Hens Stuffed with Rice and Fruit (page 241), Puerto Rican Chicken, Rice, and Sausage Stew (page 242), and Chicken or Turkey Pozole (page 240) all show how sausage can provide a country's characteristic flavors in a dish and liven up regional staples.

The great advantage of using sausage in cooking is its ability to act as a kind of "flavor bomb." Add Italian sausage to lentils and you have an Italian dish, Moroccan sausage to rice and it's North African in an instant. And sausage not only adds flavor but, when you make it yourself or buy from an artisan producer, it is a good source of protein with very little fat—just what you need for a main course when paired with starches and/or vegetables.

Creative chefs these days are also using sausages in new and exciting ways, often departing from traditional recipes and combinations—Salmon Sausage in Champagne Sauce (page 225), for example, or Fish Sausage *en Papillote* with Mustard and Tarragon Butter (page 226). The possibilities are endless here; use your imagination to create new sausages or try out combinations that appeal to your fantasies and taste buds.

A Note on Ingredients

In our recipes we suggest you use the following:

- **butter** Unsalted unless otherwise specified. It tastes better, is generally fresher, and lets you control the amount of salt in the recipes more exactly.
- **salt** Kosher salt. It has fewer impurities than table salt and a less salty taste. If you only have ordinary table salt, then use about 2 1/2 teaspoons for every 1 tablespoon of kosher that we call for in the recipe.
- **stock** Homemade stock from beef, chicken, or other poultry or meats. It has more taste than most canned or frozen stock, and doesn't contain high levels of salt and MSG. You can substitute canned stock, but you should cut back on the salt in the recipe to compensate.
- **tomatoes** We suggest using fresh tomatoes, peeled, seeded, and chopped in many dishes. But if you can't get good, fresh, vine-ripened tomatoes, you are better off using Italian-style canned tomatoes.
- **herbs** Use fresh herbs whenever they are available. We'll often give proportions of fresh to dried herbs (in general, use half as much dried herbs as fresh), but if we just specify marjoram or oregano, for example, we mean dried herbs.

Chapter 6

BREAKFAST ALL DAY

BREAKFAST AND SAUSAGE—THE TWO WORDS SEEM TO GO TOGETHER. SAGE-based breakfast sausage is the classic American breakfast sausage, but breakfast sausage doesn't have to be limited to the old standby. Some of our spiciest sausages can be used to create original and mouth-awakening breakfasts. Our Huevos con Chorizo (page 128) and Green Chile Sausage Soufflé (page 132) give breakfast a southwestern flavor. Our Sausage and Creamy Eggs in Popovers (page 130) and the Sheepherders' Omelet of Wild Greens, Potatoes, and Basque Chorizo (page 129) provide flavorful hints of the Mediterranean. Or you could try a Cajun breakfast with our Andouille Hash (page 125).

Many of our breakfast dishes also make delicious lunches or first courses for a dinner party, including our Bette's Diner Corn Cakes with Spicy Louisiana Sausage (page 136) or Chilaquiles de Chorizo (page 126).

Quick and Easy Breakfasts

Sausage and eggs are an obvious combination, but you might want to vary the usual black pepper and sage sausage with other types of sausages. Try dicing smoked sausage and mixing it with scrambled eggs or use a precooked sausage as part of an omelet filling with sautéed mushrooms or cooked spinach. Make a French toast sandwich with 2 slices of French toast and a mild sausage such as Bockwurst (page 57) or Chicken and Apple Sausage (page 34) in between (see French Toast Stuffed with Chicken and Apple Sausage, page 133). Serve this with sautéed apples or fruit syrup. Dice up bits of smoked sausage and add to pancake, biscuit, or waffle batter. Roll sausages in brioche, biscuit, or bread dough and eat hot out of the oven with some home-fried potatoes.

Cheese and Sausage Biscuits

Makes 2 dozen

THESE ZESTY BISCUITS ARE DELICIOUS TO NIBBLE ON THROUGHOUT A LONG and leisurely breakfast and also make great appetizers. Match with a malty, highly hopped beer like Sierra Nevada, Anchor Steam, or Samuel Adams for hors d'oeuvres or half-time snacks. You can use our recipe as a basic guide but get creative and use your own favorite biscuit recipe, or add herbs or use a different cheese. In fact, you can use whatever you happen to have lurking in the back of the refrigerator, but don't forget to add the sausage!

¼ pound (½ cup) Spicy Fresh
  Country Sausage (page 27)
  or other spicy bulk sausage
2 cups all-purpose flour
1 tablespoon baking powder
¾ teaspoon salt
¾ teaspoon sugar

4 tablespoons (½ stick) cold
  unsalted butter
¼ cup vegetable shortening
½ cup grated sharp Cheddar cheese
¾ cup plus 2 tablespoons
  buttermilk
½ teaspoon baking soda

Preheat the oven to 450°.

Fry the sausage in a small heavy skillet over medium-high heat for 5 minutes, breaking the meat up with a fork as it cooks. Drain through a sieve and cool on paper towels.

In a large bowl, mix together the flour, baking powder, salt, and sugar. Cut in the butter and shortening. Mix the sausage and grated cheese into the dough. Combine the buttermilk and baking soda, pour into the dry ingredients, and stir until a soft dough forms. Turn onto a lightly floured surface and knead gently for 10 to 20 seconds to form a ball. Roll or pat the dough to a thickness of ½ inch. Cut into 1½-inch rounds and arrange on a lightly greased cookie sheet.

Bake for 10 to 15 minutes, until lightly browned. Serve warm.

Variations

You can vary this formula as you wish by using smoked or fresh sausage, and different types of cheese, such as Asiago, Parmesan, and smoked Gouda. You might also want to add a teaspoon or two of chopped fresh herbs, such as thyme or oregano, or a couple of teaspoons of chopped garlic, green onions or scallions, and/or chopped red bell pepper.

Somewhere in Iowa

We're somewhere in Iowa, driving east just before dawn, the first light glimpsed through the tall corn that lines the road. It's definitely time for coffee and breakfast after a long night on the road, but will anything be open at 4:00 A.M. on a summer morning?

The sun's just coming up as we enter the town: neat brick houses, carefully tended lawns, trees shading quiet streets. There's no problem finding someplace open for breakfast at this early hour. Here on the main street, four cafés are bustling. Pickup trucks fill the lots and streets in front; there are men in overalls and baseball caps sitting on fenders and talking, crowded at tables just inside the windows.

The smell of sweet cinnamon rolls and frying pork sausage billows out onto the street from the air conditioners. We sniff our way to the most crowded (and most fragrant) restaurant. The neon signs says "Home Style Cooking—Buffet."

Inside it's all friendly pandemonium with purposeful, smiling women in flowered aprons keeping everyone happy and all the coffee cups filled. Flats of eggs are stacked neatly beside grills almost hidden under mounds of home fries. Sausage patties sizzle next to constantly depleted and replenished stacks of pancakes. Trays of hot, sticky cinnamon rolls emerge with regularity from the ovens. This is the heartland. We have arrived in breakfast country. A waitress waves us to a table. As we sit down, suddenly the day looks better, and the journey not so long.

THIS SPICY EGG DISH IS NOT ONLY GOOD FOR BREAKFAST, BUT MAKES AN excellent lunch or light supper. It is a good example of the Spanish influence on Creole cooking. Best served warm and not hot directly from the oven, this is ideal for a party buffet or brunch.

18 3- to 4-inch green beans (about ¼ pound)
1 tablespoon olive oil
1 pound Cajun-Style Andouille (page 44), Smoked Country Sausage (page 32), Pickled-Pork Sausage (page 50), or other smoked sausage, cut into ½-inch rounds
¼ cup finely chopped onion
6 green onions or scallions, white parts finely chopped, green tops thinly sliced

2 teaspoons minced garlic
½ cup diced green bell pepper
¼ cup dry sherry
6 plum tomatoes, fresh or canned, peeled and quartered
½ teaspoon ground cayenne pepper
Salt and pepper
6 large shrimp (20 to 25 count), peeled and cooked (optional)
1 pimiento or red bell pepper, cut into ¼-inch strips
6 eggs

Bring 4 quarts of salted water to a boil. Add the green beans and blanch for 5 minutes, until they are tender but still crunchy. Drain and cool under running water. Set aside.

In a large heavy skillet, heat the olive oil over medium heat. Add the sliced sausage and fry until browned on both sides, about 5 minutes. Add the onion, the finely chopped white parts of the green onions, and garlic, and sauté slowly for about 5 minutes, until soft. Add the green bell pepper and cook for an additional 2 to 3 minutes. Add the sherry, tomatoes, and cayenne and cook for 10 minutes. Season this sauce with salt and pepper to taste.

Preheat the oven to 450°. Spread the sausages and tomato sauce evenly over the bottom of a 13 by 9-inch gratin or baking dish. Arrange the green beans, shrimp, and the pimiento strips on top. Break the eggs one at a time onto the sauce, arranging them evenly over the dish and taking care not to break the yolks. Garnish with the green onion tops, and bake until the egg whites are set, about 10 to 12 minutes. Serve at once or at room temperature.

Andouille Hash

Makes 6 to 8 servings

IF **FLAKY BISCUITS, POACHED OR FRIED EGGS, AND THIS SAVORY HASH MAKE A** marvelous combination for breakfast or lunch.

4 tablespoons (½ stick) unsalted
    butter
2 pounds red potatoes, cut into
    ½-inch dice
1 large onion, cut into ¼-inch dice
1 pound Cajun-Style Andouille
    (page 44) or smoked ham,
    cut into ½-inch dice
½ cup diced red bell pepper
    (¼-inch pieces)

½ cup diced green bell pepper
    (¼-inch pieces)
¼ teaspoon kosher salt
½ teaspoon freshly ground black
    pepper
¼ teaspoon ground cayenne pepper
¼ cup finely chopped green onions
    or scallions

In a large skillet, melt the butter over medium heat. Add the potatoes and onion and fry for 15 minutes. They should be light brown on the outside and soft in the center. Add the diced sausage, bell peppers, salt, black pepper, and cayenne. Continue frying until potatoes and sausage are nicely browned, about 5 minutes. Taste for salt and pepper, sprinkle with the green onions, and serve.

Chilaquiles de Chorizo (Tortilla and Chorizo Pie)

Makes 5 to 6 servings

ᵀ᷀ORTILLAS ARE AN ESSENTIAL PART OF THE MEXICAN AND SOUTHWESTERN diet, so they are never thrown away, even when stale. The challenge is finding ways to use up leftover tortillas, and chilaquiles is the usual answer. This substantial and delicious dish is often served with scrambled eggs for breakfast on Sunday morning to use up the last of the week's tortillas, but it is good any time for lunch or dinner with a salad. Serve chilaquiles with plenty of fresh salsa.

2 tablespoons olive oil
3 to 4 fresh Anaheim or other
  mild green chiles
6 to 8 tomatillos, or 1 (16-ounce)
  can
2 onions
4 cloves garlic
1 bunch (4 to 6 ounces) fresh
  cilantro
1 or more cups chicken stock
Salt and pepper

1½ pounds Chorizo (page 74)
  or other fresh southwestern
  sausage (pages 75 to 78),
  in bulk or removed from
  casings
2 cups finely chopped onions
16 corn tortillas, cut into sixths
Oil for deep-frying
6 cups shredded Jack cheese

Garnishes
Avocado slices
Fresh cilantro sprigs

To make a sauce, coarsely puree the olive oil, chiles, tomatillos, onions, garlic, and cilantro in a food processor. Combine with 1 cup of the chicken stock in a saucepan and simmer for 5 minutes. Taste for salt and pepper, and reserve.

Fry the chorizo in a large heavy skillet over medium-high heat, breaking up the meat with a fork, for about 5 minutes. Pour off all but about 2 tablespoons of the fat, add the finely chopped onions, and cook another 5 minutes, until the onions are soft.

Meanwhile, deep-fry the tortilla wedges in batches in hot oil (350° to 375°) for 1 to 2 minutes, until they are crisp but not brown. Drain well on paper towels.

To assemble the chilaquiles, oil a 3- to 4-quart casserole. Make layers of tortilla chips, chorizo, all but 1 cup of the cheese, and sauce. Repeat until all the ingredients are used. Press down with a plate, making sure all the solids are covered with liquid. Otherwise, add more stock. Cover with foil and refrigerate overnight so that the tortillas absorb the liquid.

The next day, preheat the oven to 350°. Remove the plate from the chilaquiles and sprinkle the top with the remaining shredded cheese. Bake, covered, for 45 minutes. Garnish with avocado slices and cilantro sprigs and serve hot.

··

Use any recipe for sage sausage in this book, or any high-quality store-bought bulk sausage. This simple egg preparation makes a great brunch or hearty breakfast.

<table>
<tr><td>⅔ pound bulk sage sausage,
store-bought or homemade
(pages 27–34)
4 eggs</td><td>2 tablespoons heavy cream
¼ cup grated sharp Cheddar cheese
1 tablespoon chopped chives
(optional)</td></tr>
</table>

Shirred Eggs and Sausage

Makes 2 servings

Preheat the oven to 350°. Form the sausage into 4 patties about 3 inches in diameter.

In a large heavy skillet over medium heat, fry the sausages for about 5 minutes on each side until they are nicely browned. Drain on paper towels, and place 2 patties each into two individual ramekins or shallow bowls. Gently break the eggs over the sausage patties. Pour the cream over the eggs and sprinkle with grated cheese.

Set the ramekins in a pan of hot water and bake for 15 to 20 minutes, or until the eggs are set and the topping has begun to brown. Sprinkle with chives, and serve.

Huevos con Chorizo

Makes 2 to 3 servings

THIS HEARTY BREAKFAST IS A FAVORITE IN FINE RESTAURANTS AND GREASY spoons from Texas to California. Served with refried beans and hot tortillas, Huevos con Chorizo makes a substantial brunch or light supper. Depending on your preference, you can let the eggs set in the pan to make an omelet or you can stir them to make scrambled eggs. Accompany with refried beans, with cheese melted on top, and with warm tortillas.

Use any of the spicy fresh sausages with a southwestern flavor, homemade, or a good store-bought chorizo. Be sure to drain the sausage thoroughly before mixing it with the eggs.

½ pound Chorizo (page 74) or other spicy sausage, in bulk or removed from casings

2 tablespoons chopped green onions or scallions

1 mild green chile, such as Anaheim or poblano, fire-roasted and chopped (page 73), or 1 canned fire-roasted green chile, chopped

3 to 4 eggs, lightly beaten

Garnishes
Sour cream
Salsa cruda

Fry the chorizo in a small heavy skillet for 5 minutes over medium-high heat, crumbling the meat as it cooks. Add the green onions and chile, and cook for 2 more minutes. Pour off all but about 2 tablespoons of the fat and transfer the chorizo mixture to an omelet pan. Add the eggs over high heat, and scramble them until done to your taste, or let them set, then fold over into an omelet. Serve on a warm platter, garnished with sour cream and salsa.

THIS TYPE OF THICK OMELET MADE WITH POTATOES, SAUSAGES, AND THE other ingredients is called a tortilla in Spain. It is enjoyed hot or cold, and is perfect for hors d'oeuvres when cut into small wedges or squares. Basque sheepherders typically prepare omelets like this with a few eggs, a piece of cherished smoked chorizo, and some wild greens gathered from the hillsides. A tortilla makes a satisfying one-dish meal and is a delicious leftover, eaten cold for lunch, or as a tapa. If you can't find Spanish chorizo, substitute a good quality pepperoni.

Tortillas or Spanish omelets are a great way to use whatever's on hand in the refrigerator or garden. Artichokes, pimientos, bell peppers, spinach, and leftover ham or chicken are all delicious in omelets, but always include a little Basque Chorizo or other spicy sausage such as Linguiça (page 89), Cajun-Style Andouille (page 44), or pepperoni to liven things up.

Sheepherders'
Omelet of
Wild Greens,
Potatoes, and
Basque
Chorizo

Makes 4 main-course
or 6 to 8 appetizer
servings

6 tablespoons olive oil
1 onion, thinly sliced
½ pound Basque Chorizo
    (page 91), cut into ½-inch
    rounds
3 cups thinly sliced red potatoes
4 cloves garlic, chopped

4 cups chopped wild greens, such as
    dandelion, milkweed, or lamb's
    quarter, or bitter greens, such as
    arugula, curly endive, escarole,
    or watercress
Salt and pepper
8 eggs, lightly beaten

Heat 3 tablespoons of the olive oil in a large heavy skillet over medium-high heat. Add the onion and sauté for 3 minutes. Add the sausage rounds and cook for 2 minutes, turning them once. Add the potatoes and cook for 10 to 15 minutes, shaking the pan and turning the potatoes frequently until they are tender. Stir in the garlic and greens and season to taste with salt and pepper.

Mix the potatoes, greens, and sausages with the eggs in a large bowl. Heat the remaining 3 tablespoons of olive oil in a clean 12-inch omelet pan or nonstick frying pan. Pour in the egg and potato mixture and cook over low heat until the eggs have almost set, about 5 minutes. Invert the omelet onto a plate or pan lid, slide back into the pan, and cook the other side until done, about 5 minutes more. Transfer to a platter. Let the tortilla rest for 5 minutes, and then slice into wedges and serve.

Sausage and Creamy Eggs in Popovers

Makes 6 servings

This popover recipe comes from Julie and Gary Wagner, who make wonderful breakfasts for the many friends who visit their Napa Valley home. Julie is a popover wizard and even had a special glazed pottery pan made to produce giant, airy popovers. Julie has two important tips for perfect popovers: Use only whole milk (not skim or low fat) and make sure you whisk the batter by hand, as an electric mixer can overbeat the batter and prevent it from rising.

Wagner's Puffy Popovers

8 eggs
2⅔ cups whole milk
2⅔ cups all-purpose flour
1 teaspoon kosher salt
8 tablespoons (1 stick) butter, melted

Filling

½ pound Chicken and Apple Sausage (page 34) or other fresh breakfast sausage, in bulk or removed from casings
½ stick (4 tablespoons) butter
8 eggs
3 ounces cream cheese, at room temperature
Salt and freshly ground black pepper
¼ cup chopped chives or green onions

To make the popovers, preheat the oven to 375°. Beat the eggs in a deep bowl and beat in the milk until well blended. In another bowl, combine the flour and salt. Using a fork or pastry blender, stir the butter into the flour. Then gradually add the flour and butter mixture to the eggs, blending well with a whisk—not an electric mixer. Thoroughly butter six ¾-cup custard cups or ¾-cup popover cups. Fill each with ½ to ⅔ cup of batter, place them directly on the oven rack, and bake until golden, 55 to 60 minutes. Remove the popovers from the oven and let stand for at least 5 minutes before filling.

To make the egg and sausage filling, fry the sausage in a 10- to 12-inch nonstick skillet over medium heat in 1 tablespoon of the butter for 4 to 5 minutes, breaking it up as it cooks. In a bowl, beat together the eggs and cream cheese. Add the remaining butter to the skillet with the sausage and melt it over medium heat. Pour in the egg and cheese mixture and, as the eggs begin to set on the bottom and sides of the pan, gently lift the cooked portion so that the uncooked egg can coat the bottom and side. Repeat, but don't stir the eggs constantly.

They are done when all the eggs have thickened, but are still quite moist. Season with salt and pepper to taste.

Cut off the top of each popover. Spoon out any uncooked batter remaining in the center, and fill generously with the sausage and egg mixture. It's okay if some of the mixture runs over the side of the popover. Sprinkle with chives, replace the top, and serve.

··

STUFFED FRENCH TOAST MAKES A SATISFYING AND SIMPLE BREAKFAST. IT IS basically a French toast sandwich stuffed with lightly browned Chicken and Apple Sausage patties and topped with sautéed apples in an apple cider syrup.

French Toast Stuffed with Chicken and Apple Sausage

Makes 4 servings

1 pound Chicken and Apple
  Sausage (page 34) or other
  mild breakfast sausage, formed
  into 8 patties
Sautéed Apple Slices (page 132)
3 eggs

2 cups milk
1 tablespoon ground cinnamon
1 teaspoon ground nutmeg
8 slices French bread or egg bread
2 tablespoons butter or more

In a large nonstick skillet, panfry the sausage patties over medium heat for 6 to 7 minutes, turning once or twice. Cut into a patty to test for doneness; there should be no pink showing. Cover and keep warm while you sauté the apples and make the French toast.

Prepare the apples according to the recipe directions and keep warm.

Whisk together the eggs, milk, cinnamon, and nutmeg in a large bowl. Soak the bread slices in the egg mixture for 2 to 3 minutes per side.

Melt the butter on a griddle or nonstick skillet, and fry the bread slices in batches over medium-high heat, turning once or twice, until nicely browned.

Place a slice of French toast on each plate and coat it with apples and their syrup. Cover with 2 patties of cooked sausage. Cover the patties with the second piece of French toast, and spoon more apples and syrup over the top.

Sautéed Apple Slices
Makes about 4 cups

Our favorite apple for this dish is a firm tart apple, such as Granny Smith or pippin. The sautéed apples are also delightful on pancakes and waffles or on ice cream, with grilled pork chops or sausages, or with baked ham. They also make a great topping for ice cream.

1 tablespoon butter
4 cups sliced, peeled, and
    cored apples (Granny Smith
    or pippin)

3 cups apple cider
Pinch of ground cloves

In a large, heavy skillet, melt the butter over medium heat. Add the apples and sauté until they are slightly soft, about 3 minutes. Add the cider and cloves and boil for 5 minutes over high heat, or until the apples and cider form a syrup. Serve warm. The apples in syrup will keep, covered in the refrigerator, for a 7 to 10 days. They also freeze well.

Green Chile Sausage Soufflé

Makes 4 servings

A POPULAR DISH IN MANY MEXICAN RESTAURANTS IS *chiles rellenos*, MILD green chiles stuffed with cheese, coated with a thick egg batter, and fried. In the hands of an accomplished cook, *chiles rellenos* can be light and delicious. But all too often they are made up in the morning and served later in the day. The result is heavy and greasy, often with a warmed-over flavor. In addition, preparation is difficult and time-consuming. A much easier but no less satisfying dish is this green chile casserole, using our Southwest Green Chile Sausage, whole green chiles, mild cheese, and eggs. It is painless to make and has far less fat and calories than the traditional fried version. An added plus is that it can be rewarmed with satisfactory results, although it also tastes pretty darn good cold. Other southwestern flavored sausages would also work in this dish. Warmed corn tortillas and refried beans make the perfect accompaniment.

2 (4-ounce) cans whole, fire-roasted
green chiles, drained, or 8 fresh
Anaheim or poblano chiles,
fire-roasted and peeled
(page 73)
6 ounces jack cheese, cut into ½
by 3-inch strips
½ pound Southwest Green Chile
Poultry Sausage (page 77),
removed from casings

½ cup all-purpose flour
½ teaspoon kosher salt
Pinch of ground nutmeg
4 large eggs, separated, plus 2 egg
whites
2 cups milk

Garnish
Salsa cruda
Chopped fresh cilantro

Preheat the oven to 350°. Oil a 9 by 13-inch baking dish.

Cut a lengthwise slit in each chile, insert a strip of cheese into each chile, and place in the dish. Fry the sausage in a nonstick skillet over medium-high heat for 4 to 5 minutes, breaking it up as it cooks. Distribute the sausage over the top of the chiles.

In a food processor or large bowl, mix the flour, salt, and nutmeg with the egg yolks and milk until smooth. In a separate large bowl, beat the egg whites until they form firm peaks. Fold the yolk mixture into the whites until no white areas remain. Spoon the egg mixture over the chiles.

Bake until a toothpick inserted in the center comes out clean, 12 to 15 minutes. Using a metal spatula, cut out and serve 2 chiles per person. Garnish with salsa cruda and chopped cilantro.

Bette's Puffy Pancakes

Makes 4 servings

HUGE, PUFFY SOUFFLÉ PANCAKES ARE FAVORITE BREAKFAST TREATS AT Bette's Diner in Berkeley and are the basis for our sausage-topped version. But don't start getting nervous about the word *soufflé*. Unlike traditional soufflés, these pancakes are almost foolproof (or more exactly, fall-proof). Bette's method is to start the pancakes on top of the stove and then finish them under the broiler until they are beautifully puffed and browned. Your challenge as chef and host is to make sure your guests are already seated and ready at the table, so you can present them with the airy masterpiece before it begins to deflate. Watch the pancake carefully during the last couple of minutes of cooking so that you don't overcook it. An overcooked soufflé pancake will fall immediately, while a properly cooked version will stay nice and puffy all the way to the table. Then, instruct your happy diners that the proper way to eat a soufflé pancake is from the edge toward the center, because the center will continue to cook as the pancake cools. These delicious pancakes are perfect for an autumn brunch or luncheon. Use tart apples such as pippins, Granny Smiths, or Winesaps.

Sausage and Apple Topping

2 teaspoons butter
½ pound Chicken and Apple
    Sausage (page 34) formed
    into 8 patties
1 cup peeled, cored, and sliced tart
    apples (about 1 medium apple)

¼ teaspoon ground cinnamon
1 tablespoon sugar

Puffy Pancakes

4 egg yolks
1 cup half-and-half
½ cup all-purpose flour
1½ tablespoons butter
2 teaspoons granulated sugar

½ teaspoon kosher salt
6 egg whites
Powdered sugar and ground
    cinnamon for dusting

To make the topping, melt the butter in a heavy skillet over medium-high heat, and fry the sausage patties, turning once, until lightly browned on both sides, about 7 minutes total. Remove and reserve patties. Add the apples to the skillet and sprinkle with the cinnamon and sugar. Reduce the heat to medium and cook the apples, stirring occasionally, until they are just soft, about 5 minutes. Set aside and keep warm while you prepare the pancake batter.

To make the pancake batter, beat the egg yolks with the half-and-half in a large bowl. Slowly add the flour, stirring just to combine. In a 10-inch nonstick skillet with an ovenproof or removable plastic handle, melt the butter. (This saves greasing the pan for pancakes later.) Stir the melted butter, sugar, and salt into the egg batter. In another large bowl, beat the egg whites until they form soft peaks and fold them into the batter.

Preheat the broiler.

Heat your already greased skillet over high heat until it begins to smoke. Add ½ of the batter, reduce the heat to medium, and cook until the bottom is lightly browned and the batter has begun to firm up, about 5 minutes. Arrange four of the sausage patties and half of the cooked apples over the top of the pancake.

Place the skillet 4 to 5 inches away from the heat and broil until the top is browned and the center of the pancake is just set, but still soft, 4 to 5 minutes. Slide the pancake onto a serving platter, dust with powdered sugar and cinnamon, and bring it to the table pronto. Cut into 4 wedges to serve. Repeat the process for the second pancake.

Bette's Diner Corn Cakes with Spicy Louisiana Sausage

Makes 4 main-course or 6 to 8 appetizer servings

BETTE KROENING AND SUE FARLEY ARE TWO OF THE ORIGINAL PARTNERS OF the twenty-year-old Bette's Diner in Berkeley, which is known nationwide for its fantastic breakfasts. Although their buttermilk pancakes and buckwheat pancakes are classics, their corn cakes have always been among our favorites. Bette has served these delectable corn cakes to her delighted patrons over the years (former Senator Jacob Javits was a special aficionado of the crisp cakes). She has also recently packaged the mix for home use. It is available from specialty stores or direct from Bette's (see Sources, page 307). The corn cakes are delicious as is, but also they are wonderfully easy to embellish and turn into satisfying sausage dishes.

2 teaspoons vegetable oil
½ pound Spicy Louisiana Poultry
    Sausage (page 39), removed
    from casings
2 cups water
2 tablespoons butter
¼ teaspoon kosher salt
1 tablespoon sugar
1 cup yellow cornmeal
2 eggs
½ cup milk
¼ cup stone-ground whole wheat
    flour or all-purpose flour

¼ cup cake flour
2 teaspoons baking powder
½ cup uncooked sweet corn kernels
    (fresh or frozen)
¼ cup chopped, seeded, and
    deveined red bell pepper
    (optional)
½ cup chopped green onions or
    scallions, white and green parts
Butter, berry or maple syrup,
    and warmed honey for
    accompaniment

Heat the oil in a skillet over medium-high heat. Add the sausage and fry for 3 to 4 minutes, breaking it up as it cooks. Remove with a slotted spoon. Drain sausage on paper towels while you prepare the batter.

In a small saucepan, bring the water and butter to a boil. Stir in the salt and sugar and pour over the cornmeal in a large bowl. Stir to combine and thoroughly moisten the cornmeal. Cover and let the mixture rest for 10 minutes.

In another bowl, lightly beat the eggs, stir in the milk, and quickly mix in both flours and baking powder. *Do not overmix.* Add the egg-flour mixture to the cornmeal along with the reserved sausage, corn, bell pepper, and green onions. Stir just enough to combine.

Heat a lightly oiled griddle or heavy skillet over medium-high heat. Pour ¼ cup of batter onto the hot surface to form a 4- to 5-inch cake. Cook 3 or 4 cakes at a time, being sure not to crowd them. When bubbles come to the surface of the pancake and the underside is lightly browned, turned and cook for an additional 2 to 3 minutes, until the other side is lightly browned. Serve with butter, syrup, or warmed honey.

Chapter 7

SAUSAGE STARTERS

Appetizers and Salads

WITH A FEW PACKAGES OF OUR VARIOUS SAUSAGES IN THE FREEZER, YOU'LL never have to worry about an impromptu party or the last-minute arrival of unexpected guests. Each sausage is packed with flavor. With some condiments and a little imagination, you can put together a party without a lot of fuss and with very little lead time.

Sausages make tasty and interesting appetizers or first courses that will perk up the taste buds of your friends and family. Tiger Prawns Stuffed with Asian Sausage (page 140) and Savory Thai Seafood and Sausage Dumplings (page 154) make a great beginning for a wonderful Asian banquet.

Spicy Empanadas (page 148), Beef and Sausage Piroshki (page 150), and My Pot Stickers (page 153) are all tasty wraps to get your guests ready for an exciting meal.

It might seem odd to be adding sausage to salads. Fatty commercial sausage is just too greasy to eat cold, and when you add a dressing with oil, the fat content might be a bit much. But with our sausages you can perk up your salads by adding tasty little morsels of flavor without adding excess fat.

There really is no need to make up the salads beforehand since the preparation is so simple and quick. And since many of the salads are eaten warm or at room temperature, ingredients like rice, pasta, or lentils do not get starchy as they would after spending a night in the refrigerator. The sausage provides much of the flavor interest, and most of the salads only take a few minutes to assemble.

Use these salads as luncheon main courses or for buffets, picnics, or barbecues. Some of the salads, such as Thai Sausage Salad (page 158) and Priscilla's Wilted Salad of Savory Cabbage, Pears, and Sausage (page 159) make great first courses for an elegant meal.

Tiger Prawns Stuffed with Asian Sausage

Makes 4 servings

We USED ASIAN TIGER PRAWNS FOR THIS UNUSUAL AND MOUTHWATERING appetizer, but any large shrimp or even small lobster tails would do as well. The trick is to stuff the curve of the prawn's belly with a spicy sausage, and then bake in a hot oven. We used our Thai Chicken and Turkey Sausage, but our Chinese Black Bean and Shiitake Mushroom Sausage or another flavorful fresh sausage would also be delicious. Let your guests dip the prawns into a homemade sauce or a commercial Thai sauce such as Sriracha chili sauce.

16 large raw prawns (about ¾ pound total), peeled and deveined
½ pound Thai Chicken and Turkey Sausage (page 100), removed from casings, or Chinese Black Bean and Shiitake Mushroom Sausage (page 98)

Nancy's Asian Dipping Sauce (page 152) or Korean Dipping Sauce (page 155)

Preheat the oven to 450°.

Coat a baking sheet with peanut oil. Arrange the prawns on the baking sheet so that they form semicircular "C" shapes. Place about 1 tablespoon of the sausage within the semicircle of each prawn. Pack the sausage tightly and make sure the filling is even with the sides of the prawn. You can secure the tips of the prawn with wooden tooth-picks, if you like, but there is really no need. As the prawns cook, they will tighten up to secure the filling.

Bake until the prawns are pink and the sausage meat is firm, about 10 minutes. Serve at once with the dipping sauce.

THIS SIMPLE AND DELICIOUS RECIPE CAN BE SERVED AS AN APPETIZER OR entrée. The same technique works with large sea scallops. If you don't have tasso, use Westphalian or country ham cut into paper-thin slices.

¼ pound Tasso (page 49), very
thinly sliced
1 pound large shrimp (20 to 25
count), peeled and deveined,
tails left on

1 recipe Creole Mustard Butter
(below)

Prepare a hot fire in the grill.

Cut the tasso slices into strips ½ to ¾ inch wide. Wrap the tasso around each shrimp in a spiral pattern. Secure the tasso with a wooden toothpick or skewer. Brush with the mustard butter and grill for 2 to 3 minutes per side over hot coals, or until the shrimp are firm and pink. Remove the shrimp from the grill and brush generously with more mustard butter before serving.

Creole Mustard Butter
Makes about 2 cups

This mustard butter is also excellent on grilled fish, chicken, or meat. It freezes well, so you can keep some on hand for last-minute inspirations or drop-in guests.

$^1/_2$ pound (2 sticks) unsalted
butter
4 tablespoons minced garlic
6 to 7 tablespoons Creole or
other spicy mustard
3 teaspoons Worcestershire
sauce

2 teaspoons Tabasco sauce
$^1/_3$ cup freshly squeezed lemon
juice
Salt and pepper to taste

Melt the butter over low heat, add the garlic, and cook for 1 minute. Whisk in the mustard, Worcestershire sauce, Tabasco, and lemon juice. Taste for seasonings. Use hot or chilled. Keeps 1 week in the refrigerator, or 2 months in the freezer.

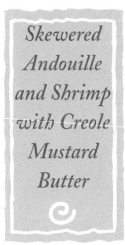

Skewered Andouille and Shrimp with Creole Mustard Butter

Makes 8 appetizer or 4 main-course servings

THIS SIMPLE SKEWER CAN BE SERVED AS AN HORS D'OEUVRE OR A MAIN course. The delicate flavors of shrimp with the spicy, smoky sausage and the piquant mustard-flavored butter always bring cheers from grateful diners.

1 red bell pepper, cut into 1-inch chunks
1 red onion, cut into 1-inch chunks
1 pound Cajun-Style Andouille (page 44), cut into ½-inch rounds

1 green bell pepper, cut into 1-inch chunks
1 pound large (20 to 25 count) shrimp, peeled and deveined, tails left on
Creole Mustard Butter (page 141)

Soak 25 small (6-inch) bamboo skewers in water for 30 minutes. Prepare a hot fire in the grill or preheat the broiler.

Thread a piece of red bell pepper and a piece of red onion on each skewer. Thread a chunk of andouille onto each skewer, pushing the skewer through the casing so the cut edge is parallel to the skewer. Then thread on another piece of red onion, followed by a piece of the green bell pepper, a shrimp skewered lengthwise, another piece each of red bell pepper and onion, and another chunk of andouille. Finish each skewer with one more piece each of onion and red bell pepper.

Brush each skewer generously with the mustard butter and grill over a hot charcoal fire for 2 to 3 minutes on each side, until the shrimp is firm and pink and the sausage is lightly browned. Serve with a small ramekin of the mustard butter on the side.

Serve these appetizing stuffed baguettes with cocktails at dinner parties, or cut the baguettes into sandwich-sized pieces and have them for lunch or as a simple dinner with a green salad. We prefer to use andouille in this easy-to-make appetizer because it is lean, spicy, and deliciously smoky, but any good-quality smoked sausage will work.

Makes 32 appetizer or
4 to 6 main-course
servings

½ bunch chard, about 6 to 8 ounces
2 baguettes or other French bread
½ pound Cajun-Style Andouille (page 44) or other lean smoked sausage, diced

2 to 3 cloves garlic, minced
3 green onions or scallions, finely chopped
1 cup ricotta cheese
Grated Parmesan cheese to taste, about ½ cup

Strip the leaves of the chard from the stems and discard stems. Chop leaves coarsely. Steam over boiling water until wilted, 5 to 7 minutes. Plunge into cold water to stop the cooking. Drain well. Squeeze handfuls of the leaves to remove as much water as possible.

Preheat the oven to 375°.

Cut a thin slice off the top of each baguette and hollow out the center. Save the top to use for bread crumbs.

Combine the sausage, garlic, and onions in a food processor fitted with the metal blade and chop finely. Pour into a bowl and add the ricotta and cooked chopped chard. Reserve a little Parmesan to sprinkle over the top and mix the rest into the sausage-chard mixture. Stuff the loaves with the mixture and place them on a baking pan. Sprinkle with the remaining Parmesan cheese

Bake for 15 to 20 minutes, until the tops have begun to brown and the cheese has melted. Cool for a couple of minutes and cut into 1½-inch slices for hors d'oeuvres or into 6-inch pieces for sandwiches. Serve warm.

Marty's Marvelous Marin Mushrooms

Makes 6 to 8 servings

MARIN COUNTY EPITOMIZES CALIFORNIA'S LAID-BACK LIFESTYLE WITH shingled cottages tucked away among the eucalyptus groves, redwood decks, and hot tubs, and, of course, the ever-popular peacock feathers. While not everyone has peacock feathers, a lot of people who appreciate food, wine, and the good life live in Marin, and Marty's Parties of Marin helps them enjoy themselves. Marty Rosenbloom and his wife, Betsy, run a catering operation that is well-organized and professional, and provides genuinely original, delicious party food. This stuffed mushroom recipe from Marty is a favorite appetizer or party snack.

24 large mushroom caps
4 tablespoons olive oil
4 cloves garlic, minced
4 green onions or scallions, finely
   chopped
2 tablespoons mirin (sweet cooking
   sake) or medium-sweet Madeira
   or sherry
½ teaspoon coarsely ground black
   pepper

2 teaspoons freshly squeezed lemon
   juice
1 pound mild Italian sausage,
   removed from casings
¼ cup dried bread crumbs
6 tablespoons freshly grated
   Parmesan cheese
¼ cup fresh goat cheese (optional)

Clean the mushrooms with a damp cloth, and carefully remove and chop the stems. Heat 2 tablespoons of the olive oil in a skillet over medium-high heat. Add the chopped mushroom stems, garlic, and green onions and sauté for about 5 minutes, stirring frequently. Add the mirin or wine and cook until it evaporates. Transfer the stuffing to a bowl and sprinkle with the black pepper and lemon juice.

In the same pan, fry the sausage meat for about 5 minutes, crumbling it with a fork, until it is no longer pink. Add this to the bowl. Stir in the bread crumbs and all but 2 tablespoons of the Parmesan cheese, along with the goat cheese. Divide the mixture into 24 equal portions and stuff the mushrooms, mounding the stuffing up and pressing it lightly into the cavities with your fingers. At this point the mushrooms can be wrapped and refrigerated until you are ready to bake them.

Preheat the oven to 375°.

Brush the mushrooms with the remaining 2 tablespoons of olive oil and sprinkle with the rest of the Parmesan cheese. Bake for 10 minutes, until the mushrooms soften and the tops begin to brown. Place the mushrooms under a broiler for 1 to 2 minutes to finish browning the tops and serve at once.

Quick and Easy Appetizers

Sausages make the perfect easy appetizer. All you have to do is make sure they are cooked and cut them into bite-sized pieces. Your guests can serve themselves with toothpicks or fingers, and dip the savory bites into interesting sauces, mustards, chutneys, or flavored mayonnaises. You can be more elaborate, if you wish, arranging the sausages on skewers with aromatic vegetables, meats, or seafoods. Or you can use sausage meat as a savory filling for pastries, empanadas, small tamales, and other hors d'oeuvres.

Sausage bites coated with crisp bread crumbs make a delicious appetizer or cocktail snack. Use a mildly flavored, precooked sausage such as Smoked Bratwurst (page 54), Minnesota Potato Sausage (page 69), or Chicken and Apple Sausage (page 34). Cut the sausage into 1-inch chunks, brush generously with a sweet mustard, roll in dried bread crumbs, and broil 3 to 4 inches from the flame for 2 to 3 minutes, turn, and broil 1 to 2 minutes more until crisp and brown.

Asparagus and Sausage Tourtière

Makes 10 to 12 appetizers or 6 main-course servings

Loni Kuhn, one of the *grandes dames* of our San Francisco cooking scene, held a cooking school in her home for years. Although she taught everything from Mexican to Moroccan, her first love was always Italian food. She liked to entertain, and this savory pizzalike custard makes a perfect appetizer or light main course. Use real Italian fontina; it will really make a difference in the flavor of the dish.

2 pounds pencil-thin asparagus
8 tablespoons (1 stick) butter, softened
1 loaf day-old, chewy white bread, such as San Francisco sourdough or Italian bread, crusts removed and thinly sliced
¾ pound mild Italian sausage, such as Italian Sweet Fennel Sausage (page 84) or Tuscan Sausage (page 84), removed from casings

12 to 14 ounces Italian fontina cheese, sliced, rind removed
4 egg yolks
1 cup heavy cream
¼ teaspoon kosher salt
¼ teaspoon white pepper
Pinch of freshly grated nutmeg
Freshly grated Parmesan cheese

Butter two 14-inch pizza pans. Trim the asparagus to fit the radius of the pan.

Bring 3 to 4 quarts of salted water to a boil. Add the asparagus and cook until crisp-tender, about 2 minutes. Plunge them into cold water, drain, and pat dry.

Butter the bread slices and, buttered side down, completely cover the bottom of the pans, fitting the pieces together like a jigsaw puzzle *with no gaps.*

In a large, heavy skillet over medium-high heat, fry the sausage. Use a fork to crumble the meat as it browns. After about 5 minutes, remove and drain. Discard the grease.

Place a thin layer of sliced fontina over the bread, and then a layer of asparagus, arranged like the spokes of a wheel with the tips facing toward the center. Top with another layer of fontina. Divide and sprinkle half the sausage on the top of each pan. You can prepare the tourtières several hours ahead to this point.

Preheat the oven to 375°.

Beat the egg yolks, cream, salt, pepper, and nutmeg together

Spicy Empanadas

Makes 36 small or 12
large empanadas

Tʜᴇsᴇ sᴘɪᴄʏ ᴍᴇᴀᴛ-ꜰɪʟʟᴇᴅ ᴛᴜʀɴᴏᴠᴇʀs ʜᴀᴠᴇ ᴍᴀɴʏ ᴠᴀʀɪᴀᴛɪᴏɴs ᴀɴᴅ ʜᴀᴠᴇ become a very popular snack throughout the Southwest. They are great at parties or before dinner served with an array of Mexican beers or a sparkling wine from Spain or California. In this version we suggest a piquant chorizo, raisin, and potato stuffing. You should feel free to experiment with fillings depending on your tastes and what you have on hand. Just make sure that the turnovers are packed with plenty of spice and flavor. Make empanadas ahead of time, freeze, and then bake them directly from the freezer. Add an extra 5 minutes or so to the baking time. The empanada filling also works well in tamales, tacos, or enchiladas.

1½ pounds Chorizo (page 74)
    or other southwestern-style
    sausage (pages 75 to 78),
    removed from casings
2 cups finely chopped onions
1 cup diced potatoes (¼-inch dice)
¼ cup red wine vinegar
½ cup Tex-Mex Red Enchilada
    Sauce (page 273)

½ cup raisins
½ cup chopped fresh cilantro
    (optional)
1 recipe Edy's Foolproof Pie Dough
    (page 149)
1 egg mixed with 2 tablespoons
    water for egg wash

In a heavy, large skillet, fry the sausage meat and onions together for 5 to 7 minutes over medium-high heat, until the onions are soft and the fat is rendered. Pour off most of the fat. Add the potatoes, vinegar, enchilada sauce, and raisins. Decrease the heat to medium, simmer, and cook until the potatoes are tender and most of the sauce has been absorbed, about 15 minutes. Add a little water if the potatoes are not quite done by the time the sauce is absorbed, and cook a bit longer. Skim any fat from the surface and cool the mixture in the refrigerator completely before assembling the empanadas. The filling can be made up a day ahead of time and refrigerated.

To assemble the empanadas, stir the cilantro into the filling. Make the dough according to the recipe directions. Roll out the dough to a thickness of ⅛ inch. For large empanadas, cut out 6-inch circles and place about ⅓ cup of filling in the center of each. For hors d'oeuvre–sized empanadas, cut 3-inch circles, and use 1 to 2 tablespoons of filling. Fold the dough over the filling to make half-moon-shaped turnovers and crimp the edge well with a fork or dough crimper. Place the empanadas on an ungreased baking sheet.

Preheat the oven to 400°. Brush the empanadas with the egg wash. Bake until the dough is golden and the empanadas give off a wonderful aroma, about 20 minutes, regardless of size. Serve warm.

Edy's Foolproof Pie Dough

Makes enough dough for a 10-inch two-crust pie, two 9-inch single-crust pies, or 36 small or 12 large empanadas

ur good friend and master chef Edy Young makes a simple-to-prepare dough that is always tender and flaky.

*¹/₂ pound (2 sticks) chilled
  salted butter, cut into
  ¹/₂-inch pieces
3 cups all-purpose flour
1 large egg yolk*

*Enough milk to make a total
  volume of ¹/₂ cup when
  combined with the egg yolk*

In a food processor fitted with the metal blade, process the butter and flour until the mixture looks like coarse meal. Add the combined egg yolk and milk through the feed tube and process in short bursts until the dough just begins to ball up.

Remove the dough, divide it in half, and form each piece into a ball. You can use the dough immediately, or wrap in plastic wrap and refrigerate until you are ready to use it (up to 2 days), or freeze for up to 2 months.

MY GRANDMOTHER ALWAYS SERVED PIROSHKI, SAVORY RUSSIAN TURNOVERS, with cabbage borscht. When I was growing up, it was one of my favorite meals. I would get excited as soon as I stepped into my grandmother's house because the appetizing aroma of piroshki baking is overwhelming. As soon as they came out of the oven and were put out on a board to cool in the kitchen, I'd sneak around the back door and grab one. I'd eat it while it was much too hot and burn my mouth. I still love piroshki, and with the simple cream cheese pastry in this recipe, they are easy to make and foolproof. —B.A.

Easy Cream Cheese Dough
8 ounces cream cheese
½ cup (1 stick) unsalted butter
2 cups unbleached all-purpose flour

Pinch of salt
1 egg beaten with 1 tablespoon
   water, for egg wash

Filling
2 tablespoons butter
2 onions, finely chopped
1 pound lean ground beef
1 pound Fresh Kielbasa (page 63),
   or other mild fresh sausage,
   removed from casings

2 hard-boiled eggs, chopped
2 teaspoons chopped fresh dill or
   1 teaspoon dried
2 tablespoons rich chicken or beef
   broth
Salt and pepper

To make the dough, in an electric mixer cream the cream cheese and butter together. Blend in flour and salt. Form the dough into a ball, cover, and chill for an hour before using.

Preheat the oven to 450°.

To make the filling, melt the butter in a large skillet over medium heat. Add the onions and sauté until they are soft and translucent, about 5 minutes. Combine in a bowl with the beef, kielbasa, eggs, dill, and broth. Season with salt and pepper. Mix thoroughly.

Roll out the dough to ⅛-inch thickness. Cut out circles 4 inches in diameter. Place 2 tablespoons of filling to one side of the center of each circle. Brush the edges lightly with the egg wash. Fold the dough over and press the edges together. Piroshki can be frozen at this point.

Brush each finished piroshki with the egg wash. Bake for 30 minutes or until lightly browned. Cut into one to make sure the meat is completely cooked. Serve warm.

Savory Crab Turnovers

Makes 30 small or 14 large turnovers

THIS RECIPE IS BEST MADE WITH FRESH CRABMEAT FROM THE ATLANTIC BLUE crab, the "beautiful swimmers" (*Callinectes sapidus*) of Chesapeake Bay and the Gulf Coast. If you can't find blue crab, you can use Dungeness or any other fresh lump crabmeat. Don't bother with canned or frozen crab, which often has the flavor and texture of wet, shredded cardboard. The pastry here is almost foolproof: simple to make, but wonderfully rich and buttery.

Pastry

8 ounces cream cheese
½ cup (1 stick) unsalted butter
½ teaspoon salt

2 cups all-purpose flour
1 egg beaten with 1 teaspoon
    water, for egg wash

Crab and Sausage Filling

4 tablespoons unsalted butter
½ pound smoked sausage, such as
    Cajun-Style Andouille (page
    44) or Smoked Country
    Sausage (page 32), finely
    diced
1 cup finely chopped onions
¼ cup thinly sliced green onions or
    scallions

1½ cups heavy cream
¼ cup freshly grated Parmesan
    cheese
½ teaspoon Tabasco sauce
1½ teaspoons Worcestershire sauce
2 egg yolks
1 pound cleaned fresh lump
    crabmeat

To make the pastry, cream the cream cheese and butter together in an electric mixer. Add the salt and flour, and blend thoroughly. Gather the dough into a ball, cover, and chill for at least an hour. (At this point, the dough can be frozen for later use.)

Roll out the dough onto a well-floured surface to about ⅛-inch thickness. For hors d'oeuvre–sized turnovers, cut into 30 3-inch circles. For larger turnovers, make 14 5-inch circles. Overlap the pastry circles on a sheet pan and refrigerate them until they are ready to be filled. Freeze any excess dough for a later use.

To make the filling, melt the butter in a heavy skillet over medium heat. Add the sausage and fry for 5 minutes, and then drain off all but about 1 tablespoon of the fat. Add the onions and cover the pan. Cook over moderate heat for about 10 minutes or until the onions are quite soft. Add the green onions, along with the cream, Parmesan, Tabasco, and Worcestershire sauce. Bring to a boil and cook, uncovered, stirring until the cream begins to thicken, about 10 minutes. Remove from the heat.

Beat the egg yolks in a bowl. Gradually stir in 1 cup of the hot cream and cheese mixture, being careful not to curdle the eggs. Return this mixture to the skillet while off the heat, and stir until all is blended together. Fold in the crabmeat, taste for seasoning, and cool for at least an hour or overnight in the refrigerator.

To assemble the turnovers, place 1 to 2 tablespoons of the filling on the small pastry circles or ¼ cup on the large. Flip one half of the circle over onto the other to make a half-moon shape. Crimp and seal the edges. At this point the turnovers can be frozen for baking later.

To bake, preheat the oven to 375°. Brush the turnovers with the egg wash, and bake for 20 to 25 minutes (25 to 30 minutes if frozen), until lightly browned. Serve warm.

Nancy's Asian Dipping Sauce

This delicious and easy-to-prepare sauce was created at the Boulevard restaurant in San Francisco by Nancy Oakes. It's a fantastic dipping sauce for seafood and can also be used as a quick dressing for a Thai salad. Sriracha Thai sauce, Asian hot chili oil, and Southeast Asian fish sauce are available at Asian groceries or by mail order (page 307).

½ cup Sriracha Thai chili sauce	¼ cup finely chopped green onions
¼ cup rice vinegar	or scallions, white and green parts
¼ cup Southeast Asian fish sauce	1 tablespoons finely chopped fresh
or soy sauce	ginger
Juice of 1 lime	Asian hot chili oil (optional)

Mix together the chili sauce, vinegar, fish sauce, lime juice, green onions, and ginger. Add chili oil to taste. The sauce will keep covered in the refrigerator for 7 to 10 days.

POT STICKERS ARE A POPULAR APPETIZER OR PARTY SNACK AND MAKE A GREAT accompaniment to soup. If you have some sausage in the fridge, as I usually do, they are quick and easy to put together. Any of our Asian-style sausages will work well here. They are delicious served with Nancy's Asian Dipping Sauce (page 152). —B.A.

**Makes 20 to 24
dumplings**

½ pound Asian-style sausage such
  as Chinatown Crépinettes
  (page 96), Chinese Pork and
  Shrimp Sausage (page 99), or
  Chinese Black Bean and
  Shiitakie Mushroom Sausage
  (page 98), removed from
  casings
2 cups finely shredded Napa or
  green cabbage

½ cup chopped fresh cilantro
¼ cup finely chopped green onions
  or scallions
1 teaspoon Chinese brown bean
  paste (optional)
20 to 24 round pot sticker
  (wonton) wrappers
3 tablespoons peanut oil
⅔ to 1⅓ cups water or stock

Thoroughly mix together the sausage, cabbage, cilantro, green onions, and bean paste. Put 1 tablespoon or more of this filling in the center of a wrapper, and fold it over to make a half moon. Brush the edges with a little water and pinch the edges together. Make 4 or 5 small pleats along the curved side, then pinch the two pointed ends together tightly to seal.

Heat the oil in a heavy 12-inch nonstick or cast-iron frying pan over medium heat. Add the pot stickers, seam side up, and fry for 2 to 3 minutes until the bottoms are lightly browned. Pour in ⅔ to 1 cup water or stock and cover the pan. Cook the pot stickers over medium heat for 10 to 15 minutes, until the liquid has evaporated. Check to see that the bottoms of the pot stickers are nicely browned and the dough is tender. If they are not brown, fry them, uncovered, for 1 or 2 more minutes. If the dough isn't tender, add another ⅓ cup of liquid, cover, and cook until the liquid has evaporated. Serve at once.

Savory Thai Seafood and Sausage Dumplings

Makes 6 servings
(20 to 25 dumplings)

●●

THESE SAVORY DUMPLINGS ARE ABSOLUTELY SIMPLE TO MAKE AND DOWN-right irresistible. Using premade round wonton wrappers, you can turn out these tasty dumplings quicker than a professional dim sum chef, and with just as good results. Just tuck the sausage mixed with seafood in the wrappers and steam the dumplings to perfection in a few minutes. Make up some of Nancy's Asian Dipping Sauce or Korean Dipping Sauce for a dim sum feast, and serve with a bottle of Tsing-Tao or Sapporo beer on the side. Use the seafood of your choice, alone or in combination. Raw shrimp, rock shrimp, or scallops are all delicious, as are lobster or crawfish tails. The seafood should be impeccably fresh and peeled and deveined, if necessary.

1 cup coarsely chopped seafood
2 cups (about ½ pound) Thai
  Chicken and Turkey Sausage
  (page 100), Chinese Black
  Bean and Shiitake Mushroom
  Sausage (page 98), or other
  spicy fresh sausage, removed
  from casings

20 to 25 round wonton wrappers
Nancy's Asian Dipping Sauce
  (page 152) or Korean
  Dipping Sauce (page 155)

In a large bowl, mix together the seafood and sausage. To make the dumplings, press a wonton wrapper into the curved palm of your hand. Scoop about 1 tablespoon of the filling into the small cup made in the center of the wrapper. Using the fingers of both hands, gently gather and fold the sides of the wrapper to make natural pleats. Squeeze the tops and sides of the wrapper together to make sure it forms around the filling. Tap the dumpling on a flat surface so that it can stand upright. Repeat until all wrappers and stuffing are used.

Place in a bamboo steamer or on an oiled plate over boiling water in a covered pot, and steam until the filling is firm, 15 to 20 minutes. Serve at once with one or both of the dipping sauces.

Korean Dipping Sauce

Makes about 1 cup

This tart, nutty sauce makes a great sauce for grilled shrimp or pot stickers.

¹/₄ cup chopped fresh cilantro
   (optional)
¹/₄ cup finely chopped green onions,
   white and green parts
¹/₄ cup soy sauce
2 tablespoons rice vinegar or cider
   vinegar

1 tablespoon grated fresh ginger
2 teaspoons toasted sesame seeds
   (pages 156–157)
2 teaspoons Asian sesame oil
2 teaspoons sugar

In a glass jar or bowl, combine the cilantro, green onions, soy sauce, vinegar, ginger, sesame seeds, sesame oil, and sugar. Shake or stir to mix thoroughly. This versatile dipping sauce will keep in the refrigerator in a sealed jar for 1 week.

Cold Chinese Noodles and Sausage with Sesame Dressing

Makes 4 to 6 servings

Cold noodle salad with sesame dressing and savory tidbits is a favorite snack in Chinese and Japanese restaurants all along the West Coast. In fact, it is so popular that you are sure to find some type of cold noodle dish in just about every gourmet deli in California. We used our Chinese Black Bean and Shiitake Mushroom Sausage here, but you could also use any Asian-flavored links or mild Italian sausage.

Noodle Salad

10 dried shiitake mushrooms

¼ pound snow peas or sugar snap peas, with stems removed

12 whole green onions or scallions, cut on the diagonal into 2-inch lengths

1 pound Chinese Black Bean and Shiitake Mushroom Sausage (page 98)

1 tablespoon peanut oil (optional)

2 eggs, beaten (optional)

Pinch of salt

2 tablespoons sesame seeds

½ pound fresh thin Chinese egg noodles or ¼ pound dried vermicelli

1 cup coarsely chopped cilantro

Sesame Dressing

2 tablespoons Chinese black vinegar or Japanese rice wine vinegar

1 tablespoon soy sauce

2 teaspoons sugar

6 tablespoons sesame oil

Pour boiling water over the shiitake mushrooms. Cover and soak for at least 30 minutes or for up to several hours. Remove the tough stems and slice the caps into thin shreds.

Bring a large pot of lightly salted water to a boil. Add the snow peas and green onions and blanch for 30 seconds. Drain under cold running water in a colander and set aside.

Fry the sausages whole in a heavy covered frying pan over medium heat until they are lightly browned and firm to the touch, about 10 minutes. Remove them from the pan, and when they are cool enough to handle, cut the sausages into thin rounds.

Heat the peanut oil in a medium omelet pan. Add the eggs, beaten with a pinch of salt, to make a thin omelet. Fry until set, turn over, and fry 1 minute more. Transfer the omelet to a plate and when it is completely cool, cut it into thin shreds about 2 to 3 inches long.

In a small dry frying pan, roast the sesame seeds over low heat,

Quick and Easy Salads

With its varied flavors and textures, sausage combines beautifully with many different vegetables, greens, and pasta to make easy yet dramatic and delicious salads. They are very versatile and can serve as appetizers or first courses, lunch or buffet dishes.

It's critical to use high-quality, lean sausages in salads. Homemade are best, but some lean commercial poultry sausages will also work well. Serve these salads warm, cold, or at room temperature. The possible variations are endless.

Combine cooked sausages with seasonal vegetables: asparagus and young lettuce in the spring, sweet corn and red peppers in the summer, cauliflower and broccoli in the fall, and cabbage and potatoes in the winter. Use leftovers as your inspiration: cold pasta; leftover roast chicken, meat, or fish; assorted cheeses; yesterday's cooked vegetables—all combine well with sausages to make delightful salads.

For dressings, try a Ginger-Mustard Dressing (page 159) or a Sesame Dressing (page 156).

shaking the pan continuously until they are light brown and aromatic, about 5 minutes. Transfer them to a small bowl.

Bring a large pot of lightly salted water to a boil. Add the fresh noodles and cook for 1 minute, just until they are tender. Cook dried vermicelli according to directions on package. Taste one to see if they are cooked to your taste. Drain and cool them under running water in a colander. Run your hand through the noodles as they rinse to make sure they are cool and to help wash off the starch.

To make the dressing, mix together the vinegar, soy sauce, and sugar in a small bowl. Gradually whisk in the oil.

To assemble the salad, place the noodles in a large bowl with the mushrooms, snow peas, green onions, sausage, and all but ¼ cup each of the shredded omelet and the cilantro. Mix in the dressing until everything is well coated. Transfer the salad to a shallow bowl or platter. Scatter the remaining cilantro and egg over the surface and sprinkle the sesame seeds over all.

Thai Sausage Salad

Makes 4 to 6 servings

Thai food is characterized by lively flavors, very little fat, and substantial heat levels from pepper and chiles. These appealing qualities are most clearly shown in the many salads found on Thai tables. Cold salads of squid or shrimp or grilled beef, pork, or chicken are found all over Thailand and in many Thai restaurants in America. The chewy seafood or meat is contrasted with crisp ingredients like red onions and lettuce, with all the flavors tied together by tangy limes and hot chiles. Thai salads make delightful first courses and can also serve as main dishes when paired with other Thai dishes.

1 pound Thai Chicken and Turkey
   Sausage (page 100) formed
   into 2-inch patties, ½ inch thick
⅓ cup freshly squeezed lime juice
2 tablespoons soy sauce
2 to 3 teaspoons Sriracha Thai
   chili sauce or Tabasco sauce
Pinch of sugar

20 fresh mint leaves
1 tablespoon thinly sliced
   lemongrass (center stalks only)
½ red onion, thinly sliced
1 medium head iceberg lettuce,
   large outer leaves removed and
   kept whole, remaining leaves
   thinly sliced

Garnish
Cilantro sprigs

In a large nonstick skillet, panfry the sausage patties over medium heat until lightly browned and cooked through, 5 to 7 minutes. Set the sausage aside and reserve the pan drippings.

In a small bowl, combine the drippings from the sausage pan with the lime juice, soy sauce, chili sauce, and sugar. Add the mint leaves, lemongrass, and sliced onion to this dressing and stir well.

Lay the large lettuce leaves on a platter and cover with the shredded lettuce. Arrange the sausage patties over the lettuce. Spoon the dressing all over the salad, and garnish with cilantro sprigs.

Priscilla Yee is a grand-champion recipe-contest winner who lives in California. Much of her spare time is spent developing delicious recipes for the cooking contests that she wins with great frequency. From this recipe you can see why. This wilted salad typifies Priscilla's cooking style: quick and easy, with fresh ingredients and ethnic touches from her Asian heritage. It's wonderful for lunch or a light summer supper.

Priscilla's Wilted Salad of Savoy Cabbage, Pears, and Sausage

Makes 4 servings

Salad

8 ounces Asian-style sausage (pages 96 to 101) or mild Italiansausage

2 ounces snow peas, trimmed (about 24)

1 large red bell pepper, cut into julienne strips

4 cups shredded savoy cabbage (½-inch strips)

1 cucumber, peeled, seeded, and sliced

1 firm ripe pear, cored and sliced

2 tablespoons chopped fresh cilantro

Ginger-Mustard Dressing

¼ cup salad oil, preferably peanut

3 tablespoons freshly squeezed lemon juice

1 tablespoon minced fresh ginger

2 teaspoons light soy sauce

2 teaspoons Dijon mustard

1 teaspoon sugar

Garnish
Cilantro sprigs (optional)

Fry the sausages whole in a heavy covered skillet over medium heat until they are browned and firm to the touch, about 10 minutes. Set aside to cool while you prepare the dressing.

Whisk the oil, lemon juice, ginger, soy sauce, mustard, and sugar together in a small bowl. Slice the sausage into ¼-inch rounds.

Drain off all but 2 tablespoons of the drippings from the skillet and heat over medium-high heat. Add the snow peas, bell pepper, cabbage, cucumber, and Ginger-Mustard Dressing. Stir just until the cabbage starts to wilt, 1 to 2 minutes. Stir in the pear, cilantro, and sliced sausage. Spoon the salad onto 4 plates and garnish with cilantro sprigs.

Chapter 8

SAUSAGE-BASED SOUPS

Soups are typical of the generous, hearty, and nutritious foods that make country cooking so satisfying. Soups also provide a lot of nourishment for little money, and they don't have to be high in fat or calories.

With a few vegetables, some dried beans or lentils, and an assortment of our tasty sausages in the freezer, you can turn out delicious soups quickly and with very little effort. Each sausage gives a soup its own flavor profile: All you have to do is fry up a little sausage, add some onions, carrots, celery, a cup of precooked or canned beans, some homemade or canned stock, and within 45 minutes you can call out "Soup's on!" and watch the family come running.

Some of the soups in this chapter are somewhat more involved, such as Braised Stuffed Lettuce Soup (page 174), but none requires complicated procedures or long, drawn-out cooking. A plus is that many soups like Cajun-Style Pea Soup (page 165) and Polish Sausage, Mushroom, and Barley Soup (page 168) improve with a day or two of aging in the refrigerator. So you can let them cook on Sunday while you are reading the paper on the deck. Then heat them up later in the week for quick and delicious dinners.

CORN CHOWDER IS A POPULAR SOUP ALL THROUGH THE HEARTLAND, AND IN New England and the South as well. Recipes often contain bacon and salt pork, but we've substituted a highly smoked sausage instead. Use any flavorful smoked sausage, such as smoked kielbasa.

The key to this dish is the freshness of the corn. Ideally you should try to make this chowder at the height of the corn season when the ears can be freshly picked and are perfectly sweet. Use fresh corn if you can and be sure to scrape the cobs with the dull side of a knife after you slice the kernels off to get all that delicious milky juice into the chowder. When making this soup out of season, use frozen corn rather than imported fresh corn, because the frozen has a sweeter flavor.

2 tablespoons butter
½ pound smoked sausage, such as Cajun-Style Andouille (page 44), Smoked Bratwurst (page 54), or Smoked Kielbasa (page 64), diced
1 onion, finely chopped
½ cup chopped celery
1 fresh pimiento, red bell, or other sweet red pepper, seeded and chopped
2 red potatoes, peeled and diced
4 cups chicken stock
2 bay leaves

⅛ teaspoon ground cumin
2 sprigs fresh thyme or ½ teaspoon dried
4 cups garden-fresh corn kernels (from about 4 ears) or frozen corn
2 cups half-and-half
2 egg yolks
2 tablespoons cornstarch
1 cup buttermilk
Salt and freshly ground black pepper
Tabasco sauce

Garnish
2 tablespoons butter
Chopped chives

In a large pot or Dutch oven, melt the butter over medium heat. Add the sausage and fry for 3 minutes. Add the onion and celery, and cook until soft, about 10 minutes. Add the fresh pimiento and potatoes, and sauté briefly. Pour in the stock. Bring to a boil, decrease the heat, and simmer. Add the bay leaves, cumin, and thyme, and simmer for 5 to 10 minutes, until the potatoes and peppers are tender. Add the corn and any milky juices, along with the half-and-half.

Cook for 1 to 2 minutes, until the corn is tender but still full of flavor. Remove the soup from the heat.

Whisk the egg yolks and the cornstarch into the buttermilk. Stir ½ cup of the soup into this mixture, and then add back to the soup in the pot, stirring well.

Return the soup to the stove. Heat without boiling to thicken. Taste for salt, pepper, and Tabasco. Serve with a bit of butter and chopped chives in each bowl.

Quick and Easy Soups

With ½ to ¾ pound of sausage and 6 cups of good beef or chicken stock you have the basis for many fine soups. The sausage may be smoked or raw. If you wish, it can be precooked and drained to get rid of some of the fat.

For a delicious vegetable soup, add 3 cups of a mixture of chopped potatoes, carrots, leeks, and celery to the stock and sausage and cook gently until the vegetables are done. Another delicious soup: Add 3 cups of chopped broccoli, a chopped onion, and a few garlic cloves chopped and sautéed briefly in olive oil to the stock and sausage, along with some freshly cooked macaroni. Cook gently until the broccoli is just done.

To make a satisfyingly thick soup, add ¼ pound chopped smoked sausage, 2 cups diced zucchini, and 1 cup of cooked rice to the sausage/stock mixture. Cook gently until the zucchini is just tender and puree everything in a food processor. Add a little lemon juice and taste for salt and pepper.

The possibilities are endless. Put together whatever combinations of vegetables, stock, and sausages appeal to you—you'll soon find that a flavorful soup, served with a good crusty bread and a glass of wine, makes an easy and satisfying meal for family or guests.

Red Bean and Sausage Soup

Makes 8 servings

Serve these beans up with Cheese and Sausage Biscuits (page 122) and some steamed turnip or mustard greens for a stick-to-the-ribs country dinner. A big, full-bodied Zinfandel from California's Amador County or a high-hopped ale like Anchor Liberty or Canada's Black Horse would wash everything down right nicely. If you haven't the time to make our Country Ham and Pork Sausage, you can use any good-quality smoked sausage with these tangy beans.

1 pound red beans (about 2½ cups)
4 quarts beef or chicken stock
2 ham hocks (about 1½ pounds)
½ pound Country Ham and Pork Sausage (page 30) or smoked sausage, chopped
2 cups chopped onions
1 cup chopped celery
½ teaspoon freshly ground black pepper

1 bay leaf
1 teaspoon dried thyme
½ pound Smoked Country Sausage (page 32) or other smoked sausage, sliced into ¼-inch rounds
¼ cup red wine vinegar
Salt and freshly ground black pepper
Tabasco sauce

Garnish
3 hard-boiled eggs, chopped (optional)

½ cup finely chopped green onions or scallions

Place the beans in enough water to cover by 2 to 3 inches and soak overnight.

In a 6- to 8-quart pot, bring the stock to a boil. Drain and rinse the beans and add them to the pot along with the ham hocks, chopped Country Ham and Pork Sausage, the onions, celery, pepper, bay leaf, and thyme. Decrease the heat to a low boil and simmer, stirring occasionally, for 2 hours, until the beans are tender.

Remove the ham hocks. Chop the meat and skin coarsely and return them to the pot. Discard the bones. Add more stock if the soup is too thick. Add the rounds of Smoked Country Sausage to the pot, and cook for 10 minutes more. Add enough wine vinegar to produce a slightly tangy flavor. Adjust the salt and pepper, and add a couple of healthy jolts of Tabasco.

To serve, ladle the soup into bowls and garnish with chopped egg and green onions. Your guests can add more Tabasco to taste.

Cajun-Style Pea Soup

Makes 6 to 8 servings

On cold, gray winter days, nothing satisfies more than a bowl of hearty pea soup. This Cajun pea soup is simple to prepare, but substantial enough to serve as a one-course meal with biscuits or cornbread.

8 cups beef or chicken stock
2 large ham hocks (about 1½ pounds)
1 pound split green peas (about 2 cups)
2 cups chopped onions
2 carrots, chopped
4 ribs celery, chopped
½ green bell pepper, chopped
1 leek, thinly sliced (optional)
2 cloves garlic, minced
1 teaspoon ground sage
1 teaspoon dried thyme

1 teaspoon ground cayenne pepper
2 bay leaves
1 pound Cajun-Style Andouille (page 44) or other good-quality smoked sausage, sliced into ½-inch rounds
2 teaspoons filé powder (optional)
1 cup chopped fresh parsley
½ cup finely chopped green onions or scallions
Salt and freshly ground black pepper

In a heavy 4-quart pot, bring the stock to a boil and add the ham hocks. Decrease the heat to a simmer and cook for 1 hour.

Add the split peas, onions, carrots, celery, green bell pepper, leek, garlic, sage, thyme, cayenne, and bay leaves. Simmer, covered, for 45 minutes, until the peas are falling apart.

Add the sausage and simmer for 10 minutes more. Stir in the filé powder, parsley, and green onions. Season to taste with salt and pepper. Serve in large bowls.

Ciambotta

Makes 12 to 15 servings

•••

THIS "RECIPE" WAS A FAMILY FAVORITE OF PAUL CAMARDO'S, CO-OWNER OF Bucci's Restaurant in Emeryville, California. It is a hearty soup/stew that can be inspired by leftovers. Use whatever is lurking around the refrigerator—scraps of prosciutto, salami, or ham, some tasty sausage, vegetables, etc. A great way to use up leftovers—come up with your own mix of ingredients. Ham bones or rinds, celery root, leeks, just about any kind of greens can all be tossed into the pot.

4 quarts beef or chicken stock
1 pound leftover pieces of
    prosciutto, coppa, ham, or salt
    pork, coarsely chopped
2 tablespoons fennel seeds
3 boiling potatoes, cut into 1-inch
    chunks
1 onion, coarsely chopped
4 ribs celery, cut into 1-inch
    chunks
½ head cabbage, coarsely chopped
2 carrots, coarsely chopped
2 pounds Italian Sweet Fennel
    Sausage (page 84) or other
    mild Italian sausage, cut into
    1-inch rounds

2 bunches (about 2 pounds) of
    greens (mustard, kale, turnip,
    chard, spinach, etc.), coarsely
    chopped
½ pound green beans, cut into
    1-inch pieces
1 whole head garlic, chopped
4 tablespoons chopped fresh basil or
    2 teaspoons dried
Salt and freshly ground black
    pepper
Freshly grated Parmesan cheese

Bring the stock to a boil and add the meat and the fennel seeds. Decrease the heat and simmer for 1 hour, uncovered. Add the potatoes, onion, celery, cabbage, and carrots, and cook for 20 minutes more.

Place the sausage chunks in a large skillet and brown for 10 minutes over medium heat to render some of the fat. Add the sausage to the pot along with the greens, green beans, garlic, and basil. Add salt and pepper to taste. Cook for an additional 10 minutes, until all the vegetables and meats are tender.

Serve in large individual bowls. Sprinkle with Parmesan cheese and enjoy.

We call this recipe New Year's Eve Borscht, because its bright red and green colors are reminiscent of the Christmas/New Year's holidays. It makes a delicious, hearty one-pot meal at a New Year's gathering. Borscht is popular throughout Eastern Europe. Depending on the region and nationality, ingredients and spellings may differ, but the flavor is always satisfying. Use a garlicky smoked sausage, such as smoked kielbasa, German garlic sausage, or Cervelat. If beet greens aren't available, use chard, kale, or other greens.

New Year's Eve Borscht

Makes 12 to 16 servings

2 pounds beef chuck, cut into
    1-inch chunks
12 cups beef stock
2 cups coarsely chopped onions
2 cups chopped Italian-style
    canned tomatoes
1 medium head cabbage (2 pounds),
    coarsely shredded
3 to 4 boiling potatoes (1 pound),
    coarsely diced
4 carrots, coarsely chopped
4 ribs celery, coarsely chopped
4 parsnips, diced

2 leeks, coarsely chopped
1 celery root, peeled and cut into
    julienne strips
4 beet roots, diced, and greens
    sliced
1 pound garlicky sausage, such as
    Smoked Kielbasa (page 64)
    or Garlic, Pork, and Ham
    Cervelat (page 60)
2 teaspoons caraway seeds
Salt and freshly ground black
    pepper
Red wine vinegar (optional)

Garnish
1 cup sour cream
Fresh or dried dill

In a large soup pot, bring the meat and stock to a boil. Decrease the heat and simmer, uncovered, for I hour. Add the onions, tomatoes, cabbage, potatoes, carrots, celery, parsnips, leeks, celery root, and diced beets. Simmer for 30 minutes. Add the sausage and cook for 5 minutes. Add the beet greens and the caraway seeds and simmer vigorously for 5 more minutes. Season to taste with salt and pepper, and add a little red wine vinegar if you like a slight tang.

Serve in large soup bowls, garnished with sour cream and dill.

Polish Sausage, Mushroom, and Barley Soup

Makes 6 to 8 servings

My MOTHER MADE A BIG DEAL ABOUT SCOTCH BROTH, A MEAT AND BARLEY soup that she'd make up in prodigious quantities every two years or so and freeze. That was my first experience with barley soup, and after a while I somehow lost my enthusiasm.

Many years later in a Polish neighborhood restaurant in Toronto, I ate a barley and mushroom soup that was included with the dinner (I wouldn't have ordered it if it wasn't). It was spicy, satisfying, and wonderfully rich. From then on I was hooked on barley soups, especially ones that used dried mushrooms and kielbasa.—B.A.

Either smoked or fresh kielbasa works well in this recipe. You could also use a mild but flavorful sausage like bockwurst or bratwurst. Some recipes for this popular Eastern European soup call for beef, but we prefer to use chicken gizzards, and of course, sausage.

1 ounce dried Polish or porcini
    mushrooms
½ cup pearl barley
¼ pound chicken gizzards, finely
    diced, or ¼ pound beef stew
    meat, diced
1 bay leaf
½ teaspoon dried marjoram
8 cups chicken or beef stock
1 onion, finely chopped
1 cup thinly sliced leeks

1 carrot, diced
1 rib celery, diced
½ pound fresh mushrooms, sliced
½ pound Fresh Kielbasa (page 63)
    or Smoked Kielbasa (page 64)
    or other mild sausage, chopped
2 eggs
1 cup sour cream
Salt and freshly ground black
    pepper

Garnish
Fresh dill

About 30 minutes before you plan to start cooking, combine the dried mushrooms with 3 cups boiling water and set aside to soak for 30 minutes or more.

Combine the barley, gizzards, bay leaf, and marjoram with the stock in a large pot and simmer for 45 minutes. Add the onion, leeks, carrot, and celery.

Add the soaked mushrooms and their liquid. Make sure that you leave any sand from the mushrooms behind, by either decanting the

Tortilla, Vegetable, and Chorizo Soup

Makes 8 servings

SOUPS GARNISHED WITH FRESHLY FRIED TORTILLA STRIPS ARE VERY POPULAR in Mexican-American neighborhoods throughout the Southwest. This soup was never officially a recipe when I made it at Poulet—I just put it together with whatever vegetables were on hand. The only constants were the chicken broth, chorizo, and the fried tortillas. Depending on the season and what we had in the refrigerator, we used zucchini, green beans, spinach, crookneck squash, cabbage, or even shredded lettuce. But no matter what ingredients we used, everybody seemed to love the soup.

2 pounds Chorizo (page 74) or
    other southwestern or Mexican
    sausage, removed from casings
4 onions, chopped
6 cups chicken stock
1 (28-ounce) can peeled whole
    tomatoes and liquid, coarsely
    chopped, or 3½ cups peeled and
    chopped fresh tomatoes
1 (16-ounce) can garbanzo beans,
    rinsed and drained
1 teaspoon dried oregano
1 teaspoon ground cumin

2 Anaheim chiles, fire-roasted,
    peeled, and chopped (page 73)
1 red bell pepper, fire-roasted,
    peeled, and chopped (page 73)
1 tablespoon chopped garlic
4 cups diced zucchini
1 (10-ounce) box frozen corn or
    about 2 cups fresh corn, cut
    from the cob
Juice from 3 to 4 limes (about
    1 cup)
Salt and freshly ground black
    pepper

Garnish

4 corn tortillas, cut in half and
    each half cut into ½-inch-wide
    strips
Oil for frying
2 cups grated jack cheese

½ cup chopped green onions or
    scallions
32 to 40 fresh cilantro leaves
    (optional)
Lime wedges

Brown the sausage in a heavy large pot or Dutch oven over medium-high heat until the fat is rendered, 5 to 7 minutes. Remove all but 3 tablespoons of the fat from the pan, and add the onions. Sauté for 3 to 5 minutes, until they are translucent and soft.

Pour in the chicken stock, and add the tomatoes and their liquid, the garbanzos, oregano, and cumin. Bring to a boil, then decrease the heat to a simmer. Add the chiles, bell pepper, garlic, zucchini,

Deep-Dish Chicken and Sausage Pie with Biscuit Crust (*page 234*)

Rolled Flank Steak with Italian Sausage, Basil, and Swiss Cheese *(page 260)*

Stacked Cheese and Chorizo Enchiladas (*page 272*)

Hot Potato and Sausage Salad (*page 294*)

Winter
Vegetable,
Sausage,
and
Chestnut
Soup

Makes 6 to 8 servings

Tʜɪs sᴀᴛɪsғʏɪɴɢ sᴏᴜᴘ/sᴛᴇᴡ ᴄᴏᴍʙɪɴᴇs ᴛʜᴇ ʜᴇᴀʀᴛʏ ғʟᴀᴠᴏʀs ᴏғ ᴡɪɴᴛᴇʀ vegetables, such as celery root and squash, with the exotic flavor of black mushrooms and chestnuts and the smoky tang of ham hocks and sausages. Dried chestnuts are just as good as fresh, and for this soup they are a whole lot less work to prepare. They can be purchased in Chinese groceries or Italian delis in most large cities. If you can't find them, use fresh chestnuts. Similar to the popular Chinese hot and sour soup, this is a bit richer, with a subtle, smoky flavor. If you prefer it spicier, stir in some Tabasco or hot chili oil. Like most of the hearty stews and soups in this book, it tastes even better the next day.

1 cup dried chestnuts or 1½ pounds fresh chestnuts
8 cups beef or chicken stock
1 pound ham hock, sawed into 2-inch pieces
1 pound spicy smoked sausage such as Hot Links (page 43) or Cajun-Style Andouille (page 44), sliced into ¼-inch rounds
6 Chinese black mushrooms or Japanese shiitakes, soaked in hot water to cover
1 leek, well washed and chopped
1 parsnip, peeled and cut into 1-inch cubes
1 celery root, peeled and cut into 1-inch cubes

¾ pound white turnip or rutabaga, peeled and cut into 1-inch cubes
½ teaspoon ground cayenne pepper
1 bay leaf
1½ pounds butternut squash, peeled and cut into 1-inch cubes
1 tablespoon soy sauce
3 tablespoons white or cider vinegar
2 tablespoons cornstarch
Salt and freshly ground black pepper
Tabasco sauce

Soak the dried chestnuts in water overnight and drain. If using fresh chestnuts, preheat the oven to 450°. Cut a deep cross on one side of each chestnut. Roast for 15 minutes, or until the shells begin to open. Remove the shells and outer skin. Bring 2 cups water to a boil in a medium pot. Add the chestnuts, decrease the heat to low, and simmer until tender, about 20 minutes. Drain.

Bring the stock to a boil in a large pot or Dutch oven. Add the ham hocks and about ¼ pound of the sausage. Decrease the heat and

Braised Stuffed Lettuce Soup

Makes 4 main-course
or 6 to 8 appetizer
servings

THE SALINAS VALLEY NEAR MONTEREY IS OFTEN CALLED THE LETTUCE BOWL of America. Although we are used to eating lettuce raw in salads, it can also make a delicious cooked vegetable. Many of the Italian immigrants who settled and farmed the Salinas Valley used cooked lettuce in family dishes, and the recipe below is inspired by this tradition.

Several varieties of lettuce and greens work well in this dish, including iceberg, escarole, romaine, green leafy lettuce, and Swiss chard. You can vary the sausage according to your taste; any mild-flavored fresh sausage will contribute its own flavor. Try a fresh Asian-style sausage or mild Italian, or other fresh mild sausage. Since the sausage meat doesn't have to be stuffed into casings, you can easily make up a batch in the food processor for this recipe. Depending on the size of the portion, this soup can be used as an appetizer or main dish.

15 large outer leaves from romaine,
    iceberg, escarole, or Swiss chard
¾ pound Chinese Pork and Shrimp
    Sausage (page 99) or other
    mild-flavored fresh sausage such
    as mild Italian, in bulk or
    removed from casings
¾ cup fresh bread crumbs
½ cup chopped watercress
1 egg, beaten

½ teaspoon salt, or more to taste
6 cups chicken stock
½ cup dry white wine
1 teaspoon minced garlic
1 tablespoon olive oil
1 tablespoon lemon juice, or more
    to taste
2 teaspoons cornstarch
Freshly ground black pepper
Lemon wedges

Blanch the lettuce or chard leaves by dipping for 30 seconds in boiling water to make them soft and pliable. Drain and set aside.

In a bowl knead together the sausage, bread crumbs, watercress, egg, and ½ teaspoon salt. Mound 2 to 3 tablespoons of the mixture on the edge of each leaf. Fold in the sides like an envelope, and roll to form a package. Place the rolls, seam side down, in a nonreactive Dutch oven or heavy casserole. Pour in the stock and wine, along with the garlic, olive oil, and 1 tablespoon lemon juice. Bring to a simmer and cook, covered, for 35 minutes, until the rolls are quite tender and the filling cooked. Transfer 3 rolls each to 4 soup bowls.

Season to taste with salt, pepper, and lemon juice. Pour the soup over the rolls and serve, garnished with lemon wedges.

It's hard to imagine soup being popular in a climate as hot and humid as Thailand's, but spicy soups are some of the favorite dishes of this exciting cuisine and among the most delicious. Our Thai Sausage Soup is simple to make because most of the seasoning and flavor come from the sausage, which is simmered in chicken stock with vegetables and a little coconut milk. The coconut milk provides richness and a lightly sweet exotic undertone. It's available canned in most Asian groceries or by mail order (page 307), but if you can't find any, substitute condensed milk in equivalent amounts.

1 tablespoon peanut oil
½ pound Thai Chicken and Turkey
    Sausage (page 100), removed
    from casings
½ cup chopped onion
½ cup thinly sliced celery
6 cups chicken stock
6 bamboo shoots, diced

10 medium-sized fresh mush-
    rooms, sliced
½ cup coconut milk or condensed
    milk
1 tablespoon fresh lime juice
Salt and freshly ground black
    pepper

Garnish
¼ cup chopped green onions or
    scallions, white and green parts
Cilantro leaves

Heat the oil in a large pot over medium heat. Add the sausage and stir-fry for 3 minutes, breaking it up as it cooks. Add the onion and celery and stir-fry for 5 more minutes. Add the chicken stock, bring to a boil, decrease the heat, and simmer for 10 minutes. Add the bamboo shoots, mushrooms, and coconut milk. Simmer for 2 more minutes. Add the lime juice and taste for salt and pepper. Serve garnished with green onions and cilantro leaves.

Chapter 9

SAUSAGE SANDWICHES AND PIZZAS

WHAT COULD BE SIMPLER OR TASTIER THAN A JUICY, FLAVORFUL SAUSAGE tucked into a roll with some sliced onions, peppers, hot mustard, and whatever else you might have on hand? There are unlimited possibilities for sausage sandwiches, so experiment and try them on your family and friends. Instead of mustard, dress the sandwich with a vinaigrette; combine sausage with seafood, sautéed eggplant, or grilled vegetables. Let your leftovers and your imagination be your guide.

The hot dog on a bun, America's favorite sausage sandwich by far, has its own regional variations. In New York, it is eaten on steamed rolls with sauerkraut, raw onions, and brown mustard. In Chicago, it is consumed with mustard, chopped tomato, chopped pickles, onions, and cheese. In Los Angeles it is preferred cut open, grilled, and eaten with chili, cheese, and onions. Take your pick or make up your own favorite hot dog.

Pizza and sausage seem made for each other. Tangy Italian sausage with herbs and garlic and tomatoes and cheese is the perfect topping for any type of pie, from classic thin-crust New York style to the thick and gooey pan pizza favored by Chicago pizza fanatics.

ONE OF NEW ORLEANS' GREATEST SPECIALTIES, THE PO' BOY SANDWICH, can be made with such humble ingredients as fried potatoes, or with elegant fillings like fried oysters or soft-shelled crab. Some of the best are made with chaurice, or "hot sausage" as it's called in New Orleans.

What makes a great po' boy? First, the bread. It must be very fresh, soft inside with a slightly chewy crust. The crust can't be too hard or the filling will come oozing out with the first bite. And then, there's the fixin's. Usually the sandwich maker will ask how you want your po' boy. "Fully dressed" means the works—finely shredded lettuce or cabbage, mayonnaise, Creole mustard, sliced dill pickles, and sometimes tomatoes, along with very thinly sliced red onions.

Creole Mustard–Mayonnaise Sauce

6 tablespoons Creole or Dijon mustard
3 tablespoons homemade or good commercial mayonnaise

½ teaspoon Worcestershire sauce
Tabasco sauce or other hot sauce

Po' Boy

4 (6-inch) sections French bread
4 links Chaurice (page 45) or other spicy fresh sausage, such as New York–Style Spicy Hot Italian Sausage (page 82)
3 cups finely shredded cabbage or lettuce

12 to 15 dill pickle slices
½ red onion, thinly sliced (optional)
1 large tomato, sliced (optional)

To make the sauce, combine the mustard, mayonnaise, and Worcestershire sauce in a small bowl. Add Tabasco to taste. Set aside.

Preheat the oven to 350°. Warm the French bread for 10 minutes.

In a heavy skillet, fry the sausages for 15 minutes over medium heat, turning the links so they brown evenly.

Slice the bread in half lengthwise, and spread generously with mustard-mayonnaise sauce on both sides. On one side, heap the shredded cabbage and lay over it the pickle slices, onion, and tomato. Place split hot sausage on top, close up the sandwich as best you can, and get to work.

STREET FOOD IN BANGKOK IS SOME OF THE BEST IN THE WORLD. SIDEWALKS are crowded with vendors offering grilled meats and fish, spicy salads, sandwiches, snacks, soups—all bursting with the bright and lively flavors that make Thai cooking so appealing. Our Thai Chicken and Turkey Sausage has plenty of those flavors—Thai green curry, garlic, basil, cilantro. In this tasty sandwich, we wrap the zesty sausage in a flour tortilla and add our gingery Mango Vinaigrette to wake up the taste buds. Wash it all down with a cold Singha beer.

Makes 4 servings

Mango Vinaigrette

½ ripe mango, peeled and cut up
⅓ cup vegetable oil
2 tablespoons white wine vinegar
2 tablespoons packed fresh mint leaves
½-inch piece fresh ginger, peeled and chopped

Freshly grated zest of ½ lemon
1 clove garlic
Sriracha Thai chili sauce
Salt and freshly ground black pepper

Sandwiches

4 links Thai Chicken and Turkey Sausage (page 100)
4 flour tortillas

4 to 8 green onions, white and green parts, thinly sliced lengthwise
Cilantro sprigs (optional)

To make the vinaigrette, combine the mango, oil, vinegar, mint, ginger, lemon zest, and garlic in a food processor or blender. Process until smooth. Add a dash or two of the chili sauce and salt and pepper to taste. Set aside.

Preheat the oven to 300°.

Panfry the sausage in a large, heavy skillet over medium-high heat for 3 to 5 minutes on each side until browned and cooked through. Set aside and keep warm.

Wrap the tortillas in aluminum foil and warm in the oven for 10 minutes.

To assemble the rolls, place a sausage in a tortilla, top with a tablespoon or two of Mango Vinaigrette, some green onions, and sprigs of cilantro. Roll up and serve. Repeat with the remaining sausages and tortillas.

Italian Grilled Sausage and Vegetable Rolls

Makes 4 to 6 servings

WHILE IT'S NICE TO WANDER DOWN MULBERRY STREET DURING THE FESTA di San Gennaro sampling the grilled sausages as you go, you can come pretty close in your own backyard, on the deck, or in the kitchen with this Italian sausage and vegetable barbecue. We suggest a mix of half hot and half mild Italian sausages, but you can cook any types that you, your family, and friends prefer.

Offer both white and red wines to your guests: a spicy pinot bianco from the Alto Adige region in Italy's Alps and an earthy Chianti Colli Senesi or California zinfandel.

Marinade

¼ cup freshly squeezed lemon juice
½ cup olive oil
3 cloves garlic, minced
2 tablespoons chopped fresh basil or
  1 tablespoon chopped fresh
  marjoram

½ teaspoon salt
½ teaspoon freshly ground black
  pepper

Sausage and Vegetables

1 red bell pepper, quartered
  lengthwise and seeded
1 green bell pepper, quartered
  lengthwise and seeded
1 yellow bell pepper, quartered
  lengthwise and seeded
4 Japanese eggplants, split
  lengthwise

1 large red onion, cut into
  ½-inch slices
4 Italian sweet fennel sausages
4 spicy hot Italian sausages
8 crusty French or Italian rolls

Prepare a medium fire in a covered barbecue kettle or preheat the broiler.

Whisk together the lemon juice, olive oil, garlic, basil, salt, and pepper in a large bowl. Toss the bell peppers, eggplant, and onion into the bowl and rub them with the marinade so they are generously coated. Remove the vegetables, shaking off any excess marinade into the bowl. Save the marinade.

Grill the vegetables over medium coals in a covered barbecue kettle or under a broiler. Place the sausages on the grill and cover immediately. If any flaming occurs, douse the flames with a spray of water. Turn the sausages and vegetables frequently. The vegetables are done when they are tender but still firm. Transfer them to a serving platter when they are cooked. Serve the vegetables warm or at room temperature. The sausages are done when firm or when an instant-read thermometer inserted through the end registers 155° to 160°. Transfer the sausages to the platter and keep warm.

Cut the rolls in half and brush with the reserved marinade. Pour the remaining marinade over the platter of sausages and grilled vegetables. Have your guests make their own sandwiches, choosing their own sausage and vegetable combination.

Cucumber and Yogurt Sauce

Makes 1³/₄ cups

Fresh cucumbers and tangy yogurt are very refreshing with hot foods such as our Thai Green Curry (page 247) or spicy salads like our Thai Sausage Salad (page 158). This dill-accented sauce also makes an excellent condiment with our Spicy Lamb, Pine Nut, and Sundried Tomato Sausage (page 92) and Spicy Louisiana Poultry Sausage (page 39), and is a flavorful addition to grilled fish or chicken. This sauce is delicious with our Middle Eastern Vegetable Pancakes (page 296).

1 cucumber, peeled, seeded, and
   cut into ¹/₂-inch dice
1 cup high-quality plain whole-milk
   yogurt
1 tablespoon or more freshly
   squeezed lemon juice

1 tablespoon chopped fresh mint
1¹/₂ teaspoons chopped fresh dill or
   ¹/₂ teaspoon dried dill
1 small clove garlic, minced
Salt and freshly ground black
   pepper

To make the sauce, mix together the cucumber, yogurt, lemon juice, mint, dill, and garlic in a bowl. Add salt and pepper to taste and additional lemon juice if needed. The sauce keeps overnight covered in the refrigerator, but should be used up within a day or so.

Pita with Mediterranean Flavored Sausage

Makes 4 servings

Street food is one of our passions. Some of the spiciest and tastiest food imaginable is found on the crowded streets of the great cities: New Orleans, Naples, Bangkok, Hong Kong to name a few. And in New York, Chicago, and Athens—any place with a substantial Greek population—you're likely to find street vendors hawking spicy sausages or bits of roast lamb tucked into pita bread with tart and flavorful sauces. The sauces are the key to these delicious snacks. They are often family secrets handed down from generation to generation and usually include favorite Mediterranean flavors like garlic, lemon, capers, and olive oil. Pair Loukanika or Spicy Lamb, Pine Nut, and Sundried Tomato Sausage and our refreshing Cucumber and Yogurt Sauce for a piquant and satisfying sandwich. Serve it with Greek pickled banana peppers and a Greek salad of onions, tomatoes, olives, and crumbled feta cheese for a substantial lunch or light dinner.

4 links Loukanika (page 88); Spicy Lamb, Pine Nut, and Sundried Tomato Sausage (page 92); Chicken or Turkey Merguez (page 93); or other spicy sausage, such as New York–Style Spicy Hot Italian Sausage (page 82)

4 pita rounds
Cucumber and Yogurt Sauce (page 181)
1 cup coarsely chopped ripe tomatoes
½ cup coarsely chopped fresh cilantro (optional)

Preheat the oven to 300°.

Panfry or grill the sausage over medium-high heat for 3 to 5 minutes on a side until browned and cooked through. Set aside and keep warm.

Wrap the pita breads in aluminum foil and warm in the oven for 10 minutes. Cut the top off the pita and open up the round to form a pocket. Fill the pocket first with the sausage. Spoon in a couple of tablespoons of the sauce, the chopped tomatoes, and cilantro. Repeat with the remaining pitas and sausages.

Tortas are Mexican sandwiches served on soft chewy rolls called *bolillos*, filled with chicken, *carnitas* (small bits of fried pork), beef, or cheese. The sandwich is then dressed with lots of condiments: mayonnaise, guacamole, salsa, onions, etc. If you don't live near a Mexican bakery, fresh French or Italian sandwich rolls will do just fine. Use any southwestern or Mexican flavored sausage for this sandwich.

*1 pound Southwest Green Chile
    Sausage (page 77), formed
    into 4 oblong patties about the
    size of the rolls, or any south-
    western flavored sausage link
4 bolillos or other rolls, split*

*Mayonnaise
1 cup Guacamole (page 184)
½ cup or more Lime Pickled
    Onions (below)
4 tablespoons good commercial salsa
2 cups shredded lettuce*

Panfry the sausage patties in a large heavy skillet over medium-high heat for 3 to 5 minutes on each side, until browned and cooked through. Set aside and keep warm.

Spread each half of the rolls with mayonnaise, place a patty on the bottom halves, and cover with a layer of guacamole, some pickled onions, and a spoonful of salsa cruda. Put a layer of shredded lettuce on the other half, and squeeze the halves together gently. Cut each in half and serve.

Lime Pickled Onions
Makes about 1 cup

Quesadillas, Mexican tortas or sandwiches, and many other Southwest dishes are wonderful with these tangy onions. They are also great on meat loaf sandwiches and with our Southwest Green Chile Sausage (page 77), Spicy Louisiana Poultry Sausage (page 39), Chicken and Turkey Merguez (page 93), and Thai Chicken and Turkey Sausage (page 100).

*1 large red onion, thinly sliced
¹/₂ teaspoon salt
Juice of 1 lime (about ¹/₄ cup)*

Combine all the ingredients in a small bowl. Cover and marinate at least 3 hours at room temperature or overnight in the refrigerator. Keeps 3 to 4 days refrigerated.

Guacamole

Makes about 2 cups

Guacamole is not only a traditional condiment for Mexican dishes such as tortas, tacos, and beans, but is also very tasty with grilled Thai Chicken and Turkey Sausage (page 100) and Chinese Black Bean and Shiitake Mushroom Sausage (page 98). It makes a great dip for tortilla chips and is delicious on nachos or as a sauce for grilled or poached fish.

2 large avocados (preferably Hass variety), peeled and pitted

$^1/_2$ cup good commercial salsa

$^1/_4$ cup chopped fresh cilantro

$^1/_4$ cup finely chopped onion

Fresh lime juice and salt to taste

In a bowl, using a fork or potato masher, mash avocados to a coarse, lumpy texture. Stir in the salsa, cilantro, and onion. Season with lime juice and salt to taste. Use as soon as possible after making to avoid discoloration.

WISCONSIN IS JUSTIFIABLY FAMOUS FOR ITS BRATWURST AND ITS BEER. And it's no coincidence that these two hearty German specialties go well together. There are as many recipes for braising bratwurst in beer as there are types of bratwurst, and many call for sweet spices like cloves, allspice, or some sugar in the braising liquid. These can be very tasty, but we prefer the flavors of coarse German mustard and onions with the sausages.

Another popular variation is to cook the sausages for 10 to 15 minutes until the beer evaporates, and then brown the brats in the pan or grill them over charcoal.

Makes 4 servings

1 pound Sheboygan Brats (page 56), Hunter's Sausage (page 58), or other mild sausage	*12 ounces dark German beer*
	2 bay leaves
1 large onion, sliced	*1 tablespoon coarse German-style mustard*
	4 kaiser or other hard rolls

Over medium heat, brown the bratwurst for about 10 minutes in a heavy skillet large enough to hold all the sausages at once, turning them occasionally as they brown. Remove the sausages and all but 3 tablespoons of the fat. Add the onion, cover the skillet, and cook over medium-high heat for 10 minutes, stirring frequently until light brown. Pour in the beer and scrape up any brown bits clinging to the bottom of the pan. Return the sausages to the pan, and add the bay leaves. Partially cover and cook over moderate heat for 15 minutes. Stir in the mustard, and cook until the liquid has begun to thicken slightly.

To serve, split the brats down the middle and place on a roll with the onions and sauce. Pass a pot of hot mustard on the side.

Quick Pizza

Makes 2 to 3 main-
course or 6 to 8
appetizer servings

Now that prebaked pizza crusts like Boboli are available at the local supermarket, you can whip up a tasty pizza any time with a little sausage from the freezer, some grated cheese, a few veggies, and a tangy tomato sauce. These quick pizzas can feed the family any night of the week, make great lunches, or can be cut into wedges for delightful appetizers or party snacks. What follows is a basic method for turning out delicious pizzas using our sausages and the time-honored pizza toppings of shredded cheese and tomato sauce. We have added some tart variations to the basic theme by suggesting different types of cheese, sausages, sauce, and other toppings. But you should feel free to improvise. Don't limit yourself and your family to Italian ingredients only. Roam the world and your pantry, and let your imagination, your sense of adventure, and the availability of ingredients be your guide.

1 prebaked pizza crust (about
   12 inches)
1 cup shredded cheese
½ pound sausage, removed from
   casings and formed into ½-inch
   chunks, or sliced

2 ripe tomatoes, sliced, or ½ cup
   good commercial tomato sauce

Preheat the oven to 450°. Sprinkle the crust with the cheese. Over the cheese, arrange chunks of sausage. Cover this with sliced tomatoes or drizzle with sauce. Add other toppings, if you like, suggested in the following variations. Bake until cheese is melted and the sausage is fully cooked, about 10 minutes. Cut into wedges and serve.

Variations

ITALIAN (OF COURSE): Italian sausage (any type), mozzarella cheese, thinly sliced fresh mushrooms, tomato and basil sauce.

SICILIAN: Italian sausage, pinch or more of red pepper flakes, chopped garlic, pitted Sicilian black olives, chopped anchovies, capers, chopped fresh tomatoes.

PROVENÇAL: Spicy Lamb, Pine Nut, and Sundried Tomato Sausage (page 92) with sliced tomatoes, fresh goat cheese, chopped fresh oregano, pitted Niçoise olives.

Tex-Mex: Southwestern flavored sausage (pages 74 to 78), mixture of jack and Cheddar cheese, salsa cruda, fresh corn kernels. Add chopped cilantro after pizza comes out of the oven.

Cajun: Cajun-Style Andouille (page 44); chopped red onions; small oysters, clams, or shrimp; mozzarella cheese; chopped green onions or scallions and garlic. No tomatoes.

All-American: Chicken and Apple Sausage (page 34) or sage-flavored sausage; Sautéed Apple Slices (page 131); sliced sweet onions; mixture of jack and mozzarella cheese. No tomatoes.

Thai: Thai Chicken and Turkey Sausage (page 100), chopped red onions, jack cheese, fire-roasted green chiles (page 73), yellow cherry tomato halves. Add chopped fresh mint or basil after pizza comes out of the oven.

Chinese: Chinese Black Bean and Shiitake Mushroom Sausage (page 98) or other Asian flavored sausage, sliced bamboo shoots, chopped green onions or scallions, mozzarella cheese, Chinese straw mushrooms. No tomatoes.

Chapter 10

LOTSA PASTA

(and Sausage)

LIKE HAM AND EGGS, OR BEER AND PRETZELS, OR COUNTRY MUSIC AND cheatin' hearts, sausages and pasta seem made for each other. Pasta, let's face it, is basically a paste of flour and water, and there's nothing duller, in our minds, than a plate of pasta without sauce. Lots of substance, but no spice. So spice is what you need with pasta and that means sausage in our book. The big advantage of sausages is that they pack a lot of flavor in a small package. Add some Italian-style sausage to a platter of capellini along with lemon, garlic, and basil and you've got a dish that takes pasta to new heights (see Capellini with Sausage, Lemon, and Basil, page 190).

Most of our recipes for pasta feature Italian-style sausages like our New York–Style Spicy Hot Italian Sausage (page 82) or Tuscan Sausage (page 84). But feel free to use other sausages with the pasta of your choice. Spicy Lamb, Pine Nut, and Sundried Tomato Sausage (page 92) is great with couscous; Chinese Pork and Shrimp Sausage (page 99) goes with Asian noodles; and Smoked Bratwurst (page 54) is delicious with spaetzle.

Capellini with Sausage, Lemon, and Basil

Makes 4 to 6 servings

WE ENJOYED A LEMONY PASTA LIKE THIS ONE BRIGHT SPRING AFTERNOON on a terrace near Trento in the foothills of the Alps. A glass of fresh, crisp pinot bianco from the vineyards on the hills above picked up the light citrus flavors and fresh herbs in the pasta with the fruity olive oil and earthy sausage providing bass notes. Sometimes you wonder what all those Italian angels are singing about in the paintings—and then suddenly you know!

1 pound dried capellini or other thin pasta
1 tablespoon extra-virgin olive oil
½ pound Italian Turkey and Sundried Tomato Sausage (page 85) or other good-quality Italian sausage, removed from casings
Zest of 2 lemons, cut into fine julienne strips

5 tablespoons freshly squeezed lemon juice
20 fresh basil leaves, shredded
5 tablespoons minced fresh parsley
Salt and freshly ground black pepper
Freshly grated Parmesan cheese (optional)

Cook the capellini in a large pot of salted boiling water until al dente, about 5 to 6 minutes. Drain.

Meanwhile, in a large skillet, heat the olive oil over medium heat. Add the sausage and sauté for 4 to 6 minutes, breaking it up as it cooks. Add the lemon zest, lemon juice, basil, and parsley. Cook for 1 minute more.

When the pasta is ready, toss with the sausage mixture until well coated. Season with salt and pepper and sprinkle with Parmesan.

Quick and Easy Pastas

S ausage and pasta are a perfect match. You can pair virtually any type of sausage with any of the fresh or dried pastas available today. Each sausage provides a unique flavor, and the different shapes and forms of pasta offer endless combinations.

If unexpected guests show up for dinner or you are tired after a long day, all you need is some sausage in the freezer and some dried pasta on the shelf, and you can whip up a simple but delicious meal in minutes.

For 1 pound of dried pasta (enough to feed 4 people generously), you'll need $^1/_2$ to $^3/_4$ pound of sausage removed from the casings and chopped coarsely. While you are cooking the pasta, fry the sausage in a skillet until it is no longer pink. Drain off and discard the grease. To make a quick and easy sauce, add some liquid ($^1/_2$ cup wine or 1 cup cream or 1 cup stock or 1 cup chopped tomatoes), perhaps a few sundried tomatoes, sliced mushrooms, or blanched spring vegetables, or any combination of the above. Cook the sauce down over a high flame until it just begins to thicken. Taste for salt and pepper and mix the sauce with the cooked, drained pasta. Sprinkle with some freshly grated Parmesan cheese on top and enjoy!

More Quick Pasta Ideas
Follow directions above.

- Sauté $^1/_2$ pound of chopped smoked sausage, and add 1 cup of peas and 1 cup of cream.
- Sauté $^1/_2$ pound of Italian sausages with 1 cup of chopped parboiled crookneck squash or zucchini or broccoli, and 1 cup of chicken stock.
- Fry $^1/_2$ pound of spicy sausages with 1 cup of chopped beet greens, a chopped garlic clove, and 2 tablespoons of olive oil.
- Fry $^1/_2$ pound of spicy sausages with a chopped garlic clove and 1 cup chopped broccoli rabe.

Pasta with Sausage and Beans

Makes 4 servings

Thıs hearty dish is based on one of Italy's most famous and nutritious soup/stews, *pasta e fagioli*, also known as *pasta fa'zool*. Mixing pasta with beans (*fagioli*) sounds a bit starchy, but this simple peasant dish has plenty of flavor and is a good choice for a fall football party or a New Year's Day buffet. Our version is easy, and it combines precooked white beans (preferably cannellini) with orecchiette. You can cook the beans yourself or use some of the excellent canned beans (Progresso brand is quite good). We prefer to use New York–Style Spicy Hot Italian Sausage or Barese-Style Sausage for this dish.

½ pound dried orecchiette, bow ties (farfalle), pinwheels, or large twisted pasta

3 tablespoons olive oil

½ pound New York–Style Spicy Hot Italian Sausage (page 82), Barese-Style Sausage (page 86), or other good-quality Italian sausage, removed from casing

1 cup chopped onion

1 cup chopped carrot

2 cups chopped, peeled, and seeded fresh tomatoes or drained and chopped canned Italian-style tomatoes

2 cups cooked white beans (cannellini, Great Northern, or navy bean)

2 fresh sage leaves or ½ teaspoon dried sage

Salt and freshly ground black pepper

½ cup freshly ground Parmesan cheese

Cook the pasta in a large pot of salted boiling water until al dente, as directed on the package. Drain.

Meanwhile, in a large deep skillet, heat 2 tablespoons of the olive oil over medium-high heat. Add the sausage and cook for 3 minutes, breaking it up as it cooks. Add the onion and carrot and cook until the onion is translucent, about 5 minutes, stirring often. Add the tomatoes, cooked beans, and sage, cover, and cook until the carrots are just tender, about 10 minutes.

Mix in the pasta and taste for salt and pepper. Transfer to a shallow serving bowl, and drizzle with the remaining tablespoon of olive oil. Serve in shallow bowls, garnished with Parmesan cheese.

Spaghetti
with
Sausage
and Fresh
Tomato
Sauce

Tʜɪs ʙᴀꜱɪᴄ ʀᴇᴄɪᴘᴇ ᴄᴀɴ ʙᴇ ᴇᴍʙᴇʟʟɪꜱʜᴇᴅ ᴡɪᴛʜ ᴅɪᴄᴇᴅ ʀᴏᴀꜱᴛᴇᴅ ᴇɢɢᴘʟᴀɴᴛ, zucchini, peas, or other cooked vegetables such as broccoli, cauliflower, asparagus, or green beans. You could even add diced leftover chicken for extra richness. For a bit of crunchiness and added flavor, garnish the pasta with toasted nuts such as pine nuts, walnuts, or pecans. Other sausages that would do well here are Tuscan Sausage (page 84) and Spicy Lamb, Pine Nut, and Sundried Tomato Sausage (page 92).

1 pound dried spaghetti or other
    long pasta (such as linguine or
    fettuccine)
1 tablespoon olive oil
1 pound Italian Turkey and
    Sundried Tomato Sausage
    (page 85) or other good-
    quality Mediterranean sausage,
    removed from casings

¾ cup white wine
2 tablespoons tomato paste
2 ripe tomatoes, diced
25 basil leaves, chopped

Cook the spaghetti in a large pot of salted boiling water until al dente, about 8 to 9 minutes. Drain.

Meanwhile, heat the olive oil in a skillet over medium heat. Add the sausage and brown for 4 to 5 minutes, crumbling it as it cooks. Add the wine and tomato paste, stir well, and cook for 5 minutes more. Add the diced tomatoes and cook for 2 minutes more. (At this point you could add cooked vegetables, diced chicken, nuts, etc.) Add the chopped basil.

Toss the drained cooked pasta with the sauce. Transfer to a platter and serve.

Rotini with Broccoli Rabe, Sausage, and Balsamic Vinegar

Makes 4 to 6 servings

Broccoli rabe is a variety of broccoli with smaller heads and a pleasantly bitter flavor. Use it in this recipe, or use regular broccoli with heads trimmed and separated into florets (discard thick stalks). Balsamic vinegar—the aged, sweet vinegar made in the northern Italian town of Modena—gives this dish a pleasant sweet/sour character. If you can't find it, use red wine vinegar and add a pinch of sugar or a dash of sweet sherry. Use any homemade or store-bought Italian sausage of your choice.

1 pound broccoli rabe or broccoli, heads trimmed and separated into florets
¾ pound dried rotini, rotelle, fusilli, or other curly pasta
1 tablespoon olive oil
½ pound mild or spicy Italian sausage, homemade or good-quality store-bought, removed from casings
1 onion, chopped
1 red bell pepper, seeded, deveined, and chopped
4 cloves garlic, chopped
¼ teaspoon red pepper flakes
¼ cup balsamic vinegar
Salt and freshly ground black pepper
Freshly grated Parmesan cheese, for garnish

In a small amount of salted boiling water in a tightly covered saucepan, steam the broccoli rabe or broccoli for 2 to 3 minutes. Be sure not to overcook; the broccoli should be bright green and very crisp. Cool under cold running water, drain, and reserve.

Cook the pasta in a large pot of salted boiling water until al dente, about 9 to 10 minutes, drain, and reserve.

Meanwhile, heat the oil in a large skillet over medium heat. Add the sausage and fry for 3 minutes, breaking it up as it cooks. Add the onion, bell pepper, garlic, and red pepper flakes, and sauté for another 5 minutes, stirring frequently. Add the cooked broccoli rabe or broccoli and the balsamic vinegar and stir well to mix everything together. Cook for another 3 to 4 minutes, stirring occasionally, until the broccoli is tender, but still crisp. Taste for salt and pepper.

Transfer the sausage-broccoli mixture to a large serving bowl. Toss with the pasta, sprinkle with Parmesan cheese, and serve hot or at room temperature.

THIS SIMPLE AND SATISFYING DISH TASTES GREAT SERVED OVER A GOOD-quality dried Italian pasta. We prefer tagliarini or spaghetti, but just about any will do as well. Our Italian Sweet Fennel Sausage is a perfect match for the earthy flavors of dried mushrooms, but almost any Italian sausage is delicious here. Accompany this with a salad of bitter greens, bruschetta—French bread toasted and rubbed with garlic and extra-virgin olive oil—and a bottle of Dolcetto d'Alba or California sangiovese.

1 ounce dried porcini mushrooms
1 tablespoon olive oil
1½ pounds Italian Sweet Fennel Sausage (page 84), New York–Style Spicy Hot Italian Sausage (page 82), or other good-quality Italian sausage
½ cup beef stock
1 cup dry wine, white or red
4 cloves chopped garlic

1 pound ripe tomatoes, peeled, seeded, and roughly chopped, or 2 cups canned Italian-style tomatoes, drained and chopped
2 tablespoons chopped fresh basil or 1 teaspoon dried basil
Salt and freshly ground black pepper
1 pound dried pasta
Freshly grated Parmesan cheese

Pour 2 to 3 cups of boiling water over the porcini. Cover and let the mushrooms steep for at least 30 minutes or up to several hours. Drain, and reserve liquid.

In a large heavy skillet, heat the oil over medium heat. Add the sausage and fry, turning them occasionally, for 10 to 15 minutes until nicely browned. Transfer the sausage to a plate and pour off the accumulated fat. Pour the stock and wine into the pan, and bring it to a boil, scraping up any brown bits from the bottom of the pan. Add the garlic, tomatoes, and basil, and bring to a boil. Cut the sausage into ¼-inch rounds and add it and the porcini. Strain the reserved porcini liquid through a paper towel or coffee filter into the pan, taking care to keep out any dirt or sand. Reduce the heat to a simmer, and cook, uncovered, for 30 minutes, until the sauce begins to thicken slightly.

Meanwhile, cook the pasta in a large pot of salted boiling water until al dente. Drain.

Taste the sauce for salt and pepper, and serve over the cooked pasta. Garnish with grated Parmesan.

Baked Penne with Sausage, Tomatoes, and Ricotta

Makes 4 to 6 servings

THIS SIMPLE BAKED PASTA HAS THE FLAVOR AND CHARACTER OF LASAGNA without all the work and with a lot less fat. You can make it up the night before a party or special dinner, refrigerate it, and bake it the next day. This recipe can be varied easily. You can mix in a half cup of fresh goat cheese, such as Laura Chenel's. Or to give this dish a Middle Eastern note, use our Chicken and Turkey Merguez (page 93), mix a half cup of feta cheese with the ricotta, and substitute fresh or dried Greek oregano for the basil.

1 pound dried penne or other tubular pasta
2 tablespoons extra-virgin olive oil
¾ pound Italian-style sausage, such as Barese-Style Sausage (page 86) or Tuscan Sausage (page 84), removed from casings
2 to 3 cups coarsely chopped spinach

½ pound fresh tomatoes, coarsely chopped
½ pound low-fat ricotta cheese
10 fresh basil leaves, sliced into ¼-inch ribbons
Salt and freshly ground black pepper

Preheat the oven to 350°.

Cook the penne in a large pot of salted boiling water until al dente, about 10 minutes, and drain.

Meanwhile, heat the olive oil in a large skillet over medium heat. Add the sausage and sauté for 4 to 5 minutes, breaking it up as it cooks. Add the spinach and cook until wilted.

In a large mixing bowl, mix together the sausage and spinach with the tomatoes, ricotta, and basil. Add the cooked, drained penne and mix well. Taste for salt and pepper.

Transfer the pasta mixture to a shallow greased 9 by 13-inch baking dish and bake until the cheese is bubbly, about 20 minutes. Serve hot.

SLOWLY ROASTING TOMATOES IS A GREAT WAY TO ENHANCE FLAVOR, EVEN with not-so-wonderful, out-of-season tomatoes. The results are really fantastic, though, if you use vine-ripened tomatoes at the height of the season. Once roasted, the tomatoes can be packed into containers and refrigerated or frozen to be used as a simple and delicious tomato sauce. Covered, they will last in the refrigerator for about a week, frozen for up to 3 months. We prefer the exotic flavors of our Chicken and Turkey Merguez sausage with this eggplant and tomato dish, but you could also use other spicy Italian-style sausage. If you can't find penne in your neighborhood, use elbow macaroni instead. We prefer to roast eggplant in the oven, rather than sauté it in oil, because the eggplant cooks more evenly and you won't need as much oil.

Roasted Tomatoes

2 pounds Italian-style (plum) tomatoes, each tomato sliced into 2 or 3 thick slices lengthwise

2 tablespoons olive oil

2 tablespoons finely chopped garlic

2 tablespoons chopped fresh herbs (such as basil, oregano, or thyme) or 2 teaspoons dried herbs (use individual herbs or combine)

Salt and freshly ground black pepper

1 large unpeeled eggplant (1½ to 2 pounds), diced

¼ to ½ cup olive oil

Salt and freshly ground black pepper

1 pound Chicken and Turkey Merguez Sausage (page 93) or other spicy or mild sausage, removed from casings

12 ounces dried penne or elbow macaroni

½ cup freshly grated Parmesan or Romano cheese

Preheat the oven to 250°. Spread the sliced tomatoes on baking sheets or roasting pans. Drizzle with olive oil and sprinkle with garlic, herbs, salt, and pepper. Roast until the juices given off by the tomatoes have begun to thicken, about 1 hour. Using a spatula, scrape the tomatoes and all the juices into a nonreactive container.

Increase the oven temperature to 400°. In a large bowl, toss the eggplant in ¼ cup of the oil and sprinkle with salt and pepper. Spread the eggplant on a baking sheet or roasting pan and bake for 10 minutes. Check the eggplant: If the pieces seem dry, brush with more oil and stir thoroughly. Bake for about 10 minutes more, or until all the eggplant pieces are quite soft and beginning to brown. Remove from the oven, set aside, but do not turn off the oven.

In a large heavy skillet over medium-high heat, heat 2 tablespoons of the olive oil. Add the sausage and cook for 5 minutes, stirring occasionally, leaving the sausage in fairly large pieces. Add the roasted tomatoes and eggplant, taste for salt and pepper, and set aside.

Meanwhile cook the pasta in a large pot of lightly salted boiling water until al dente, 10 to 12 minutes, and drain. Mix together the pasta, the sauce, and all but 2 tablespoons of the cheese. Spoon the pasta into a shallow baking dish, sprinkle the top with the remaining cheese, and bake until the cheese is golden brown, about 10 minutes. Serve at once.

Pastitsio (with a Sausage Surprise)

Makes 8 to 10 servings

• •

Pastitsio—Greek macaroni and cheese—is one of the basics of Greek country cooking. If you can't find Loukanika and you don't feel like making your own, just substitute some sweet fennel or other mild Italian sausage. This makes a substantial lunch or dinner with a salad of tender lettuce and bitter greens with Greek olives and marinated red onions—a great dish for a crowd. Serve with cold retsina or a crisp Mâcon Blanc or California Chardonnay.

Pasta and Sausage

1 pound Italian ziti or dried elbow macaroni
4 tablespoons olive oil
¾ pound Loukanika (page 88) or Italian Sweet Fennel Sausage (page 84) or other Italian sausage, removed from casings
1 pound lean lamb shoulder, cut into ½-inch dice
Salt and freshly ground black pepper

2 cups chopped onions
5 ripe tomatoes, peeled, seeded, and chopped, or 2 cups canned Italian-style tomatoes
1 cup tomato puree
1 teaspoon chopped garlic
⅛ teaspoon ground cinnamon
⅛ teaspoon ground allspice
½ cup fresh bread crumbs
1 egg, lightly beaten

Cream Sauce

2 tablespoons butter	*Pinch of freshly grated nutmeg*
½ cup all-purpose flour	*6 eggs, beaten until frothy*
4 cups milk	*1 cup grated Kefalotiri, Asiago,*
½ teaspoon salt	*Kasseri, or other sharp cheese*

Cook the pasta in plenty of water until it is al dente. Drain it in a colander, and cool under running water. Coat the pasta with about 1 tablespoon of olive oil to keep it from sticking together while you make the sauce.

For the tomato and sausage sauce, heat the remaining 3 tablespoons of olive oil in a heavy skillet over medium-high heat. Add the sausage and brown, breaking up the meat with a fork as you go. After about 5 minutes, when it is nicely browned, remove the sausage with a slotted spoon and drain on a paper towel. Add the lamb to the hot fat, and sprinkle lightly with salt and pepper. After it is lightly browned, about 5 minutes, toss in the onions and cook for another 5 minutes, or until they are soft and translucent. Add the tomatoes and tomato puree. Bring to a boil, then decrease the heat to a simmer. Add the garlic, cinnamon, allspice, meat, and sausage. You can add a little tomato juice or water if the sauce is too thick. Cook for 30 minutes over low heat, then remove the pan from the heat. Stir in ¼ cup of the bread crumbs along with the beaten egg.

While the tomato sauce is cooking, you can prepare the cream sauce. In a heavy saucepan, melt the butter over medium heat. Stir in the flour and cook for 1 or 2 minutes, until the flour and butter are smoothly blended together. Remove from the heat and whisk in the milk, salt, and nutmeg. Return to the heat and continue to whisk until the sauce is thick and creamy, about 5 minutes. Remove from the heat and gradually whisk in the 6 beaten eggs.

Preheat the oven to 375°. Oil a large casserole or 9 by 13-inch baking dish with olive oil. Sprinkle the bottom with the remaining ¼ cup bread crumbs. Spread half the pasta over the crumbs and cover it with all of the tomato-sausage sauce. Cover this with half the cream sauce and sprinkle with half the grated cheese. Make another layer of the remaining pasta. Pour over the rest of the cream sauce and the remaining cheese.

Bake, uncovered, for 45 minutes, until the top is lightly golden and bubbly. Cut the pastitsio into squares and serve.

Thai Noodle Stir-Fry

Makes 4 servings

Tᴴᴇꜱᴇ ꜱᴡᴇᴇᴛ ᴀɴᴅ ꜱᴏᴜʀ ɴᴏᴏᴅʟᴇꜱ ᴀʀᴇ ᴄᴀʟʟᴇᴅ *pad Thai* ɪɴ Tʜᴀɪ ʀᴇꜱᴛᴀᴜ-rants, and some version or other of this dish is found on every Thai menu we've ever seen. Our recipe uses our Thai Chicken and Turkey Sausage instead of the more usual shrimp. However, our Chinese Pork and Shrimp Sausage (page 99) or other Asian-style sausage would also work well. Quick, simple, light, and delicious, these noodles should prove very popular with family and friends.

1 pound dried flat rice stick noodles
3 tablespoons peanut oil
2 tablespoons sliced garlic
2 teaspoons chopped fresh ginger
½ pound Thai Chicken and
    Turkey Sausage (page 100) or
    other Asian sausage, removed
    from casings
2 eggs, beaten
¼ cup Southeast Asian fish sauce

1 tablespoon light soy sauce
1 tablespoon sugar
2 tablespoons ketchup
⅓ cup chopped dry-roasted peanuts
4 cups bean sprouts
10 green onions or scallions, white
    and green parts, cut into
    2-inch lengths
2 limes, cut into wedges

Cover the rice stick noodles with warm water and soak until very limp and white, at least 20 minutes. Drain and set aside.

Heat 1 tablespoon of the oil in a large wok or heavy nonstick skillet over medium-high heat. Add the garlic and ginger and stir-fry for 30 seconds, taking care not to burn the garlic. Add the sausage and stir-fry for 3 minutes, breaking the sausage up as it cooks. Remove from the pan to a bowl.

Add 1 tablespoon of the oil to the wok and pour in the eggs. Tilt the pan to spread the eggs out evenly to form a thin omelet. As soon as they begin to set, stir-fry to scramble the eggs coarsely. Add the eggs to the sausage mixture.

Heat the remaining tablespoon of the oil in the wok over high heat and add the soaked, drained noodles. Using a spatula, spread the noodles into a thin cake and then fold them back into a clump. Repeat this process until the noodles soften and curl, about 3 minutes. Stir in the fish sauce, soy sauce, sugar, ketchup, and peanuts. Toss for 30 seconds to coat noodles.

Put 3 cups of the bean sprouts and the green onions in the wok with the noodles, and add the sausage and egg mixture. Stir-fry and toss for 1 minute over high heat. Transfer the noodles to a shallow bowl or platter and garnish with the remaining bean sprouts and the wedges of lime.

Chapter 11

BETTER BEANS AND GRAINS

For centuries, cooks all over the world have added sausages to beans and grains. Sausages liven up these often bland foods, adding protein and juiciness along with spice and extra flavor. Classic peasant dishes, such as Italian polenta (see page 206) and Cuban black beans (see page 208), are examples of recipes vastly enhanced by the addition of traditional sausages.

Cotechino with Lentils

Makes 6 to 8 servings

ⅇARTHY LENTILS AND AROMATIC COTECHINO SEEM MADE FOR EACH OTHER. Serve this combination with a full-bodied California Nebbiolo and plenty of sourdough French bread. The sauce is an old recipe of chef Franco Dunn's family. (Franco is a Sonoma County restaurateur and old friend.) It is easy to make up the sauce the day before—it's even better reheated.

Franco's Bagnet Piemontese

3 cloves garlic

1 (2-ounce) can anchovies

6 sundried tomatoes packed in olive oil

2 bunches (4 to 6 ounces each) Italian flat-leaf or regular parsley

1 to 1½ cups extra-virgin olive oil (the best you can afford)

¼ cup high-quality balsamic vinegar

Salt and freshly ground black pepper

Lentils

2 Cotechino sausages (see page 87) (1½ to 2 pounds total)

5 cups chicken or beef stock

1 cup dry white wine

1 pound brown lentils (about 2 cups)

2 cups canned Italian-style tomatoes, chopped

2 bay leaves

2 to 3 sprigs fresh rosemary or 2 teaspoons dried

2 onions, chopped

1 carrot, chopped

1 rib celery, chopped

1 tablespoon chopped garlic

Salt and freshly ground black pepper

½ cup chopped fresh parsley

To make the sauce, combine the garlic, anchovies, and sundried tomatoes in a food processor. Process for 30 seconds. Add the parsley and pulse to chop roughly. Add the olive oil and balsamic vinegar, and pulse to blend in. Don't puree. Taste for salt and pepper. The sauce can be made in advance and will keep for 5 to 7 days refrigerated in a closed jar.

Place the sausages, stock, and wine in a large pot or Dutch oven. Bring to a boil. Add the lentils, tomatoes, bay leaves, and rosemary. Simmer, uncovered, for 30 minutes. Add the onions, carrot, celery, and garlic, and continue to simmer until the lentils are tender, another 30 minutes. Taste for salt and pepper. Remove and discard the rosemary sprigs and bay leaves.

Cut the Cotechino into ¼-inch slices. Place the lentils in a shallow serving bowl, and mix in the Cotechino and parsley, arranging a few slices on top. Ladle some Bagnet Piemontese over the slices and pass the extra at the table.

Moroccan Rice with Fruit and Almonds

Makes 4 side dish servings

THIS PILAF IS INSPIRED BY THE COOKING OF MOROCCO, WHERE THE SWEET taste of dried fruit is often combined with rice, meat, and poultry. It makes a wonderful side dish for grilled or roast chicken, duck, or lamb, and is delicious as a stuffing for chicken or game hens.

1 tablespoon olive oil
½ pound Mediterranean flavored sausage, such as Spicy Lamb, Pine Nut, and Sundried Tomato Sausage (page 92) or Chicken and Turkey Merguez (page 93), in bulk or removed from casings
½ cup chopped onion
¾ cup uncooked medium-grain white rice
1¼ cups chicken stock (preferably homemade)

¼ cup golden raisins
¼ cup diced pitted prunes
1 cup peeled, cored, and diced apple (preferably Golden Delicious)
¼ cup toasted almonds
1 tablespoon freshly squeezed lemon juice
1 egg, beaten lightly
Salt and freshly ground black pepper to taste

Preheat the oven to 350°.

Heat the oil in a large, heavy skillet over medium heat. Add the sausage and onion and fry for 3 minutes, breaking up the sausage as it cooks. Add the rice and stir until it is coated with the mixture. Pour in the chicken stock, bring to a boil, and decrease the heat to a simmer. Cover and cook until the rice is tender and the liquid is absorbed, about 20 minutes.

Spoon the rice into a large bowl. Stir in the raisins, prunes, apple, almonds, lemon juice, and egg. Mix together well. Taste for salt and pepper.

Place the rice mixture in an oiled casserole, cover with aluminum foil, and bake for 30 minutes. Serve hot.

Pilaf Stuffing
This recipe makes enough pilaf to stuff four 1-pound Cornish game hens. Prepare the pilaf but do not bake. Stuff the hens with the mixture instead of the usual bread stuffing.

Braised Sausage with Polenta

Makes 6 to 8 servings

THIS RECIPE COMES FROM OUR FRIEND EDY YOUNG, WHO NOT ONLY COOKS A mean Chinese meal, but turns out some of the best Italian food this side of Tuscany. She made this savory polenta with our Italian Turkey and Sundried Tomato Sausage, but we also like it with our Tuscan Sausage (page 84) or any good store-bought Italian-style sausage.

Polenta
2 cups polenta meal (coarse cornmeal)

8 cups water
2 teaspoons salt

Sausage
2 tablespoons olive oil
2 pounds Italian Turkey and Sundried Tomato Sausages (page 85) or Tuscan Sausages (page 84), left whole
1 onion, chopped
2 large cloves garlic, minced

2 carrots, chopped
1 celery root, peeled and chopped
2 parsnips, chopped
1½ cups white wine
2 tablespoons tomato paste
Salt and freshly ground black pepper
¼ cup chopped fresh basil

To prepare the polenta, mix the polenta and 2 cups of the water in a large, heavy saucepan. Stir over medium-high heat, gradually adding the salt and the remaining water. Bring to a boil and reduce the heat to low, stirring constantly until thickened. Cover and cook, stirring occasionally, until the polenta is soft and creamy, 30 to 40 minutes.

While the polenta is cooking, heat the olive oil in a large skillet or Dutch oven over medium heat. Add the sausages and fry for 5 minutes on each side. Remove and reserve.

Add the onion and garlic to the fat remaining in the skillet and sauté until slightly browned, about 3 minutes. Add the carrots, celery root, parsnips, wine, and tomato paste. Stir well and bring to a boil. Decrease the heat, place the sausage carefully on top of the vegetables, cover, and cook gently for about 20 minutes. Taste for salt and pepper.

Transfer the polenta to a large platter or dish, spoon the wine and vegetable mixture over the top, and arrange the sausage around the outside of the dish. Sprinkle with the chopped basil.

Cholent

Makes 6 to 8 servings

THIS SUBSTANTIAL MEAT AND BEAN DISH CAME ABOUT BECAUSE OF THE strict Jewish observance of the Sabbath that prohibits any cooking from sunset Friday to sunset Saturday. Orthodox Jewish cooks would prepare the cholent on Friday and bring it down to the village or neighborhood baker before sunset. Left in the warm oven overnight, the cholent would be ready for the noonday Sabbath meal. It can be made with just beans and flavorings, but it usually includes meat of some sort, most often beef or lamb.

2 tablespoons chicken fat
    (schmaltz) or olive oil
1 pound Romanian Jewish Beef
    Sausages (page 59)
4 lamb shanks, each cut into
    4 pieces across the bone
Salt
1 teaspoon freshly ground black
    pepper
Pinch of ground ginger
Pinch of cumin
2 teaspoons sweet Hungarian
    paprika

3 large onions, coarsely chopped
1 rib celery, coarsely chopped
2 bay leaves
4 cups chicken stock
3 to 4 cups dry white wine
½ pound dried lima beans
    (1¼ cups), soaked overnight,
    rinsed, and drained
½ pound dried brown lentils
    (1 cup)
1 cup uncooked pearl barley

Preheat the oven to 250°. In a 4- to 6-quart Dutch oven with a tight-fitting lid, heat the chicken fat over medium heat. Add the sausages and cook them for 5 minutes, turning them to brown evenly. Don't worry if they are not completely cooked. Remove the sausages, and add the lamb shanks to the fat in the pan. Lightly sprinkle them with some of the salt, pepper, ginger, cumin, and paprika. Brown for 10 minutes or so, turning often. Remove the lamb and add the onions and celery. Cover and cook until the onions begin to brown, about 10 minutes, stirring frequently. Add the remaining spices and the bay leaves, along with the sausages and the lamb. Pour in the stock and wine. Stir in the limas, lentils, and barley. Bring to a boil. Cover the casserole, and put it in the oven.

Bake for 3½ hours. Check every hour or so to see whether the liquid has been absorbed or the beans are tender. Adjust the liquid level and cooking times accordingly. Remove the bay leaves before serving.

Makes 6 to 8 main-
course or 10 to 12
side-dish servings

A LIVELY ADDITION TO SOUTHERN COOKING COMES FROM THE LARGE CUBAN population of southern Florida. Black beans are a Cuban staple, and they are found in soups, main courses, and side dishes. A typical Cuban dinner just doesn't seem complete without black beans and rice. Black bean soup, Cuban style, is one of the most popular dishes in Miami's homes and restaurants.

1 pound dried black beans (2½ cups), picked over, soaked overnight, and drained
4 to 6 cups chicken or beef stock
1 ham hock, sawed into 3 or 4 pieces
2 pig's feet (about 2 pounds), sawed into 3 or 4 pieces (optional)
2 pounds Basque Chorizo (page 91), or other garlicky sausage, such as Cajun-Style Andouille (page 44), Portuguese Chouriço (page 90), Linguiça (page 89), or pepperoni

2 bay leaves
2 teaspoons ground cumin
2 large onions, chopped
1 tablespoon chopped garlic
1 tablespoon annato oil, if available, or a pinch of saffron and 1 tablespoon olive oil
1 small head cabbage, quartered, cored, and shredded (about 4 cups)
¼ cup dark rum
1 cup fresh or canned tomatoes, peeled, seeded, and chopped
Salt and freshly ground pepper
Malt vinegar

Garnish
Lime wedges
Chopped red onion

Chopped cilantro
Tabasco sauce

Rinse the beans well. In a heavy 4- to 5-quart pot or Dutch oven, combine the beans with enough stock to cover them by 2 inches. Bring to a boil. Add the ham hock, pig's feet, a ½-pound piece of the sausage, the bay leaves, cumin, and half the chopped onions and garlic. Decrease the heat and simmer, partially covered, for 1 to 2 hours, or until the ham hocks and pig's feet are tender and the beans are soft enough to mash against the side of the pot with a spoon. Add more stock if needed while cooking.

Heat the oil in a heavy skillet over medium heat. Slice the remaining sausage into ½-inch rounds, and fry them until lightly browned. Remove the sausage with a slotted spoon and add to the beans. In the same fat, cook the remaining onions until they are soft but not

Robin's Black Bean Chili

Makes 8 to 10 servings

Robin Cherin, who patiently and carefully tested many of the recipes in this cookbook, has contributed one of her favorites. The combination of chorizo and smoked meats gives this chili a wonderful, savory taste. Robin usually uses Tasso for the smoked meat component, but this recipe works quite well with our Hot Links. Any high-quality smoked sausage or Tasso will do just fine in this deliciously spicy chili. The chorizo should be extra-lean or use a high-quality store-bought variety. Epazote—a pungent herb found in Mexican groceries and from mail order sources (page 307)—is especially good with black beans, but is definitely an acquired taste. You can substitute oregano or leave it out altogether.

4 cups dried black beans, picked
    over, soaked overnight, and
    drained
1 bay leaf
1 teaspoon dried epazote (optional)
2 tablespoons olive oil
¾ pound Chorizo (page 74),
    removed from casings
½ pound Hot Links (page 43),
    Tasso (page 49), or other
    smoked sausage
2 large onions, chopped
4 large cloves garlic, chopped
1 red bell pepper, fire-roasted,
    peeled, and chopped (page 73)
1 green bell pepper, fire-roasted,
    peeled, and chopped (page 73)

1 Anaheim chile, fire-roasted,
    peeled, and chopped (page 73)
2 fresh jalapeño chiles, seeded
    and finely chopped, or 2
    chipotle chiles, packed in adobo
    sauce (Herdez brand
    recommended), chopped
    (optional)
1 teaspoon ground cumin
1 tablespoon sweet Hungarian
    paprika
1 tablespoon chopped fresh oregano
    or 1 teaspoon dried
3 cups canned crushed tomatoes
    in puree
Salt and freshly ground black
    pepper

Garnish
Grated cheese
Sour cream

Fresh cilantro
Salsa cruda

Rinse the beans well. In a large, heavy pot, combine the beans with water to cover by 4 to 5 inches. Bring to a boil and add the bay leaf and epazote. Reduce the heat, cover, and simmer for 1 to 1½ hours, until the beans are tender. Drain the beans, reserving 2 cups of the cooking liquid, and set aside.

In a large pot or Dutch oven, heat the olive oil over medium-high heat. Add the chorizo and smoked sausage. Stir with a fork to break up the chorizo and cook for about 5 minutes. Add the onions and garlic and cook for 5 minutes more, stirring frequently. Add the peppers and chiles, including the chipotles in adobo if you are using them, along with the cumin, paprika, oregano, and tomatoes. Add the beans and 1 cup of the reserved liquid. Bring to a boil, decrease the heat to a simmer, and cook, uncovered, for 45 minutes, until the liquid begins to thicken. If it is too thick, add more reserved bean liquid. Taste for salt and pepper.

Serve over rice. Pass the various garnishes and let your guests add their own.

Chapter 12

SAUSAGE WITH FISH AND SEAFOOD

CREOLE AND CAJUN COOKS HAVE CREATED ONE OF AMERICA'S MOST VIBRANT cuisines, utilizing sausages to infuse their food with flavor and character. Many classic Louisiana dishes mix fish and seafood with traditional sausages such as Cajun-Style Andouille (see page 44). Portuguese and Spanish dishes often blend seafood with sausages like Linguiça (see page 89) and Basque Chorizo (see page 91). Many classic Italian dishes, especially the luscious fisherman's stew, Crab and Italian Sausage Cioppino (see page 220), incorporate traditional sausages and seafood.

Shrimp, Sausage, and Potato Creole

Makes 6 to 8 servings

The first time we had a dish like this was for "brunch" at Dooky Chase's, the wonderful New Orleans Creole restaurant. "Brunch" got started about 2 P.M. (hence the quotes), and this was just one of 7 or 8 dishes at a gargantuan fast-breaker. We're not sure just when this particular "brunch" ended, but we think the sun was going down as we staggered out into the street to head on to dinner.

This recipe works best if you can find fresh Italian-style plum tomatoes. If not, you can use canned Italian plum tomatoes, available in most Italian delicatessens and quality markets. These often come packed in tomato sauce that can substitute for the tomato puree.

⅓ cup peanut oil
⅓ cup all-purpose flour
2 cups chopped onions
2 ribs celery, chopped
1 green bell pepper, cut into
　¼-inch dice
1 red bell pepper, cut into
　¼-inch dice
1½ cups thinly sliced green onions
　and scallions
3 tablespoons minced garlic
1 teaspoon dried thyme
½ teaspoon dried basil
4 bay leaves
½ teaspoon freshly ground black
　pepper
Pinch of ground allspice
½ teaspoon ground cayenne pepper
2 cups chicken stock or clam juice
1 cup dry white wine
1 cup tomato puree or juice from
　canned Italian plum tomatoes

2 pounds fresh plum tomatoes,
　skinned, seeded, and roughly
　chopped, or 1 (28-ounce) can
　Italian plum tomatoes
1½ pounds red or white boiling
　potatoes, cut into ½-inch dice
　(do not peel)
¾ pound Cajun-Style Andouille
　(page 44) or other smoked
　sausage, sliced into ½-inch
　rounds
2 pounds medium shrimp
　(30 to 35 count), peeled
½ cup chopped fresh parsley
Salt and freshly ground black
　pepper
1 tablespoon or more freshly
　squeezed lemon juice
Tabasco sauce

In a heavy 3- to 4-quart pot or Dutch oven, heat the oil over medium heat for 5 minutes. Remove from the heat and gradually stir in the flour. Return the pot to medium heat and continue to stir. The roux will turn tan colored, then light brown (the color of peanut butter).

Add the onions and celery and continue to cook, stirring frequently, for 2 to 3 minutes.

Mix together the chopped bell peppers. Add 1 cup of the bell peppers along with 1 cup of the green onions and the garlic. Cook for 5 minutes more, stirring continuously. Stir in the thyme, basil, bay leaves, pepper, allspice, and cayenne. Cook for 1 minute. Add the stock or clam juice, wine, and tomato puree. Bring to a boil while you stir well. Decrease the heat to a simmer, cover, and cook for 10 minutes.

Add the tomatoes and potatoes, and cook, uncovered, for 15 minutes more. Add the sausage and the remaining bell peppers, and cook for an additional 10 minutes, or until the potatoes are tender.

Add the shrimp and cook until firm and pink, 3 to 5 minutes.

Add the chopped parsley and remaining green onions. Taste for salt and pepper, and add lemon juice and Tabasco as desired. Serve with plain boiled rice, or as is.

Crab and Sausage Cakes with Tidewater Tartar Sauce

Makes 8 to 10 servings

Ｔʜᴇ sᴀᴜsᴀɢᴇ's sᴘɪᴄʏ, sᴍᴏᴋʏ ғʟᴀᴠᴏʀs ᴄᴏᴍᴘʟᴇᴍᴇɴᴛ ᴛʜᴇ sᴡᴇᴇᴛɴᴇss ᴏғ crabmeat. Frying in oil and butter will give them a rich, buttery quality.

Tidewater Tartar Sauce

3 tablespoons freshly squeezed
 lemon juice
2 tablespoons Creole or other
 spicy mustard
1 teaspoon salt
½ teaspoon freshly ground black
 pepper
½ teaspoon ground cayenne pepper
3 eggs, lightly beaten
1½ cups olive oil
½ cup finely chopped green onions
 or scallions

¼ cup finely chopped fresh parsley
2 tablespoons finely chopped dill
 pickle
2 tablespoons chopped fresh dill
 (optional)
1 tablespoon capers
1 teaspoon Worcestershire sauce
½ teaspoon soy sauce
1 teaspoon or more Tabasco sauce

Cakes

1 pound fresh lump crabmeat,
 picked over and cleaned
¼ pound Smoked Country Sausage
 (page 32) or other smoked
 sausage, finely chopped
2½ cups fresh bread crumbs
1 egg, lightly beaten
1 tablespoon chopped green onion
 or scallion

1 teaspoon Worcestershire sauce
1 tablespoon chopped fresh parsley
Salt and freshly ground black
 pepper
Tabasco sauce (optional)
¼ cup vegetable oil plus
 4 tablespoons butter

Garnish
Lemon wedges

Combine the lemon juice, mustard, salt, pepper, cayenne, and eggs in a food processor. With the motor running, very slowly drizzle in the oil until the mixture is completely emulsified and the oil is fully incorporated. Add the green onions, parsley, pickle, dill, capers, Worcestershire sauce, soy sauce, and Tabasco to taste. Pulse once or twice. Taste for seasonings. The sauce will keep for 1 week in the refrigerator. It tastes even better made up a day ahead to allow all the flavors to mellow.

Mix together the crab, sausage, and ¾ cup of the bread crumbs with the egg, green onion, Worcestershire sauce, and parsley. When all is well blended, stir in the 3 tablespoons of the tartar sauce. Taste for salt and pepper and add Tabasco, if desired.

Form the mixture into cakes about 3 inches in diameter and about ¾ inch thick. Coat the cakes with the remaining bread crumbs, place on a platter between sheets of waxed paper, and chill them for at least an hour.

To cook, heat the vegetable oil and butter in a frying pan over medium-high heat. When the mixture is hot, carefully add a few of the cakes to the pan. Do not overcrowd the pan. Fry the cakes for 2 to 3 minutes a side, until they are golden brown. Repeat with the remaining cakes. Serve immediately with lemon wedges and plenty of the tartar sauce.

Variation

To serve the cakes as hors d'oeuvres, form the crab mixture into cakes 2 inches in diameter and ½ inch thick. Coat with crumbs, chill, and cook as above. The recipe makes 30 cocktail-size cakes.

Steamed Clams with Linguiça

Makes 4 to 6 servings

In Portugal, this dish is called a *cataplana*, which refers to the dome-shaped pan it is traditionally cooked in. The shape of the pan is such that once the clams have opened, their juices run down into the rest of the ingredients. To accomplish the same effect without a *cataplana*, you can stir the clams thoroughly once they have opened. Use linguiça, chouriço, or a combination of the two, depending on how spicy you want the dish (chouriço is hotter).

2 tablespoons olive oil

1 pound Linguiça (page 89) and/or Portuguese Chouriço (page 90), sliced into ½-inch rounds

¼ pound smoky ham, prosciutto, or lean smoky bacon, diced

3 cups thinly sliced onions

½ cup chopped red bell pepper

2 tablespoons chopped garlic

½ teaspoon red pepper flakes

2 teaspoons Spanish or sweet Hungarian paprika

1 cup peeled, seeded, and coarsely chopped tomatoes, fresh or canned Italian-style

1 cup dry white wine

1 cup bottled clam juice or chicken stock

1 cup chopped fresh parsley (flat-leaf preferred)

2 bay leaves

2 tablespoons chopped fresh basil or 1 teaspoon dried

48 littleneck or cherrystone clams or small mussels, scrubbed

Salt and freshly ground black pepper

Tabasco sauce

Heat the olive oil in a Dutch oven or large, heavy skillet over medium-high heat. Add the sausage and ham and fry, stirring frequently, until the fat is rendered and the meat is lightly browned, about 5 minutes. Add the onions and cook, covered, for 5 minutes, stirring occasionally. Add the bell pepper and garlic and cook, covered, for 2 to 3 minutes more. Stir in the red pepper flakes, paprika, tomatoes, wine, and clam juice. Bring to a boil, and add the parsley, bay leaves, and basil. Simmer and cook for 10 minutes.

Add the clams to the pot, and cook, covered, for 10 to 15 minutes, until the shells have opened. Thicker-shelled clams will take longer. Discard any clams that don't open. Stir the pot well to distribute the clam juices. Taste for salt, pepper, and Tabasco.

Serve the clams in shallow soup bowls with plenty of sauce and soup spoons, as well as forks.

THE VIBRANT FLAVORS OF SICILIAN COOKING ARE FOUND IN THIS SPICY DISH. It makes a great main course served with large tube pasta, such as rigatoni or penne, along with a salad of bitter greens, red onions, and oranges. Any leftovers are delicious cold on thick slices of Italian bread or on crostini. We picked our Barese-style sausage but our Italian Turkey and Sundried Tomato Sausage (page 85) also works well, as would any high-quality spicy Italian sausage. Be sure to use European black olives, such as Niçoise, dried black Sicilian, or Greek kalamata olives. All are high in salt, as are the capers, so be sure to add any salt only after tasting the finished dish.

4 tablespoons olive oil
4 cloves garlic, sliced
½ pound Barese-Style Sausage (page 86), or other spicy Italian sausage, removed from casings
1 (28-ounce) can Italian-style tomatoes, drained
¼ teaspoon freshly ground black pepper

⅛ teaspoon red pepper flakes or more to taste
1 cup pitted and sliced black olives (French, Italian, or Greek)
½ cup capers, rinsed and drained
4 swordfish steaks, 1 inch thick (about 8 ounces each)
½ cup chopped fresh parsley
Salt

Heat 2 tablespoons of the olive oil in a large, heavy saucepan over medium heat. Add the garlic and sauté until lightly browned, 1 to 2 minutes. Remove the garlic and reserve. Increase the heat to medium-high heat, add the sausage, and brown, breaking it apart as it cooks, 3 to 4 minutes. Add the tomatoes, black pepper, and red pepper flakes and cook briskly over high heat for 6 to 8 minutes, crushing the tomatoes with the back of a spoon to thicken the sauce.

In a large skillet with a cover, spread half the tomato sauce and top with half the reserved garlic, ½ cup of the olives, and ¼ cup of the capers. Sprinkle with the remaining 2 tablespoons olive oil. Arrange the swordfish steaks on top of the sauce and cover with the remaining tomato sauce, garlic, olives, capers, and ¼ cup of the parsley. Cover the pan and simmer until the fish is firm to the touch, 10 to 12 minutes. Taste and add salt *only* if needed.

Transfer the swordfish steaks to plates and spoon over them any sauce remaining in the pan. Garnish with the remaining parsley.

Tʜᴇ Iᴛᴀʟɪᴀɴ ғɪsʜᴇʀᴍᴇɴ ᴏғ Sᴀɴ Fʀᴀɴᴄɪsᴄᴏ Bᴀʏ ᴀɴᴅ ᴛʜᴇ sᴜʀʀᴏᴜɴᴅɪɴɢ waters created this hearty seafood stew. It is similar to other Mediterranean fishermen's stews like cacciucco, zuppa di pesce, and bouillabaisse. All these tasty stews and soups are ways to use up bits of the catch left over at the end of the day. Most make liberal use of typical Mediterranean ingredients like garlic, tomatoes, basil, and oregano. Cioppino made with the delicious Dungeness crab of West Coast waters is a true San Francisco dish and is a favorite in Italian restaurants and homes in the Bay Area.

Although Italian sausage is not a traditional ingredient in cioppino, it adds spice and flavors that raise this wonderful peasant dish to new heights. We use hot Italian sausage, but you could add mild Italian or another flavorful sausage. If crab is unavailable, use more shrimp. If you can't find shark or halibut, substitute other firm-fleshed fish, such as swordfish or sea bass. Pay careful attention to timing and don't overcook—cooking times can vary depending on the type of fish or seafood. Taste the fish while cooking, and serve the cioppino as soon as it is done.

1 tablespoon olive oil

1½ pounds hot or mild Italian sausage links

⅓ cup diced celery

1 cup chopped onions

3 tablespoons minced garlic

1 cup thinly sliced green onions or scallions

½ cup diced green bell pepper

1 pound fresh Italian plum tomatoes, peeled, seeded, and coarsely chopped, or 2 cups coarsely chopped canned Italian-style tomatoes

¼ cup tomato paste

½ cup dry red wine such as Chianti or California zinfandel

4 bay leaves

½ teaspoon dried basil

½ teaspoon dried thyme

2 cups fish or chicken stock

1 cup bottled clam juice

¼ cup or more freshly squeezed lemon juice

2- to 3-pound Dungeness crab, cleaned and cut into 8 pieces

2 dozen clams or mussels, scrubbed

1 pound thresher or other shark, cut into 1½-inch cubes

1 pound halibut, cut into 1½-inch cubes

1 pound large shrimp, peeled and deveined

Salt and freshly ground black pepper

Garnishes
8 to 10 lemon slices
¼ cup chopped fresh parsley

In a 6- to 8-quart pot or Dutch oven, heat the olive oil over medium heat. Add the whole sausages and fry them gently for about 10 minutes, turning often, until they are firm and lightly browned. Set them aside to cool and leave 3 to 4 tablespoons of the fat in the pan. Add the celery and onions to the pan, and fry for 5 minutes, stirring occasionally. Add the garlic, green onions, and bell pepper, and cook for 2 more minutes.

Slice the sausage into 1-inch rounds and return them to the pot along with the tomatoes, tomato paste, wine, bay leaves, basil, thyme, stock, clam juice, and lemon juice. Bring to a boil, decrease the heat to a simmer, and cook for 10 minutes.

Add the crab and clams or mussels, and cook for 5 minutes, or until the shells open. Discard any clams or mussels that have not opened. Add the shark, halibut, and shrimp and cook for 5 minutes more, until the shrimp are pink and firm and the fish is cooked through. Taste for salt, pepper, and more lemon juice.

Serve at once in a large shallow bowls. Garnish each serving with a slice of lemon and a little chopped fresh parsley.

Braised Squid Stuffed with Spanish Chorizo and Prosciutto

Makes 4 to 6 main-course or 8 appetizer servings

THESE CALIMARI (OR SQUID) ARE ADDICTING. EVEN IF YOU SERVE THEM AS tapas, they always seem to end up as the main course. Either make just a few and cut your guests off in the middle of the squid binge, or give up and make enough for everybody to munch on long into the night. You can substitute pepperoni if you can't find the other recommended sausages.

Stuffed squid also make a substantial meal served over thin spaghetti or vermicelli with a salad of mixed lettuce and tangy greens. Any leftovers can be rewarmed the next day for tapas. They are also very tasty cold.

To give this Basque stuffing an Italian flavor, use a mild Italian sausage instead of Basque Chorizo and add 2 tablespoons of grated Parmesan.

Squid

1/4 cup olive oil
1/2 pound Basque Chorizo (page 91), Portuguese Chouriço (page 90), Linguiça (page 89), or other spicy sausage, finely chopped
1/2 cup finely chopped onion
1/4 pound prosciutto or smoked ham, finely chopped

1 tablespoon minced garlic
24 medium squid, cleaned, with tentacles finely chopped
1/4 cup chopped fresh flat-leaf parsley
1 cup fresh bread crumbs
1 egg, beaten
Salt and freshly ground black pepper

Sauce

1/4 cup finely chopped onion
2 shallots, finely chopped
3 cloves garlic, finely chopped
1 tablespoon sweet Hungarian paprika
3 large ripe tomatoes or 4 canned tomatoes, peeled, seeded, and chopped
1 tablespoon tomato paste

1/2 cup dry red wine
1/2 cup clam juice, fish stock, or chicken stock
1 teaspoon chopped fresh oregano or 1/2 teaspoon dried
Salt and freshly ground black pepper
Hot cooked pasta (optional)

Garnish

Lemon wedges

Heat 2 tablespoons of the olive oil in a heavy frying pan over medium heat. Add the sausage and brown for 2 to 3 minutes. Add the chopped onion and prosciutto and cook for 5 minutes. Add the garlic and the chopped squid tentacles and cook for another minute.

Transfer the contents of the pan to a large bowl, and stir in the parsley, bread crumbs, and egg. Taste for salt and pepper. Fill each squid with the stuffing and seal with a wooden toothpick. Don't pack the stuffing too tightly or the squid may burst during cooking.

Heat the remaining 2 tablespoons olive oil over medium heat. Add the squid and brown for 1 or 2 minutes, shaking the pan as they cook. Transfer them to a large platter as they brown.

Into the same pan, add the ¼ cup chopped onion along with the chopped shallots and finely chopped garlic. Cook over medium heat for 5 minutes, until they are soft. Stir in the paprika, and add the tomatoes, tomato paste, wine, clam juice or stock, and oregano, along with the reserved squid. Bring to a boil, cover, and decrease the heat to a simmer. Cook for about 45 minutes, until the squid are tender. If the sauce becomes too thick, add more wine or stock. Taste for salt and pepper.

If you plan to serve the squid as an appetizer, let them cool a bit. Otherwise, serve them hot over pasta. Garnish with lemon wedges.

Chinese Braised Stuffed Fish

Makes 4 to 6 servings

CHINESE COOKS HAVE LONG KNOWN THAT PORK AND SEAFOOD MAKE AN excellent combination. The savory aromas and rich flavors of sausage add succulence and interest to fish, whether whole, sliced, or in chunks. Out on the West Coast, rock cod is a favorite in Chinese restaurants, but you may use any whole, firm-fleshed freshwater or saltwater fish in this recipe.

The pork-sausage stuffing here adds flavor and creates more portions from a single fish. With the addition of rice and stir-fried vegetables, such as snow peas and black mushrooms or green beans, you have a very satisfying Chinese meal.

6 dried shiitake mushrooms
¾ pound Asian-style sausage, such as Chinatown Crépinettes (page 96), Chinese Pork and Shrimp Sausage (page 99), or Chinese Black Bean and Shiitake Mushroom Sausage (page 98), removed from casings or in bulk
6 peeled fresh or 4 canned water chestnuts, chopped
2- to 3-pound cleaned and scaled whole fish, head and tail still on (use rock cod, red snapper, sea bass, pike, perch, or other firm-fleshed fish)

Salt and freshly ground black pepper
Flour to coat fish
Peanut oil for frying
½ cup dry sherry or Chinese rice wine
1 cup chicken or fish stock
1 teaspoon sugar
⅓ cup Chinese soy sauce
1 teaspoon red pepper flakes
8 thin slices fresh ginger
2 cloves garlic, chopped
6 green onions or scallions, cut into ½-inch pieces
2 tablespoons sesame oil
¼ cup chopped fresh cilantro

Soak the dried mushrooms in hot water to cover for at least 30 minutes. Drain. Discard stems and chop caps. Set aside.

Mix together the sausage meat and water chestnuts. Wash the fish and pat dry. Lightly sprinkle with salt and pepper and score the skin crosswise with diagonal cuts about an inch apart. Dust the fish completely with flour and stuff with the sausage mixture, which should just fill the cavity. It is not necessary to seal the cavity.

Heat about ¼ inch of peanut oil in a heavy frying pan or wok large enough to hold the fish. When the oil is almost smoking, carefully lay the fish in the pan, taking care not to splatter the oil. Fry the fish for

5 minutes, until the skin is light brown. Gently turn over the fish, using a couple of spoons and spatulas, and brown the other side for 3 more minutes.

Pour off any excess oil, and add the sherry, stock, sugar, soy sauce, red pepper flakes, ginger, garlic, and chopped mushroom caps. Scatter half the green onions over the fish. Cover the pan and decrease the heat to a simmer. Cook for 15 minutes, then baste the fish with the braising liquid. Replace the cover, and cook for 10 to 15 minutes more, until the fish is just cooked and tender.

Transfer the whole fish to a serving platter, sprinkle with the sesame oil, and pour on the sauce. Garnish with the remaining green onions and cilantro.

Salmon Sausage in Champagne Sauce

Makes 4 servings

THIS DISH MAKES A LOVELY FIRST COURSE FOR A SPECIAL DINNER PARTY OR formal lunch. A good, midrange California or Spanish sparkling wine is fine to use in the sauce. But serve a French rosé champagne or a premium California Blanc de Noirs sparkling wine with the meal.

9 tablespoons butter
2 tablespoons chopped shallots
¼ cup chopped fresh parsley
¼ pound chopped mushrooms
1 cup good-quality sparkling wine
2 cups chicken stock
2 cups whipping cream

Salt and freshly ground black
    pepper
8 Seattle's Pike Place Salmon
    Sausages (page 117),
    Crawfish Boudin (page 114),
    or other seafood sausage

Melt 2 tablespoons of the butter in a heavy saucepan over medium heat. Add the shallots, and cook for 2 minutes, until soft. Add the parsley and mushrooms and cook for 5 minutes over medium-high heat. Pour in the wine, and boil until it is almost evaporated. Stir in the stock and cream, and cook until the liquid is reduced by half. Whisk in 6 tablespoons of the butter, piece by piece, to thicken the sauce. Taste for salt and pepper. Set aside and keep warm.

Melt the remaining 1 tablespoon of butter in a large frying pan over medium heat. Add the sausages and brown, turning occasionally, about 5 minutes. Pour off the excess fat and transfer the sausages to a platter. Pour the sauce over the browned sausages and serve.

*Fish
Sausage en
Papillote
with
Mustard
and
Tarragon
Butter*

Makes 4 servings

Cooking and serving delicate fish or fowl with aromatic herbs and vegetables in a parchment envelope is a classic technique in European kitchens. The food steams in its own juices and absorbs the flavors of the seasonings and spices. Cooking *en papillote* also provides a very dramatic presentation when you cut open the envelope and the glorious aromas steam out in a fragrant cloud at the table. These days many cooks simplify the parchment technique by using aluminum foil. The visual effect is not as elegant, perhaps, but it is a lot easier and just as fragrant and delicious.

Beside the sausages suggested below, you can use this technique with any delicately flavored precooked sausage, such as Bockwurst (page 57), Chicken and Apple Sausage (page 34), boudin blanc, or veal sausage.

Mustard and Tarragon Butter

4 tablespoons (½ stick) butter, softened

1 tablespoon coarse-grained mustard

2 teaspoons chopped fresh tarragon or 1 teaspoon dried

Sausage and Vegetables

½ leek, white part only, cut into fine shreds 2 inches long

1 carrot, cut into fine shreds 2 inches long

4 Atlantic Seafood Sausages (page 116), Seattle's Pike Place Salmon Sausages (page 117), or other delicate precooked sausages, cut into ¼-inch-thick diagonal slices

2 fresh or presoaked dried shiitake mushrooms, caps cut into thin shreds and stems discarded

In a small bowl, combine the butter, mustard, and tarragon. Set aside.

Bring 2 to 3 inches of water to a boil in a small saucepan. Blanch the leek and carrot together for 30 seconds. Drain in a sieve and cool under running water.

Cut 4 sheets of aluminum foil or parchment each measuring 12 inches square. To assemble the packets, place the slices from 1 sausage in the center of each foil or parchment sheet. Sprinkle each with one-quarter of the leek and carrot mixture and one-quarter of the shiitake mushrooms. Spread one-quarter of the mustard and tarragon butter over the top of each. Fold the foil or parchment over the food to form a 6 by 12-inch rectangle. Seal all the edges by making several thin folds and crimping tightly with your fingers.

Preheat the oven to 450°. Place the packets on a baking sheet and bake for 10 to 12 minutes. Open a packet to check. The sausage should be completely heated through and the butter melted. If not, reseal the packet and bake for another 5 minutes.

To serve, place 1 envelope on each plate. Cut open with a knife or scissors and eat at once.

Chapter 13

CACKLERS AND GOBBLERS

Poultry and Sausages

I**N VIRTUALLY EVERY REGION OF AMERICA, SAUSAGE HAS BEEN USED TO** flavor chicken- and poultry-based dishes. Whether it's in the classic Cajun stew, Chicken and Andouille Gumbo (page 232), or the Midwestern favorite, Deep-Dish Chicken and Sausage Pie with Biscuit Crust (page 234), traditional American sausage is an essential ingredient. Also some of our more exotic sausages are paired with poultry in creative new ways, such as the recipes for Thai Green Curry (page 247), Moroccan Game Hens Stuffed with Rice and Fruit (page 241), and John King's Asian Barbecue (page 248).

Chicken or Rabbit Stew with Sausage, Hominy, and Crispy Onions

Makes 4 to 6 servings

GAME HAS ALWAYS BEEN AN IMPORTANT ELEMENT IN SOUTHERN COOKING. Rabbit, squirrel, possum, and raccoon form the base of many traditional recipes and are still often found on southern tables. The spice rub is also delicious on pork or turkey. We use domestic rabbit here, but squirrel or a young possum would also be mighty tasty. And this dish is awfully good with chicken, too.

Spice Rub

½ teaspoon salt

1 teaspoon black pepper

1 teaspoon dried marjoram

Pinch of ground cloves

1 teaspoon cayenne

2 teaspoons sweet Hungarian paprika

1 teaspoon dry mustard

Stew

2- to 3-pound chicken, cut into 8 pieces, or 2-pound frying rabbit, cut into 6 pieces

1 tablespoon bacon fat or olive oil

1 pound Cajun-Style Andouille (page 44), Smoked Country Sausage (page 32), or other smoked sausage, cut into ⅜-inch rounds

4 cups thinly sliced onions

1 carrot, diced

2 mild fresh chiles (Anaheim or similar), seeded and sliced, or 1 green bell pepper, chopped

1 tablespoon chopped garlic

1 cup rich chicken or beef stock

2 cups canned Italian plum tomatoes or 2 cups peeled, seeded, and chopped fresh tomatoes

1 (16-ounce) can hominy with liquid

Salt and freshly ground black pepper

Tabasco sauce

Hot cooked rice

First, make the spice rub by combining the salt, black pepper, marjoram, cloves, cayenne, paprika, and mustard in a small bowl. Rub over the chicken or rabbit. Set it aside to season while you prepare the remaining ingredients.

In a large Dutch oven or heavy pot, heat the bacon fat or olive oil over medium heat. Add the sausage and cook until it is lightly browned, about 5 minutes. Remove from the pot and reserve. Brown the chicken or rabbit pieces in the remaining fat, turning them often to achieve a nice golden color over all. Transfer the pieces to a platter as they brown. Pour off any excess fat into a heavy skillet, and reserve, leaving about 2 tablespoons in the Dutch oven.

Add half the onions and the diced carrot to the fat remaining in the Dutch oven. Cover. Fry the vegetables for about 10 minutes over moderate heat, scraping up any brown bits. Add the chiles and garlic, and cook for 2 minutes more. Add the stock, tomatoes, and hominy with its liquid, along with any leftovers from the spice rub. Bring to a boil. Add the chicken or rabbit, along with the browned sausage. Decrease the heat, cover, and simmer the stew for about 40 minutes while you prepare the crispy onions.

Heat the skillet with the reserved fat over medium-high heat. If you haven't saved the fat, use 2 tablespoons of bacon fat or olive oil. Add the remaining 2 cups sliced onions and ¼ teaspoon salt to the hot fat. Cover the pan, and decrease the heat to medium. Cook for 15 minutes, stirring occasionally. The onions should begin to brown evenly, but not burn. Increase the heat to medium-high, and remove the lid. Brown the onions, stirring and shaking the pan frequently. Continue for another 10 to 15 minutes, until the onions are crisp and a rich mahogany brown. Drain on a paper towel.

To complete the dish, cut a small piece from the chicken wing or the rabbit's front leg and taste to see if it is tender. If not, continue to cook until done. If the sauce is watery, remove most of the meat and vegetables with a slotted spoon to a serving bowl, and reduce the liquid until it just coats a spoon. Degrease the sauce, if necessary. Taste for salt and pepper, and add Tabasco if desired. Serve the stew over rice in a shallow bowl and garnish the top with crispy onions.

Chicken and Andouille Gumbo

Makes 6 to 8 servings

Gumbo, redolent of smoky sausage and dark roux, is the best-known Cajun and Creole dish. This spicy stew is best made one or two days ahead so the flavors can mellow.

3½-pound chicken
8 cups water
1 bay leaf
1 rib celery
1 onion, unpeeled and split in half
1 carrot, cut into 2 pieces
1 cup peanut oil
1 cup all-purpose flour
3 cups chopped onions
1 cup chopped celery
1 green bell pepper, chopped into ¼-inch pieces
1 red bell pepper, chopped into ¼-inch pieces
1¼ pounds Cajun-Style Andouille (page 44) or other spicy smoked sausage, ¼ pound chopped into ¼-inch pieces, 1 pound sliced into ¼-inch rounds

1 teaspoon dried thyme
½ teaspoon dried sage
1 teaspoon ground cayenne pepper
1 teaspoon freshly ground black pepper
2 tablespoons minced garlic
1 pound okra, cut into ½-inch slices
1 cup thinly sliced green onions or scallions
Salt
Tabasco sauce
3 cups warm cooked rice
½ cup chopped fresh parsley

Put the chicken whole into the water and bring to a boil. Skim any froth from the surface, then decrease the heat to a simmer, and add the bay leaf, celery, onion, and carrot. Simmer for 40 minutes, or until tender. Remove the chicken to cool. Strain the stock, then continue to simmer the stock while you prepare the rest of the recipe.

In a heavy 3- to 4-quart pot or Dutch oven, heat the oil over medium heat for 5 minutes. Remove from the heat and gradually stir in the flour. Return the pan to the heat and cook, continuing to stir, until the roux is a deep brown color, about 20 minutes. Remove the pot from the heat and add the chopped onions and celery. The vegetables will cool the roux. Return the pan to medium heat, stirring the vegetables until they are soft, about 5 minutes. The roux will continue to darken. Add the green and red bell peppers and the ¼

Making Roux in Advance

Roux, a mixture of flour and oil, is an essential ingredient in Louisiana cooking, where it not only adds body, but also is an important flavoring ingredient, giving soups, stews, and sauces a nutty, smoky taste and aroma. Making roux is a fairly time-consuming process, so you may want to make extra. Cool it and store it in an airtight jar in the refrigerator for 4 to 6 months. Then, when you need some, spoon out the amount called for, gradually heat it, and proceed with your recipe.

To make roux, use equal amounts of flour and oil. For example, heat 2 cups of oil in a cast-iron or other heavy pan over medium heat for 5 minutes. Remove from the heat and gradually stir in 2 cups flour. Return the pan to medium heat and continue to stir.

As you cook the roux, it will go through several stages of coloring. The first stage is tan, followed by light brown (the color of peanut butter), brown, and then deep red-brown. Finally, the roux will turn black. Some cooks like to use black roux in gumbo; we think that it is too bitter and recommend stopping at the red-brown stage. If the roux begins to darken too quickly during cooking, remove it from the heat and continue to stir. Lower the heat and continue to cook until the roux is the desired color.

To stop the cooking process, remove from the heat and stir in the chopped vegetables called for in your recipe. The roux will continue to cook and darken for 2 to 3 minutes. Return the pan to low heat and cook for 5 minutes more. Make sure that your vegetables and seasoning mixtures are chopped and prepared ahead of time and are ready nearby. Depending on the color and the quantity of roux you are making, the process will take between 30 and 60 minutes to complete.

pound chopped andouille and cook for 5 more minutes. Add the thyme, sage, cayenne, black pepper, and garlic.

Measure the chicken stock that has been simmering. You should have 6 cups (add water if necessary). Stir the 6 cups chicken stock into the roux, mixing well. Bring to a boil, then simmer for 15 minutes, uncovered. Add the okra and simmer for 30 minutes. While the gumbo simmers, remove the chicken meat from the bones. Discard the skin and bones, and cut the meat into ¾-inch pieces. (The gumbo and chicken can be refrigerated separately overnight.)

If you have refrigerated the gumbo overnight, gradually bring it to a simmer. Add the sliced andouille to the simmering gumbo and cook for 10 minutes. Add the chicken meat and green onions, and simmer for 5 minutes more. Taste for salt and Tabasco.

To serve, spoon about ½ cup of warm cooked rice into a large soup bowl. Ladle the gumbo over the rice, and garnish with parsley.

Deep-Dish Chicken and Sausage Pie with Biscuit Crust

Makes 8 servings

Biscuits

To make biscuits with the crust recipe: Combine flour, baking powder, salt, and sugar. Cut in butter until mixture resembles coarse crumbs. Pour in half-and-half; blend gently. Knead the soft dough 4 or 5 times on a floured surface to form a ball. Sprinkle with flour. Roll or pat out ½ inch thick. Cut into 2½-inch circles, place on an ungreased baking sheet, and brush lightly with melted butter. Bake for 20 to 30 minutes at 425°, until golden brown.

THIS IS A SATISFYING VERSION OF A SUNDAY-DINNER FAVORITE THROUGHOUT the Midwest. The flaky baking powder biscuit crust is also a great recipe for biscuits.

Filling

4- to 5-pound stewing or roasting chicken
8 cups chicken stock
24 pearl onions or ¾ pound boiling onions, peeled
12 baby carrots or ½ pound medium carrots, cut into ½-inch pieces
3 ribs celery, cut into ¾-inch pieces
½ pound fresh or frozen peas, or ¾ pound asparagus, with tender stems cut into 1-inch pieces and tips left 2 inches long

½ pound small whole mushrooms
4 tablespoons (½ stick) butter
⅓ cup all-purpose flour
1 cup heavy cream or half-and-half
Salt and freshly ground black pepper
1 pound mild fresh sausage, such as Bockwurst (page 157), Michigan Dutch Farmer's Sausage (page 70), or Chicken and Apple Sausage (page 34), in links

Baking Powder Biscuit Crust

2 cups all-purpose flour
1 tablespoon baking powder
½ teaspoon salt
Pinch of sugar
8 tablespoons (1 stick) cold unsalted butter

¾ cup half-and-half, or ½ cup half-and-half with ¼ cup heavy cream

Combine the chicken and stock in a large pot or Dutch oven and simmer until tender, 1 to 1½ hours. Remove the chicken from the stock and cool. Add the onions, carrots, and celery to the stock. Simmer for 7 to 10 minutes. Remove and set aside. Cook the peas or asparagus and mushrooms for 2 minutes in the stock. Remove and set aside.

When the chicken has cooled, remove the chicken meat from the bones. Discard the skin and bones and reserve the meat.

Melt the butter in a saucepan, stir in the flour, and cook gently for 2 to 3 minutes. Whisk in 4 to 6 cups of the stock along with the cream or half-and-half to make a rich chicken gravy. If it is too thick, add more stock. Season with salt and pepper. Set aside.

In a large, heavy nonstick skillet, fry the sausages whole over medium heat for 5 minutes, turning often until firm and brown on all sides. Then cut into ¾-inch rounds.

Preheat the oven to 425°.

To make the biscuit dough, combine the flour, baking powder, salt, and sugar in a medium-size bowl. Cut in the cold butter until the mixture resembles coarse crumbs. Pour in the half-and-half; blend gently. Knead the soft dough four or five times on a floured surface to form a ball. Sprinkle lightly with flour.

To assemble the pie, roll out the baking powder biscuit crust ½ inch thick and large enough to cover the surface of the pie. Arrange the cooked chicken, the sliced sausage, and the parboiled vegetables in a deep casserole or baking dish. Pour in the chicken gravy. Cover with the crust. Bake for 20 to 30 minutes, or until golden brown.

Fais Do-Do: Let the Good Times Roll
with a Cajun Feast and "Ma Jolie Blonde"

Down in Cajun country, folks get together for food, music, and good times at a Fais Do-Do on the weekends. Fais Do-Do means something like "Rock-a-Bye Baby," and the hope is that the little ones are sound asleep in their cradles while the parents whoop it up with the neighbors. A Fais Do-Do can vary from a few friends playing fiddles and eating boudin on the back porch to a full-scale county-wide brouhaha that makes the bayous rock for miles. They all have a few things in common, though: plenty of good food, music, and dancing, and a sufficiency of beverages, starting with Dixie beer, and including wine, soda pop, and what you will.

You can throw your own Fais Do-Do, and you don't especially need a bayou to do it. You can come pretty close with plenty of good Cajun food, some cold beer and wine, and a tape of Michel Doucet and his band, Beausoleil, singing "Donnez-moi Pauline," or Ambrose Thibodeaux belting out "Ma Jolie Blonde" on the Cajun accordion.

Just make sure the food is hearty and hot, the beer is cold, and the music loud enough to wake the alligators three bayous down.

Italian Sausage and Pheasant Pie

Makes 4 to 6 servings

THIS IS A GREAT CENTERPIECE FOR A BUFFET OR SPECIAL DINNER PARTY. Serve this with a salad of cold broccoli and cauliflower spears, garnished with strips of roasted red bell peppers, and dressed with extra-virgin olive oil and lemon juice. A chardonnay from California or Italy's Alto Adige region is the perfect accompaniment.

½ ounce dried porcini mushrooms
4 cups chicken stock
2 tablespoons unsalted butter
½ pound Italian Sweet Fennel Sausage (page 84) or Italian Turkey and Sundried Tomato Sausage (page 85)
2- to 3-pound pheasant or chicken, cut into 6 pieces
Salt and freshly ground black pepper
½ cup all-purpose flour
1 ounce mild dry coppa or prosciutto, finely chopped
1 pheasant liver or chicken liver, finely chopped

1 small carrot, finely chopped
1 rib celery, finely chopped
3 shallots, finely chopped
1 cup finely chopped leeks, white part only
3 cloves garlic, chopped
1 cup dry white wine
½ cup crème fraîche or sour cream
1 pound puff pastry (use your favorite recipe, or frozen pastry, thawed)
1 egg mixed with 1 tablespoon water, milk, or cream for egg wash

Soak the dried mushrooms in 2 cups boiling water for at least 30 minutes or for up to 2 hours. When they are soft, strain the liquid through cheesecloth or a coffee filter into the stock, and reserve the mushrooms.

Melt the butter in a large, heavy pan. Add the sausages whole, and brown them for about 10 minutes over medium heat. Remove with a slotted spoon and set aside. Sprinkle the pheasant or chicken pieces with salt and pepper, and dredge in flour. Fry them in the fat remaining in the pan until lightly browned, about 5 to 7 minutes a side. Remove the meat, and pour off all but 3 tablespoons of the fat. Add the chopped coppa and liver to the pan, and cook over medium heat for 2 to 3 minutes. Add the carrot, celery, shallots, leeks, and garlic, and cook for 5 to 10 minutes more, until the vegetables are soft, but not colored. Pour in the wine, chicken stock, and porcini, and deglaze the pan. Bring to a simmer and add the pheasant or chicken pieces in a single layer. Cover and cook at a simmer for 20 minutes. Remove the cover, and cook for another 25 minutes, or until the bird is tender and the sauce has begun to thicken. Remove the pheasant. If the liquid in the pan is not thick enough (it should have the consistency of heavy cream), reduce it over high heat. If it is too thick, add more stock or wine. When it has thickened, stir in the crème fraîche or sour cream. Cut the sausage into 1-inch rounds and add to the pot. Adjust the salt and pepper. Return the pheasant to the sauce and cool everything thoroughly in the refrigerator for a minimum of 2 hours or overnight.

Preheat the oven to 425°.

To assemble the pie, place the braised pheasant, sausage, and sauce in an ovenproof casserole large enough to hold everything with about 2 inches to spare on top. Roll out the puff pastry ¼ inch thick and large enough for about 2 to 3 inches to drape over the sides of the casserole. Let the pastry rest on a sheet pan for 30 minutes or more in the refrigerator.

Mix together the egg wash, and paint the top 2 inches of the outside of the casserole with this mixture. Drape the pastry over the casserole, and press the overhang against the outside edge to make a seal with the egg wash. Don't press down too firmly. Brush the crust with more egg wash. Bake for 20 to 25 minutes, until the top is a deep gold in color.

To serve, spoon up a piece of pastry, some pheasant, sausage, and plenty of the delicious sauce for each person.

Turkey Pie with Chile Cornbread Crust

Makes 6 servings

THIS DISH NOT ONLY MAKES DELICIOUS USE OF LEFTOVER TURKEY OR chicken, but it tastes immeasurably better than any tamale pie you've ever tasted. It is a relative of that grammar school cafeteria favorite—but with a lot more interest and flavor. Moreover, the filling is versatile—leftover pork, veal, or duck also tastes wonderful tucked under a savory cornbread crust. To use fresh chicken or turkey thighs, poach for 45 to 60 minutes in lightly salted water or stock until tender. Cool, discard bone and skin, and coarsely chop the meat.

Filling

½ cup blanched almonds

5 cloves garlic, peeled but left whole

¾ pound Chorizo (page 74) or other spicy fresh sausage, in bulk or removed from casings

1 large onion, finely chopped

1 cup crushed tomatoes in puree

1 cup turkey or chicken stock

2 teaspoons ground coriander

Pinch of cinnamon

½ cup chopped canned green chiles or 2 fresh Anaheims, fire-roasted, peeled, and chopped (page 73)

2 tablespoons commercial chile powder (Gebhardt brand is recommended)

½ teaspoon or more salt

¼ cup dry bread crumbs

3 to 4 cups diced cooked turkey or chicken

Freshly ground black pepper to taste

Chile Cornbread Crust

1 cup yellow cornmeal

1 tablespoon baking powder

½ teaspoon salt

2 cups grated Cheddar cheese

2 eggs lightly beaten

1 cup sour cream or yogurt

1 (8-ounce) can creamed corn

4 fresh Anaheim chiles, fire-roasted, peeled, and chopped (page 73)

1 fresh jalapeño, seeded and finely chopped, or 1 (4-ounce) can green chiles, chopped

3 tablespoons melted butter

In a small heavy frying pan over medium heat, toast the almonds and garlic cloves, shaking the pan continuously until the nuts are lightly browned and the garlic is just beginning to color. Transfer to a food processor and process until finely chopped but not pureed. Set aside.

In a large heavy skillet or Dutch oven, fry the chorizo over medium-high heat for about 5 minutes, crumbling it with a fork as it browns. Add the onion and continue to cook for 5 minutes more, stirring frequently. Add the tomatoes, stock, coriander, cinnamon, chiles, chile powder, and ½ teaspoon salt. Bring everything to a boil, and then reduce to a simmer. Cook for 10 minutes. Add the toasted nuts and garlic, and just enough bread crumbs to thicken the sauce. Stir in the poultry. Taste for salt and pepper. Set aside to cool, or refrigerate overnight.

When you are ready to bake the pie, preheat the oven to 400°F. To make the topping, combine the cornmeal, baking powder, and salt in a medium-sized bowl. Stir in the cheese. In a separate bowl, combine the eggs, sour cream, corn, chiles, and butter. Add this mixture to the cornmeal mixture and stir just enough to moisten the cornmeal.

Transfer the turkey filling into a 3- to 4-quart casserole. Cover with the chile cornbread batter. Bake for 45 to 60 minutes, until the crust is golden. Serve at once. This dish rewarms well and is excellent as leftovers.

Chicken or Turkey Pozole

Makes 4 to 6 servings

THIS IS BASICALLY POZOLE, THE MEXICAN SOUP/STEW THAT'S USUALLY MADE with pork, hominy, and chiles, lightened up a bit by using chicken or turkey with our Southwest Green Chile Poultry Sausage. Depending on how much chicken stock you add, it can be a soup, stew, or even a great filler for burritos. It's easy to make, doesn't contain a lot of meat, and can feed a whole troop of starving friends without a lot of trouble. Pozole goes very well with whatever beer happens to be in the refrigerator at the time.

1 tablespoon vegetable oil
½ pound Southwest Green Chile
    Poultry Sausage (page 77) or
    other Southwestern flavored
    sausage, removed from casings
6 chicken thighs or 2 turkey thighs,
    boned and skinned, cut into
    1-inch dice (about 1½ pounds
    boneless meat)
1 cup chopped onion
1 teaspoon dried oregano
2 tablespoons good-quality chile
    powder (Gebhardt brand is
    recommended)

½ teaspoon salt
3 to 4 cups chicken or turkey stock
    (preferably homemade)
½ cup good commercial salsa or
    salsa cruda
1 (28-ounce) can white hominy,
    drained and rinsed under cold
    running water
Salt and freshly ground black
    pepper to taste

Garnish
Sour cream, for garnish

Heat the oil in a large pot or Dutch oven over medium heat. Add the sausage and fry for 3 minutes, breaking it apart as it cooks. Add the chicken or turkey and onion and cook for an additional 2 minutes, stirring well. Add the oregano, chile powder, salt, stock, salsa, and hominy. Simmer over low heat until the chicken or turkey is tender, 20 to 25 minutes. Skim any fat from the top. Taste for salt and pepper.

Serve in soup bowls with sour cream as a garnish.

THROUGHOUT NORTH AFRICA AND THE MIDDLE EAST, YOU CAN FIND POUL-try cooked in a way that is at the same time exotic and simple: exotic from the use of rare and unusual spices and ingredients, such as saffron, pickled or dried lemons and limes, dried fruits, and nuts; simple because the poultry is usually braised in one pot in a highly flavored broth of spices and onions without browning or basting. We've adapted this method to produce braised game hens or small chickens fit for a pasha, or at least the neighborhood sultan. The recipe produces quite a bit of sauce that, spooned over couscous or steamed rice, makes a sumptuous side dish.

Moroccan Game Hens Stuffed with Rice and Fruit

Makes 4 servings

1 recipe Moroccan Rice with Fruit
  and Almonds (page 205)
4 Cornish game hens or small
  chickens (about 1 pound each)
1 tablespoon olive oil
2 cups finely chopped onions
2 tablespoons minced garlic
Salt and freshly ground black
  pepper

1 tablespoon sweet Hungarian
  paprika
1 teaspoon ground ginger
½ teaspoon ground cumin
¼ teaspoon ground turmeric
Pinch of ground cinnamon
3 cups water
Steamed couscous or rice

Prepare the rice mixture according to the recipe directions but do not bake. Stuff the birds with the rice and fruit mixture, and sew or truss the cavity with string or small wooden skewers. Reserve.

Heat the oil over medium heat in a deep-sided skillet, covered, or a Dutch oven big enough to hold all 4 birds. Add the onions, garlic, and a pinch of salt, and cook until the onions are soft, about 10 minutes. Sprinkle ½ teaspoon black pepper and the paprika, ginger, cumin, turmeric, and cinnamon over the onions. Fry for 1 minute more, stirring constantly.

Place the birds on the onions and garlic, breast side up, pour in 3 cups of water, and bring to a boil. Decrease the heat to a simmer, cover, and cook the birds for 1 hour, turning them 2 or 3 times while they cook.

Remove the birds to a warm platter and keep warm while you reduce the sauce over high heat until it just begins to turn syrupy. Taste for salt and pepper and pour the sauce over the birds. Serve at once with couscous or steamed rice.

Puerto Rican Chicken, Rice, and Sausage Stew

Makes 6 servings

WE CALL THIS A STEW, BUT THE DISH IS MEANT TO BE ON THE SOUPY SIDE. Use a full-flavored, smoked sausage. This dish is wonderful with black bread spread with a fresh cheese like *queso fresco* or pot cheese and a salad of oranges and marinated red onions. This lively stew cries out for a flavorful beer such as Red Stripe or Anchor Steam, or a full-bodied Sauvignon Blanc from California.

¾ pound smoked sausage, such as Portuguese Chouriço (page 90), Linguiça (page 89), Basque Chorizo (page 91), Cajun-Style Andouille (page 44), or Smoked Country Sausage (page 32), sliced into ¼-inch rounds

2 tablespoons olive oil

1 tablespoon chopped fresh oregano or 1 teaspoon dried oregano

2 cloves garlic, chopped

1 teaspoon salt

½ teaspoon freshly ground black pepper

1 teaspoon sweet Hungarian paprika

3½-pound chicken, cut into 8 to 10 pieces (2 wings, 4 breast pieces, 2 legs, 2 thighs)

1 cup thinly sliced onion

½ cup chopped green or red bell pepper or mild chile, such as Anaheim or poblano

6 tomatoes, peeled, seeded, and chopped, or 2 cups canned Italian-style tomatoes, drained and chopped

5 to 6 cups chicken stock

2 cups converted or long-grain rice

½ pound fresh green beans, cut into 2-inch pieces

½ cup grated sharp cheese, such as Manchego, Asiago, or Parmesan

20 pimiento-stuffed green olives

1 tablespoon capers

1 canned or fresh fire-roasted pimiento (page 73), cut into ½-inch strips

Lemon wedges

Heat the olive oil in a heavy pan or 4- to 6-quart Dutch oven over medium heat. Add the sausage and brown for about 5 minutes, until the fat is rendered. Remove with a slotted spoon and set aside.

With a mortar and pestle, make a paste of the oregano, garlic, salt, pepper, and paprika. Rub this all over the chicken pieces. Reheat the fat remaining in the pan. Add the chicken and fry until golden brown, 10 to 15 minutes, turning once. Don't crowd the pan, but fry 3 or 4 pieces of chicken at a time, transferring them to a platter as they brown.

Pour off all but 2 tablespoons of the fat. Add the onion to the remaining fat and cook, stirring frequently, for about 5 minutes. Add the bell pepper, and cook for a few minutes more, until the onion is soft, but the pepper is still firm. Return the sausage to the pot along with the tomatoes, stock, and chicken. Bring to a boil, and then decrease the heat to a simmer. Cover the stew and cook for 20 minutes, until the chicken is tender.

Stir in the rice, making sure it is covered with liquid. If not, add more stock. Bring to a boil, reduce to a simmer, cover, and cook for 20 to 25 minutes.

While the rice cooks, blanch the green beans in a large pot of lightly salted water for 5 minutes. Drain, plunge into ice water to stop the cooking, and drain again.

When the rice is cooked, but the mixture is still somewhat soupy (if not, add more stock), stir in the green beans, grated cheese, olives, and capers, and simmer for 5 minutes. Adjust the seasonings. Arrange the pimiento strips on top. Cook for 2 minutes more to heat everything thoroughly. Serve right from the pot along with the lemon wedges.

Anzonini's Chicken Livers and Chorizo

Makes 4 to 6 main-course or 10 to 12 appetizer servings

Wʜᴇɴ ᴛʜᴇ ɢʀᴇᴀᴛ ꜰʟᴀᴍᴇɴᴄᴏ ꜱɪɴɢᴇʀ Aɴᴢᴏɴɪɴɪ ᴅᴇʟ Pᴜᴇʀᴛᴏ ᴄᴀᴍᴇ ᴛᴏ California from Spain, he brought with him his gypsy gusto for food, music, and life. The dishes he cooked for friends at parties and fiestas—rich with garlic, olive oil, and his spicy homemade sausages—quickly made him a patron saint of the garlic revolution in Berkeley. Filmmaker Les Blanc captured the spirit and the flavor of Anzonini's food and music in his wonderful documentary film *Garlic Is as Good as Ten Mothers*, before Anzonini died several years ago. Anzonini often served these spicy chicken livers with chorizo at his night-long celebrations of flamenco and food. They are delicious as tapas or as a main course served with saffron rice or diced potatoes fried in olive oil and garlic.

¼ cup olive oil
¾ pound Basque Chorizo (page 91) or other spicy sausage, such as Linguiça (page 89), Hungarian Paprika Sausage (Debrecini) (page 65), or pepperoni, sliced into ¼-inch rounds
1½ pounds chicken livers, divided into individual lobes
Salt and freshly ground black pepper
¼ cup dry red wine
3 small zucchini, cut into ¼-inch rounds

2 red or green bell peppers, seeded and sliced
½ cup thinly sliced red onion
6 cloves garlic, minced
8 plum tomatoes, peeled, seeded, and quartered
1 teaspoon fresh or ½ teaspoon dried rosemary
1 teaspoon fresh or ½ teaspoon dried sage
½ cup chopped fresh parsley
Lemon juice

In a large, heavy skillet, heat 2 tablespoons of the olive oil over medium-high heat. Add the chorizo and fry for 3 minutes to render some of the fat and lightly brown the sausage. Transfer the sausage to a bowl with a slotted spoon, and cook the chicken livers in the fat for 5 minutes, shaking the pan occasionally. Sprinkle the livers lightly with salt and pepper, and turn them over. Sauté them for 3 to 5 minutes more, until firm. Add to the sausage. Pour the wine into the pan and deglaze, stirring up any brown bits stuck to the bottom, then pour into the bowl.

Duck or Turkey Sausage with Apples and Onions

Makes 4 to 6 servings

Many European countries have dishes that combine sausages with apples. This savory mix works particularly well for fresh pork sausages, but it is even better with duck or turkey sausages. The addition of red onion to the apples adds a piquant note, but you can leave the onions out if you want more apple flavor. Any of our favorite mild duck sausages or wild turkey sausages will go well in this dish. It is also excellent with Chicken and Apple Sausage (page 34). To give richness to the sauce, add cream and serve over pasta. This simple dish is also delicious without the cream and served with panfried potatoes.

2 tablespoon unsalted butter
4 to 6 Duck Sausages (page 111)
   or Wild Turkey Sausages
   with Drambuie (page 109)
1 large red onion, thinly sliced
2 small green apples, cored and
   sliced

¼ cup sweet white wine, such as
   Riesling or Chenin Blanc, or
   apple cider
1 cup heavy cream (optional)
1 pound fresh pasta (optional)

Melt 1 tablespoon of the butter in a large frying pan over medium heat. Add the sausages whole and brown for 5 minutes on each side. Remove and add the remaining butter and the onion to the pan. Fry over medium heat for 5 to 7 minutes, or until the onion is soft. Add the apples and sauté for 2 or 3 more minutes. They should be cooked but still firm.

Pour in the wine or cider and reduce over high heat for 3 or 4 minutes, until the sauce is syrupy.

Decrease the heat to medium and return the sausages to the pan. Cover and cook for an additional minute and serve. Or add the optional cream, reduce by half, then return the sausage. Cook, covered, for 1 more minute. Serve over fresh pasta, if you wish.

TRADITIONAL THAI GREEN CURRIES ARE MADE WITH CHICKEN AS IN OUR recipe, but you could also use chunks of boned turkey thighs or lean pork in this zesty dish. If you already have Thai green curry paste and coconut milk in the back of your fridge from earlier recipes, you can throw this dish together in a jiffy. If not, we provide you with a recipe for making your own green curry paste. You can substitute condensed milk for the coconut milk, although the taste will not be quite the same. Serve this tangy curry over steamed rice or boiled rice noodles.

1 tablespoon peanut oil
½ pound bulk Thai Chicken and Turkey Sausage (page 100), formed into 1-inch meatballs
4 chicken thighs, boned, skinned, and cut into 1-inch pieces
1 small onion, cut into thin shreds
1 tablespoon chopped garlic
¼ cup Thai Green Curry Paste (page 249)
2 cups coconut milk
1 cup water or chicken stock (preferably homemade)
1½ tablespoons Southeast Asian fish sauce

2 teaspoons brown sugar
3 unpeeled Japanese eggplants (6 to 8 ounces each), diced
10 fresh white mushrooms, quartered
½ red bell pepper, cut lengthwise into quarters, seeded, deveined, and sliced crosswise into thin strips
Salt and freshly ground black pepper
½ cup fresh basil leaves

In a large pot or Dutch oven, heat the oil over medium-high heat. Add the sausage meatballs and lightly brown them for about 3 minutes, turning often to ensure even browning. Add the chicken and cook for 2 minutes more, stirring occasionally. Add the onion and garlic and fry for 3 minutes, stirring often. Add the curry paste, stir to coat everything well, and cook for 2 minutes. Then add the coconut milk, water or chicken stock, fish sauce, and sugar. Bring to a boil, reduce to a simmer, and add the eggplants and mushrooms. Simmer until the eggplants are soft (taste a piece), about 10 minutes. Add the red bell pepper slices, taste for salt and pepper, and add a little more curry paste, if desired.

Transfer the curry to a serving bowl and sprinkle with basil leaves.

John King's Asian Barbecue

Makes 4 servings

BERKELEY ARTIST (AND OUR GOOD FRIEND) JOHN KING SAYS HIS ASIAN-style barbecue sauce is also delicious on lamb, pork ribs, and beef (especially flank steak).

Sauce

¼ cup Japanese-style soy sauce, such as Kikkoman

¼ cup medium-dry sherry or mirin

1 cup hoisin sauce

2 tablespoons red wine vinegar

2 tablespoons Dijon mustard

2 cloves garlic, minced

1 tablespoon coarsely ground black pepper

1 teaspoon ground cumin

3 tablespoons sesame oil

1 teaspoon crushed fennel seed or 1 teaspoon dried herbes de Provence

Meat

4 boned duck breasts or 4 boned chicken breasts

4 Chinatown Crépinettes (page 96) or other mild fresh sausages

Make the sauce by mixing all the ingredients together in a small bowl. It can be stored for 2 to 3 weeks in a covered jar in the refrigerator.

Put the duck or chicken breasts (you may remove the skin if you want) in a nonaluminum bowl or baking dish. Pour in 1 cup of the barbecue sauce and massage into the meat. Cover with plastic wrap, and marinate for 2 hours or overnight in the refrigerator.

Prepare a medium fire in a covered charcoal or gas grill. Since the sauce contains a fair amount of sugar from the hoisin sauce and wine, it's best to grill over medium heat so as not to blacken the food.

Remove the poultry from the marinade, and let any excess sauce drain off. Place the breasts on the grill, skin side down if it is still attached. Put the crépinettes or other fresh sausages on the grill. Cover the grill and sear the food for 3 to 4 minutes. Baste all the food with the remaining cup of barbecue sauce. Turn the food every 3 or 4 minutes, until the poultry and sausage are firm to the touch. The poultry will take about 12 to 15 minutes, while the sausages will need about 15 minutes. Put out any flare-ups with squirts of water.

Transfer the food to a heated platter and serve at once, accompanied by 2 or 3 different salads.

Green Curry Paste

Makes ¹/₃ to ¹/₂ cup

ot chiles make this a pretty fiery sauce, so adjust the level to your tastes. And take care not to rub your eyes when handling hot chiles.

1 tablespoon coriander seeds	3 cloves garlic
¹/₂ teaspoon cumin seeds	1 shallot
3 whole black peppercorns	2 tablespoons chopped fresh hot
1 stalk lemongrass	green chiles (Thai bird's eye
1 tablespoon chopped cilantro	chiles, jalapeño, serrano, or
roots or stems	pequin), stemmed, split, and
1 teaspoon chopped fresh ginger	seeded
¹/₂ teaspoon grated lime zest	¹/₂ teaspoon salt

In a small heavy skillet, toast the coriander seeds, cumin seeds, and peppercorns over medium heat, continuously shaking and stirring the pan for 2 to 3 minutes, until the seeds become lightly darkened and fragrant. Transfer to a mortar and pestle, spice grinder, or blender, and grind to a powder.

Trim and discard the dry outer leaves of the lemongrass stalk, the grassy tops, and the roots, leaving a piece of the center about 3 inches long. Cut the lemongrass heart into ¹/₂-inch pieces. Put them into a food processor or blender along with the pulverized seeds, cilantro, ginger, lime zest, garlic, shallot, chiles, and salt. Process into a thick paste. This paste will keep for 1 week covered in the refrigerator and can be frozen for up to 3 months.

Chapter 14

RED MEAT AND SAUSAGE

Sausage can stand alone as the centerpiece of a hearty meal, such as in our Roasted Game Sausage with Mustard-Rosemary Glaze (page 284), or it can be used as a seasoning to enhance the flavors of traditional dishes, such as our Lazy Hungarian Goulash (page 261), Bigos (Polish Hunter's Stew, page 263), or Greek Braised Lamb Shanks (page 262). A spicy sausage also makes a great stuffing in our Pork Loin Stuffed with Spring Greens and Smoked Sausage (page 256) or Rolled Flank Steak Stuffed with Italian Sausage, Basil, and Swiss Cheese (page 260). And of course, sausage is featured in many classic one-pot meals, such as Pennsylvania Dutch Schnitz und Knepp (Braised Sausage, Apples, and Dumplings, page 255) and Tex-Mex Chili (page 268).

Southern-Style Barbecue

Makes 8 to 10 servings

I T'S EASY TO HOST A SOUTHERN-STYLE BARBECUE, AND YOU DON'T HAVE TO grill a shoat to do it. We suggest using a Weber or other covered barbecue, but anything from a built-in brick behemoth to a hibachi will do. We've added a couple of sauces by that fine southern chef and author of *Grilling, Barbecuing and Smoking*, Ron Clark. Use either or both, or your own favorite.

Serve with black-eyed peas, cornbread, and stewed okra, or Smothered Cabbage with Andouille and Tomato (page 291) and accompany with full-bodied, high-hopped beers, such as Anchor Steam or Sierra Nevada, or with a cool, crisp Italian Pinot Grigio.

Mixed Grill, Southern Style

*2- to 3-pound frying chicken,
    cut into 8 pieces*
*3 to 4 pounds country-style
    spareribs*

*2 to 3 pounds Smoked Country
    Sausage (page 32)*

North Carolina Basting Sauce

1 cup cider vinegar
2 tablespoons red pepper flakes

*1 teaspoon Tabasco or other hot
    pepper sauce*

Georgia Barbecue Sauce

1½ cups tomato puree
1 cup cider vinegar
½ cup vegetable oil
½ cup packed dark brown sugar
⅓ cup Worcestershire sauce

¼ cup molasses
3 tablespoons yellow mustard
2 teaspoons minced garlic
Juice of 1 lemon
Tabasco or hot pepper sauce

Prepare a medium-hot fire to one side of a covered kettle or other grill. Place a drip pan on the other side.

Make the basting sauce by combining the vinegar, red pepper flakes, and Tabasco in a small bowl.

When the fire is ready, place the chicken and ribs on the grill over the drip pan. Baste with the sauce and cover the grill. Cook by the indirect method for about 1 hour, basting and turning as needed.

Coil the sausage and secure with 2 metal skewers run through the center crosswise to hold the coil together. Place on the grill over the drip pan. Continue to swab chicken, pork, and sausage liberally with the basting sauce and keep the grill covered.

Southern Landscape, with Barbecue

We slow down for a sign saying "Narrow Bridge" about an hour from the hills toward the coast. There's a town clustered around a black iron bridge cantilevered across a stream: one store, a white clapboard church, a few houses huddled under sycamores, with cottonwoods and pines down by the creek bed. Just another small southern town to pass through this hot afternoon, when there it is—the sweet, unmistakable smell of sausages cooking.

Hot fat vaporized on the coals mixes smoke with tomatoes and spices, garlic and cayenne. Talk and good laughter rise from the creek bed, people singing, happy and loud. We pull off the road and walk down by the side of the bridge. We follow our noses to the barbecue. The path is well worn.

The creek bank is crowded with people, black and white, young and old. It seems the whole town's gathered here at the long tables, passing ambrosia and opinions. Children, raucous under a huge oak, swing on a spare tire out over the stream. Young folk flirt across the fried catfish, while two lawyers in white shirts discuss, with intensity, the nature and techniques of barbecuing sausage. A line of courtly old women edges the bank; they dip their bare feet in the passing stream, decorously conversing. Five black Baptist ladies create God's true and only harmony right there under the cottonwood, while two spiritual masters of barbecue lay chopped pig meat and sausages down on the platters as they go by.

On a huge grill propped over the hot coals, a good-sized shoat, splayed and transfixed with iron rods, drips succulent fat. The skin is swabbed from time to time with a big bunch of mint dipped into saltwater and vinegar. A washtubful of sauce and chopped meat simmers to the side, deep mahogany, redolent of tomatoes, vinegar, and peppers—sweet and secret smells. Fat links of smoked sausage sputter between the pig and the sauce, swollen with juice, red with cayenne, and flecked with black pepper. Two other washtubs hold hot water and fresh-picked corn. Pans of cracklin' bread keep warm by the fire's edge, along with pots of melted butter, casseroles of hoppin' John, red beans and rice, hominy, boiled greens, and other covered dishes brought by folks from home.

Plates are filled and we're made welcome. Southern hospitality surrounds us, warm and rich. It's like we've come home after many years, sharing food and laughter at the end of a long, hot summer day.

To make the barbecue sauce, combine the tomato puree, vinegar, oil, sugar, Worcestershire, molasses, mustard, garlic, lemon juice, and Tabasco. Glaze the chicken, pork, and sausage with the sauce during the last 30 minutes of cooking.

Depending on the grill size and distance of the meat from the coals, all the meats should be done in 1½ to 2 hours. The pork should reach an internal temperature of 160°; the chicken, 170°.

Asian Mixed Grill

Makes 6 to 8 servings

YOU MIGHT WANT TO ACCOMPANY THIS SPICY MIXED GRILL WITH A FLAVORful soup, a pasta dish, such as our Cold Chinese Noodles and Sausage with Sesame Dressing (page 156), and a Thai Sausage Salad (page 158).

Marinade

¼ cup soy sauce

2 tablespoons or more water

2 tablespoons sesame oil

2 tablespoons red wine vinegar

2 tablespoons minced garlic

1 tablespoon minced fresh ginger

1 tablespoon Chinese brown bean paste

2 teaspoons Chinese hot chili paste

2 teaspoons sugar

1 teaspoon Worcestershire sauce

½ teaspoon five-spice powder

Mixed Grill

6 to 8 chicken legs and/or thighs

6 to 8 small pork chops or country-style spareribs (2 to 3 pounds)

6 to 8 thin slices calf's liver

1 pound Chinese Black Bean and Shiitake Mushroom Sausage (page 98), formed into patties

First, make the marinade in a bowl or in a food processor by combining the soy sauce, water, sesame oil, vinegar, garlic, ginger, bean paste, chili paste, sugar, Worcestershire, and five-spice powder. The marinade should have the consistency of a thick paste. If it seems too thick, add a little more water. Place the chicken, pork, and liver (not the sausage) on a platter, spread the marinade over them, cover, and marinate for 2 hours at room temperature or overnight in the refrigerator.

Prepare a medium-hot fire in a kettle-type barbecue. Grill the chicken legs and thighs with the lid on to make sure the fire doesn't flame up. Turn the chicken pieces often and baste with any leftover marinade. After 15 minutes, add the pork and continue to baste and turn frequently for 10 minutes more. Add the sausage patties and cook for about 5 minutes on each side.

Remove pieces of chicken, pork, and sausage to a platter as they are done; the chicken should reach an internal temperature of 170°; pork and sausage are done at 160°. Once all the meats are cooked, keep them warm while you grill the liver with the lid off for about 2 minutes on each side. Serve the meats buffet-style with suggested condiments and salads.

THE ONE-POT MEAL IS ONE OF THE CLASSICS OF PENNSYLVANIA DUTCH cooking, but it is so simple, homey, and downright flavorful that it is bound to become a favorite in your family. Use any mildly flavored sausage here. Dried apples work best because they hold up better during braising and have a more intense flavor than fresh.

Pennsylvania Dutch Schnitz und Knepp (Braised Sausage, Apples, and Dumplings)

Makes 4 to 6 servings

Dumplings

2 cups all-purpose flour
1 tablespoon baking powder
½ teaspoon salt
3 tablespoons melted butter

1 egg
¾ cup milk (enough to bind the dough)

Sausage and Apples

1 pound mild fresh sausage links, such as Iowa Farm Sausage (page 31), Sheboygan Brats (page 56), Hunter's Sausage (page 58), Michigan Dutch Farmer's Sausage (page 70), or Bockwurst (page 57)

1 tablespoon butter
1 cup dried apples
2 cups apple cider
2 cups chicken stock
1 tablespoon molasses
3 tablespoons cider vinegar

To make the dumplings, mix together the flour, baking powder, and salt. Add the melted butter and egg, and mix in just enough milk to form a soft dough. Set aside.

In a large high-sided frying pan with a lid, brown the sausage links or patties in the butter over medium heat. Pour off any excess fat, and add the dried apples, cider, stock, molasses, and cider vinegar. Partially cover the pan and simmer for 10 to 15 minutes, making sure there is enough liquid to cover the sausage and apples.

Spoon heaping tablespoons of the dumpling dough over the surface of the mixture in the pan. Cover and simmer for 10 minutes more, and don't peek while they are cooking. The dumplings are done when they are firm but puffed up and fluffy. A toothpick inserted into the middle should come out clean. If they are not done, cover, and cook for an additional minute or two until ready. Serve hot.

Pork Loin Stuffed with Spring Greens and Smoked Sausage

Makes 6 to 8 servings

THE TIME TO MAKE THIS DISH IS IN THE SPRING OR SUMMERTIME WHEN THE greens are fresh and tender. It is just as good cold or hot, which makes for a tasty picnic or cold supper. Greens are easy to grow, and increasingly available at specialty and ethnic markets. Use whatever mix you can find or suits your fancy. We've listed some of our favorites below, but you'll discover your own special mixture of bitter, hot, and sweet greens after you've tried this and other recipes a few times. If you're not up to butterflying the pork loin, ask your butcher to do it for you. Most will be happy to oblige.

4 cups spring greens, loosely packed (both bitter and sweet greens, such as collard, mustard, turnip greens, and/or arugula, mixed with spinach, escarole, and/or chard)

2 tablespoons butter

1 onion, finely chopped

1 teaspoon chopped garlic

Salt and freshly ground black pepper

4- to 5-pound center cut pork loin, boned

½ to ¾ pound smoked sausage, such as Cajun-Style Andouille (page 44)

¼ cup Creole or other coarse-grained mustard

½ teaspoon ground cayenne pepper

1 teaspoon fresh sage or ½ teaspoon dried ground sage

1 teaspoon freshly ground black pepper

3 tablespoons bacon fat or butter

Carefully wash the greens, remove the stems and discard, and coarsely chop the leaves.

Preheat the oven to 350°.

In a Dutch oven over medium heat, melt the butter. Add the onion in the butter and sauté until soft, about 5 minutes. Add the greens, garlic, and a pinch each of salt and pepper, and cook, covered, until the greens are wilted, about 10 minutes, stirring occasionally.

Butterfly the boned pork loin, and spread a layer of wilted greens over the cut surface. Lay the smoked sausage lengthwise down the center of the roast, and trim the sausage to fit. Reassemble the roast by rolling the loin around the sausage and greens, and tie it in several places with kitchen string.

In a small bowl, combine the mustard, cayenne, sage, and

Joe
Molinari's
Eggplant
and
Sausage
"Lasagna"

Makes 6 to 8 servings

THIS IS A FAMILY RECIPE THAT FED A WHOLE HOUSEFUL OF ITALIAN-Americans one warm and friendly summer evening in upstate New York. Calling the dish "lasagna" is stretching the term a bit, since there are no lasagna noodles in the dish, but rather layers of eggplant, sausage, cheese, and mushrooms. But we figure if our friend Joe Molinari's family can get away with calling it lasagna, so can we! The key to success with this hearty dish is to slice the eggplants thinly, and then bake the slices until they are completely soft. Any variety of Italian sausage will do, but we think the aromatic spices of our Italian Sweet Fennel Sausage go beautifully with eggplant.

2 medium-large eggplants, peeled
   and cut into ¼-inch slices
   lengthwise
1 cup or more olive oil
2 pounds Italian Sweet Fennel
   Sausage (page 84), New
   York–Style Spicy Hot Italian
   Sausage (page 82), or other
   Italian sausage, sliced into
   ½-inch pieces
2 medium onions, chopped
4 tablespoons chopped garlic

¼ teaspoon fennel seeds or
   aniseed
2 tablespoons chopped fresh basil
   or 1 teaspoon dried basil
½ pound sliced mushrooms
2 (8-ounce) cans tomato puree
1 cup dry white wine
Salt and freshly ground black
   pepper
1 pound mozzarella, thinly sliced
½ pound Parmesan, freshly grated

Preheat the oven to 375°. Dip each eggplant slice into olive oil, drain, and place the slices on sheet pans. Bake for 20 to 30 minutes, until soft. Use more olive oil, if needed.

Meanwhile, prepare the sauce. In a large, deep skillet or Dutch oven, brown the sliced sausages over medium-high heat for 10 minutes, stirring and scraping the bottom of the pan. Remove the sausages and set aside.

Add the onions and garlic to the fat left by the sausages, and cook for 5 minutes, stirring frequently, until the onions are soft. Add the fennel seeds, basil, and mushrooms, and fry for 2 to 3 minutes more. Add the tomato puree and wine. Bring to a boil, and then decrease the heat to a simmer. Cook, uncovered, for 30 minutes. Return the sausages to the skillet. Cook for 10 minutes more, until the sauce has thickened a bit. Taste for salt and pepper.

When the eggplant is completely tender, remove from the oven. Adjust the oven temperature to 350°.

To assemble the lasagna, place a layer of eggplant on the bottom of a 9 by 13-inch baking pan. Cover with a layer of the sausage and sauce, followed by a layer of sliced mozzarella and grated Parmesan. Continuing layering ingredients, ending with a layer of cheese on top. The lasagna can be made ahead to this point and refrigerated overnight.

Bake for 20 to 30 minutes, until the sauce is bubbly and the cheese melted. Let the dish rest for 10 minutes before slicing and serving.

Rolled Flank Steak Stuffed with Italian Sausage, Basil, and Swiss Cheese

Makes 4 to 6 servings with leftovers

Sᴇʀᴠᴇ ᴛʜɪs ᴅʀᴀᴍᴀᴛɪᴄ ᴀɴᴅ ᴅᴇʟɪᴄɪᴏᴜs ᴅɪsʜ ᴡɪᴛʜ ғʀɪᴇᴅ ᴘᴏʟᴇɴᴛᴀ ᴀɴᴅ ᴀ salad, along with a *Vino Nobile di Montepulciano* or a gutsy Zinfandel from California's Sierra foothills.

1 flank steak (about 1½ pounds)
10 to 12 fresh basil leaves
4 thin slices Swiss cheese
2 to 3 links Italian Sweet Fennel Sausage (page 84) or other mild Italian-style sausages
Salt and freshly ground black pepper
3 tablespoons olive oil

1 large onion, thinly sliced
8 cloves garlic, peeled and left whole
1 cup dry red wine, such as Zinfandel
½ cup red wine vinegar
½ cup beef stock
2 bay leaves

Preheat the oven to 350°. Lay the flank steak on a flat surface and cover it with basil leaves, reserving 2 to 3 leaves for the sauce. Place slices of Swiss cheese on top, enough to cover the leaves. Place whole sausages lengthwise down the center and roll the steak around them, then tie with kitchen string. Lightly salt and pepper the roll.

Heat the olive oil in a large, heavy Dutch oven or high-sided skillet over high heat. Add the rolled steak, seam side up, and brown for 5 to 7 minutes. Remove the steak and add the onion, cover, and decrease the heat to medium. Cook the onion for 15 minutes, stirring occasionally, until it turns light brown. Add the garlic and cook for a minute more. Add the wine, vinegar, stock, bay leaves, and the remaining basil. Return the steak to the pan, seam side up. Bring to a boil, cover, and place the pan in the oven. Bake for 1 hour, or until the meat is tender.

Remove the steak to a heated platter. If the sauce is too watery, reduce it over high heat until it becomes slightly syrupy. Slice the steak into 10 to 12 slices about ¾ inch thick. Arrange on the heated platter, pour the sauce over, and serve.

THIS RICH GOULASH IS MADE IN ONE POT WITHOUT THE ADDITION OF ANY liquid. The thick, wonderful gravy comes from the natural meat juices and the vegetables alone. It is great made up a day ahead and rewarmed.

The recipe comes to us from a smart Hungarian woman who knew how to make great meals for a huge family with very little effort. The dish can be increased easily to feed a large crowd. Serve with noodles or boiled potatoes, buttered green beans, and a hearty red Syrah from the Rhône, California, or Australia, or Egri Bikaver from Hungary.

1 pound Hungarian Paprika Sausage (Debrecini) (page 65) or Smoked Kielbasa (page 64), sliced into ¾-inch rounds

2 cups chopped onions

3 pounds beef chuck, cut into 2-inch chunks

1 pound pork shoulder or butt, cut into 2-inch chunks

5 canned Italian-style tomatoes, roughly chopped

3 red, green, or yellow bell peppers, or fresh pimientos, or a combination, coarsely chopped

½ cup sweet Hungarian paprika

1 tablespoon dried marjoram

6 cloves garlic, minced

1 teaspoon salt

1 teaspoon freshly cracked black pepper

Cook the sausage in a heavy Dutch oven or casserole with a tight-fitting lid over medium-high heat for 5 minutes. Add the onions and cook for 10 more minutes, stirring occasionally. Add the beef, pork, tomatoes, peppers, paprika, marjoram, garlic, salt, and pepper. Stir well. Simmer the goulash on the stove top for 10 minutes.

Preheat the oven to 350°. Cover the pot very tightly, using foil for a seal underneath the lid. Place the pot in the oven and cook for 2 hours, stirring every 30 minutes, until the meat is quite tender and a rich gravy has been formed. Taste for salt and pepper.

This dish reheats well and is best made a day or two ahead. Remove any congealed fat before reheating and serving.

Greek Braised Lamb Shanks

Makes 4 servings

These succulent lamb shanks are a great centerpiece for a Greek meal. Serve them with rice pilaf and a Greek country salad of tomatoes, sliced onions, olives, and feta along with a dark red wine from Naousa in northern Greece or a California zinfandel.

4 lamb shanks (about 1 pound each)
Salt and freshly ground black pepper as needed
1 tablespoon olive oil
½ pound Loukanika (page 88) or mild Italian sausage, in bulk or removed from casings
1 cup chopped onions
6 cloves garlic, chopped
2 cups canned crushed plum tomatoes, drained, or whole plum tomatoes, chopped

1 cup dry red wine
1 cup beef or chicken stock (preferably homemade)
2 teaspoons dried oregano
2 teaspoons chopped fresh mint or 1 teaspoon dried mint
1 teaspoon sweet Hungarian paprika
Pinch of ground cinnamon

Garnish
Chopped fresh parsley

Trim the lamb shanks of excess fat and season with salt and pepper. In a skillet with a cover or in a Dutch oven big enough to hold the shanks, heat the oil over medium-high heat. Brown the shanks on all sides, turning often, about 5 minutes. Remove the shanks.

In the fat remaining in the skillet, fry the sausage over medium heat for 3 minutes, breaking it apart as it cooks. Add the onions and garlic and sauté for 3 minutes more. Stir in the tomatoes, wine, stock, oregano, mint, paprika, and cinnamon. Return the shanks to the skillet, bring to a boil, cover, decrease the heat, and cook over low heat until the meat is quite tender and almost falling off the bone, 1¼ to 1½ hours. Turn the shanks after about ½ hour and check the sauce occasionally; if it is too dry, add a little more wine or stock.

Remove the shanks with a slotted spoon to a platter. Skim any fat off the surface of the sauce. If the sauce is too thin, reduce it over high heat. If too thick, add a little wine or water. Taste the sauce for salt and pepper, spoon it over the shanks, and sprinkle with chopped parsley.

BIGOS IS ONE OF THE GREAT PEASANT DISHES OF THE WORLD. IT WAS ORIGINALLY a hunter's stew filled with the bounty of the forest: venison, wild mushrooms, and game birds, all cooked together with sausages, cabbage, and wine. Today, most people don't have access to such game, so bigos is most often made with store-bought ingredients. Wild mushrooms, usually dried, are an integral part of the dish even today and are available in Polish or Italian delis as dried mushrooms or porcini. Sausage is essential also, and the stew usually includes a fresh and smoked version.

Makes 6 to 10 servings

1 ounce dried porcini or Polish
    mushrooms

6 tablespoons (¾ stick) butter

1 onion, sliced

2 leeks, halved and thinly sliced

1 carrot, chopped

1 tablespoon chopped garlic

½ head cabbage, cored, quartered,
    and shredded

2 tablespoons sweet Hungarian
    paprika

½ pound Fresh Kielbasa (page 63),
    sliced

½ pound Smoked Kielbasa (page
    64), sliced

½ pound beef stew meat, cut into
    1-inch cubes

½ pound venison or lamb stew
    meat, cut into 1-inch cubes

½ pound pork shoulder butt,
    cut into 1-inch cubes

Salt

1 teaspoon coarsely ground black
    pepper

2 cups beef or chicken stock

1 cup dry red wine

1 pound sauerkraut, drained

1 cup fresh or canned peeled,
    seeded, and chopped plum
    tomatoes

4 bay leaves

2 whole allspice berries

Garnish
Sour cream

Soak the dried mushrooms in 2 cups boiling water for at least 30 minutes.

Meanwhile, in a large heavy pot or Dutch oven, melt 4 tablespoons butter. Add the onion, leeks, and carrot and sauté for 5 minutes. Stir in the garlic and cabbage, cover, and cook until the cabbage has wilted, about 5 minutes. Sprinkle with paprika and cook for 1 more minute.

In a heavy frying pan, melt the remaining 2 tablespoons butter over medium-high heat. Add the sausages and brown for 5 minutes. Remove with a slotted spoon, and reserve.

Sprinkle the beef, venison, and pork with salt and pepper. Brown the pieces of meat in batches in the fat remaining in the pan, being careful not to overcrowd—this should take about 10 minutes. Remove the meats as they brown, and add to the vegetables. Deglaze the frying pan with the stock, and add this to the vegetables along with the red wine, sauerkraut, tomatoes, the bay leaves, and allspice. Remove the mushrooms from their soaking liquid. Strain the liquid to remove any debris. Add the mushrooms and strained liquid to the pot. Bring to a boil, decrease the heat to a simmer, cover, and cook for 1 hour.

Add the reserved sausages and cook, uncovered, for 15 to 20 minutes more, or until all the meats are tender. Taste for salt and pepper.

Serve the bigos in big shallow bowls, garnished with sour cream.

· ·

Pork Chops Stuffed with Country Sausage with a Bourbon Mustard Glaze

Makes 6 servings

THE SWEETNESS AND LUSCIOUS FLAVORS OF PORK MERGE WITH THE SPICY sausage and a tangy, bourbon-flavored glaze to make this a great centerpiece for a dinner party or special gathering of friends. You might want to start off with some mint juleps and Cheese and Sausage Biscuits (page 122). Our Kentucky-Style Pork Sausage works well here, but any good sage-flavored fresh sausage will do. The bourbon-mustard glaze also makes a superb marinade for roast or grilled beef, pork, or lamb, and a tasty glaze for baked ham.

Pork Chops
6 pork chops, cut 1½ inches thick
   (3 to 4 pounds total)
Salt and freshly ground black
   pepper
2 tablespoons olive oil

Bourbon Mustard Glaze
¼ cup brown sugar
2 tablespoons molasses
¼ cup bourbon
¼ cup Dijon or Creole mustard

¼ cup soy sauce
2 teaspoons Worcestershire sauce
½ teaspoon freshly ground black
   pepper

Stuffing

1 tablespoon butter

1 rib celery, finely chopped

1 onion, finely chopped

1 cup coarse fresh bread crumbs

¾ pound Kentucky-Style Pork
   Sausage (page 28) or other
   American farmhouse bulk
   sausage

2 tablespoons dry white wine

1 egg

Cut a large pocket into each chop and season the meat with salt and pepper. Set the chops aside while you make the glaze and stuffing.

To make the glaze, combine the brown sugar, molasses, bourbon, mustard, soy sauce, Worcestershire sauce, and black pepper in a small bowl. Whisk until smooth. Set aside.

To make the stuffing, melt the butter over medium heat in a heavy skillet. Add the celery and onion and cook, covered, until soft, about 10 minutes. Transfer the onion and celery to a bowl, and mix in the bread crumbs, sausage, white wine, and egg. Knead and squeeze the stuffing until all the ingredients are thoroughly blended. Divide it into 6 equal amounts, and stuff into each chop, molding the dressing with your hands against the side.

Preheat the oven to 375°. Heat the olive oil in a large, heavy skillet over medium heat until the oil begins to haze. Brown the chops, 3 at a time, for 4 to 5 minutes on each side. Transfer them to a 9 by 13-inch pan and brush with the glaze. Bake the chops, uncovered, for 30 to 45 minutes, or until an instant-read thermometer registers 155° to 160° when inserted into the middle of the stuffing. Baste the chops generously every 10 minutes with fresh glaze. Serve at once.

Hungarian Stuffed Cabbage

Makes 10 servings, with leftovers

JUST ABOUT EVERY COUNTRY IN NORTHERN AND EASTERN EUROPE HAS A VERsion of stuffed cabbage, and recipes for this hearty peasant folk dish are like folk songs—similar in general content but wonderfully different in details. Stuffed cabbage almost always features a spicy meat or sausage filling, and most renditions are mighty tasty. But our favorite way of preparing the dish is the way the Hungarians do it—baked over sauerkraut with a tangy tomato-paprika sauce.

You can use just about any mild-flavored fresh sausage for stuffed cabbage, including Hunter's Sausage (page 58) or Sheboygan Brats (page 56). We prefer Fresh Kielbasa or Hungarian Paprika Sausage (Debreceni) in this recipe. If you have a favorite stuffed cabbage recipe of your own, try adding some fresh sausage like kielbasa or bratwurst to the stuffing. You should be pleasantly surprised by the increase in flavor and liveliness.

Cabbage Rolls
1 pound ground chuck
1 pound Hungarian Paprika Sausage (Debrecini) (page 65), Fresh Kielbasa (page 63), or other fresh sausage, removed from the casings
1½ cups finely chopped onion
2 cups cooked rice

2 eggs
3 tablespoons sweet Hungarian paprika
½ teaspoon ground caraway seeds
½ teaspoon salt
1 teaspoon coarsely ground black pepper
2 medium heads cabbage, cored

Sauce
1 cup tomato puree
1 cup beef or chicken stock
2 tablespoons sweet Hungarian paprika

½ pound Smoked Kielbasa (page 64), diced
1 to 2 tablespoons tomato paste

Sauerkraut
1½ pounds sauerkraut, rinsed briefly and drained
1 cup sour cream

Salt and freshly ground black pepper

In a large bowl, knead the ground beef, sausage, onion, cooked rice, and eggs together with the paprika, caraway, salt, and pepper until well blended.

In a large pot, bring to a boil enough water to cover the cabbage. Add the whole heads of cabbage and cook for 10 minutes. Using a large fork, stab a head of cabbage from the bottom, remove it, cool it slightly under running water, and then peel off as many leaves as you can, one at a time. Put the cabbage back in the pot, and cook for a few more minutes until it is soft enough for you to peel off a few more layers of leaves. Continue the process with both heads until you get down to the small inner leaves. Set the separated leaves and what remains of the heads aside while you make the sauce.

Combine the tomato puree, stock, paprika, and diced kielbasa in a saucepan. Bring to a boil. Stir in just enough tomato paste to give the sauce body. Reserve and keep warm.

To make the stuffed cabbage rolls, place about ⅔ cup filling in the center of each of the largest leaves. Fold in the sides, and roll the leaves up. Continue this process until all the filling is used (the smaller leaves will need less filling).

Preheat the oven to 325°. Finely shred any remaining leaves and the unused centers of the cabbage heads. Lay the shredded cabbage and sauerkraut on the bottom of a 9 by 13-inch baking pan. Put the cabbage rolls on top, seam side down. You should have 18 to 24 rolls. Pour the sauce over the rolls. Cover with foil and bake for 1½ hours, until the cabbage rolls are quite tender.

Transfer the rolls to a warm platter. Drain the juices into a saucepan and spoon the kraut and shredded cabbage over the rolls. Reduce the sauce by boiling until it is just syrupy. Off the heat, stir in the sour cream. Taste for salt and pepper. Spoon the sauce over the kraut-covered rolls and serve.

Tex-Mex Chili

Makes 8 to 10 servings

In Texas, and in other parts of the Southwest, they take their chili very seriously. Questions like whether or not to add beans, ground meat versus chopped, fresh chiles or powder can lead to strong words and high dudgeon at chili cook-offs and festivals. You don't need venison to be authentic here—beef, pork, or lamb will work just as well. Feel free to improvise with whatever comes to mind—chili cooks have been known to toss just about anything into a "bowl of red," from goat haunch to diced rattlesnake.

1½ pounds Chorizo (page 74) or other Southwestern flavored sausage, ¼ pound removed from casings

½ pound Texas Smoky Links (page 78) or other smoked sausage, diced

2 large onions, finely chopped

2 tablespoons chopped garlic

2 Anaheim, poblano, or other mild green chiles, fire-roasted, peeled, and chopped (page 73)

2 jalapeño, serrano, or other hot green chiles, seeded and minced

2 pounds venison, lamb, beef, or pork, or any combination, cut into ½-inch dice

1 (28-ounce) can whole tomatoes or crushed tomatoes in puree

1 (12-ounce) can beer

1 cup stock or water

2 to 3 tablespoons good commercial chile powder blend (Gebhardt brand is recommended)

2 teaspoons ground cumin

½ teaspoon dried oregano

1 teaspoon sugar

2 tablespoons masa harina or cornmeal

3 tablespoons or more cider vinegar

Salt and freshly ground black pepper

Garnishes
Shredded Cheddar cheese
Chopped red onion
Sliced avocado

In a large Dutch oven or heavy pot over medium-high heat, brown the ¼ pound of Chorizo that has been removed from its casing, crumbling the meat with a fork as it cooks, for about 5 minutes. Add the diced smoked sausage and cook for 2 minutes more. Reduce the heat to medium and stir in the onions. Cook until soft, about 5 minutes. Add the garlic and chiles, and cook for 5 minutes, stirring occasionally. Add the diced meat and cook over medium heat until no longer pink, stirring constantly. Pour in the tomatoes, beer, and stock, and add chile powder to taste, cumin, oregano, and sugar. Bring to a boil, decrease the heat to a simmer, and cook for 1 hour. Add more stock or beer if the chili becomes too thick.

Meanwhile, slice the remaining 1¼ pound Chorizo link sausages into 1-inch rounds and fry over medium-high heat for 5 minutes in a heavy frying pan to render some of the fat. Drain the fat and add to the chili sausage. Cook for 15 minutes, or until all the meats are tender.

In a small bowl, make a paste of the masa harina or cornmeal with the 3 tablespoons vinegar and about ½ cup of liquid from the chili. Stir this into the pot along with the sausage, and cook for 10 minutes. Taste for salt, pepper, and vinegar.

Serve immediately, or refrigerate overnight and reheat before serving.

Serve the chili over cooked rice or with cooked beans. Garnish with cheese, onions, and avocado slices.

Fiesta in the Sangre de Cristo Mountains

Two red-tailed hawks ride high in a thermal, drifting up in widening circles as we break out of the hills and down into the Chimayo Valley just north of Santa Fe. The landscape changes quickly from the hard beauty of the uplands with its piñon scrub and cactus, red rocks and arroyos, to valley fields bright with the deep brassy green of chile plants and the soft wide leaves of pumpkins, squash, and melons. Fruit trees and cottonwoods cluster near water. Nearby, adobe houses are the color of dry earth, their pale walls threaded with bright red *ristras*, strings of chiles, hanging from the eaves. Dirt roads like streams of brown water cut through the green fields. Two children riding a burro wave and laugh as we pass. The clear autumn light flavors everything like a spice.

We're on our way to a fiesta up in the foothills of the Sangre de Cristo mountains, named for how the red of the sunset seems like Christ's blood on the slopes. It's a harvest festival to honor the corn and the beans, the chiles ripening red-green under the leaves; a dance for what this hard earth gives. Apart from a good time and celebration, we're looking for the sausages we've heard about in Santa Fe and Taos. Great sausages up there in the hills, we're told—chorizos of wonderful spice and depth; sausages made from wild pigs and birds fed on piñon nuts, smoked with the aromatic woods of the high desert.

As we rise up from the valley, the sun is bright on the rocks, shadows beginning to lengthen. We turn suddenly into the village tucked in the edge of a canyon, a white church with a plaza, a cluster of houses up against the hills. In the central square, there's a riot of color, bands, and dancing, and smoke from the cooking rises up all around the edge.

The dancers swirl through the plaza: Moors and Christians, mustachioed conquistadors and warriors in masks and feathers battle across the square. We stroll among the food stands. Old women are making tortillas, cooking them quickly on *comals*, filling them with chorizo and chiles. Sausages sputter on hot grills next to salsa in bright terra-cotta bowls. *Cabritos* smoke on spits over glowing coals in the gathering dark. We order tacos and cold beer with lime, and watch the mariachis playing under the streetlights. Young girls smile and stroll around the square on the arms of their mothers. The young men are drinking beer, boisterously singing the first lines of love songs as they strut by in the other direction.

We wander around the plaza as the night goes on, sampling sausages, chiles stuffed with cheese and chorizo, bowls of steaming pozole and venison chili, spicy empanadas, and chimichangas. The *corridos* (songs of the border, danger, and love) are starting up as we drive away. We can hear them a long time as we head down the mountain under the bright, cold harvest moon.

CHILE VERDE IS USUALLY MADE BY BRAISING CHUNKS OF PORK SLOWLY WITH green chiles and tomatillos, and is often used in burritos or served over rice. This easy-to-make chile verde gains much of its flavor from the spicy sausages—it's delicious by itself or in enchiladas with sour cream.

1 pound New Mexico Chicken, Pork, and Roasted Chile Sausage (page 76) or any Southwestern flavored sausage
2 pounds pork butt, cut into 1-inch cubes
1 medium onion, finely chopped
2 cloves garlic, chopped
1 teaspoon ground cumin
1 cup chicken stock
6 canned or parboiled and peeled tomatillos, finely chopped

6 Anaheim or poblano chiles or other mild fresh green chiles, fire-roasted, seeded, peeled, and chopped (page 73), or
1 (7-ounce) can green chiles, seeded and chopped
1 bunch (4 to 6 ounces) cilantro or flat-leaf parsley
Salt and freshly ground black pepper
Lime juice

In a dry skillet over medium heat, brown the sausages whole for about 5 minutes on a side. Remove and let them cool a bit. Add the pork, brown for 5 minutes, and remove. Cut the sausage into ½-inch-thick rounds or, if you intend to use the chile verde in enchiladas, dice the sausage.

In the fat remaining in the skillet, cook the onion and garlic until soft, about 10 minutes. Mix in the cumin and add the stock and tomatillos. Bring to a boil, add the reserved pork and the chiles, and decrease the heat to a simmer.

Discard any roots from the cilantro and finely chop the stems. Add to the pot and cook for 30 more minutes, then add the sausage. Coarsely chop the cilantro leaves, reserve about ¼ cup for garnish, and add the remainder to the pot. Cook for 10 more minutes. Taste the pork to determine if it is tender; if not, cook until tender. Taste for salt and pepper, and add enough lime juice to give a tang to the sauce. Garnish with the remaining cilantro and serve.

Stacked Cheese and Chorizo Enchiladas

Makes 4 to 6 servings

STACKED ENCHILADAS ARE QUICKER AND EASIER TO PUT TOGETHER THAN THE rolled kind. You can use up stale tortillas, and you eliminate the messy (and calorie adding) step of frying the tortillas first in oil. This type of enchilada originates in the state of Sonora in northern Mexico and is very popular in neighboring New Mexico. We prefer to use New Mexico Chicken, Pork, and Roasted Chile Sausage or the Southwest Green Chile Poultry Sausage here, but Chorizo also works well. Stack the enchiladas high and cut into wedges, or use stacks of 2 to 3 tortillas for individual portions—either way is great for brunch garnished with a fried egg and salsa.

¾ pound New Mexico Chicken, Pork, and Roasted Chile Sausage (page 76), Southwest Green Chile Poultry Sausage (page 77), Chorizo (page 74), or other spicy sausage, removed from casings
1 cup chopped onions
½ cup thinly sliced green onions or scallions

3 mild green chiles, such as Anaheim or poblano, fire-roasted, seeded, and chopped (page 73)
2 cups chopped fresh cilantro (optional)
4 cups shredded jack cheese
3 cups Tex-Mex Red Enchilada Sauce (page 273)
12 corn tortillas

Garnish
Sour cream (optional)
Sliced green onions or scallions

In a heavy frying pan, fry the sausage over medium-high heat for 5 minutes, breaking the meat up as it cooks. Pour off the excess fat. Combine the cooked sausage with the onions, green onions, chiles, and cilantro. Cook for 1 minute. Remove from the heat and stir in 3 cups of the shredded cheese.

Preheat the oven to 375°. To assemble the enchiladas, heat the sauce in a 10-inch pan. Grease the bottom of a 9 by 13-inch baking dish. Dip a tortilla in the warm sauce to coat it, and place it flat in the baking dish. Spread a layer of the sausage/cheese filling over the tortilla, and top with another sauce-coated tortilla. Repeat the process until the stack is as high as you wish (6 tortillas high is about the limit). Build another stack, or make a number of stacks 2 or 3 tortillas high, depending on your preference. Sprinkle on the remaining cup of cheese. The enchiladas can be made up a day ahead and refrigerated until the final baking.

Bake until the cheese is melted. Larger stacks take more time in the oven, about 30 minutes; smaller stacks, about 20 minutes. Add an extra 7 minutes to the baking time if they start out cold. Garnish with sour cream and green onions.

Tex-Mex Red Enchilada Sauce

Makes 6 to 8 cups

ne of the foundations of Tex-Mex cooking—use for enchiladas, tacos, tamales, empanadas, etc. Make double or triple this recipe; it keeps for 2 to 3 days in the refrigerator, or you can freeze it in 1- or 2-cup batches for later use.

2 tablespoons olive oil

1 onion, chopped

2 tablespoons chopped garlic

2 tablespoons all-purpose flour

$^1/_2$ cup high-quality chile
    powder blend (Gebhardt
    brand is recommended)

1 (14-ounce) can tomato puree

1 (14-ounce) can tomato sauce

1 (28-ounce) can red chile sauce
    (also called enchilada sauce)

$^1/_4$ cup red wine vinegar

1 cup water

In a 4- to 6-quart pot, heat the olive oil over medium heat. Add the onion and garlic and cook for 10 minutes, stirring occasionally. Stir in the flour and chile powder and cook 2 minutes, scraping the pan. Add the tomato puree, tomato sauce, red chile sauce, and water. Bring to a boil, stirring. Decrease the heat to a simmer and cook, uncovered, for 30 minutes, stirring occasionally, until the sauce reaches the desired thickness.

Poblano Chiles Stuffed with New Mexico Chicken, Pork, and Roasted Chile Sausage

Makes 4 to 6 servings

POBLANO CHILES HAVE A RICH PEPPERY FLAVOR AND ARE PREFERRED FOR this dish, but you could also use Anaheim or green New Mexico chiles. If fresh chiles are hard to come by in your area, substitute green or red bell peppers. Anaheims tend to run a bit smaller than poblanos, so use two per serving. If you're fortunate enough to live near a Mexican market, use the delicious fresh Mexican cheese, *queso fresco*, instead of jack cheese.

Stuffed Chiles

6 large poblano chiles, 12 Anaheim chiles, or 6 bell peppers, tops removed
1 tablespoon olive oil
1 cup finely diced onion
1 teaspoon minced garlic
2 pounds New Mexico Chicken, Pork, and Roasted Chile Sausage (page 76), Chorizo (page 74), or El Paso Beef, Pork, and Chile Sausage (page 75), removed from casings

1 cup cooked rice
1 cup crumbled queso fresco *or* diced jack cheese
1 egg

Sauce

3 cups coarsely chopped canned plum tomatoes with juice
1 tablespoon minced garlic
2 tablespoons pure New Mexico chile powder or high-quality chile powder (Gebhardt brand is recommended)

¼ teaspoon salt
½ teaspoon coarsely ground black pepper

Garnish

1 bunch (4 to 6 ounces) cilantro, coarsely chopped (1 cup) (optional)

Blanch the chiles in a large saucepan of well-salted boiling water for 10 minutes. Remove and cool under running water. Remove any seeds. Reserve.

In a heavy frying pan, heat the olive oil over medium heat. Add the onion and fry until soft, about 10 minutes. Add the garlic. Remove from the heat and transfer to a bowl. Mix the sausage with the onion and garlic, along with the cooked rice and cheese. Add the egg and blend everything together with your hands. Let the mixture cool for 5 minutes. Stuff the cooled mixture into the chiles.

To make the sauce, combine the tomatoes, garlic, chile powder, salt, and pepper in a small nonreactive pan. Bring to a boil. Decrease the heat and simmer the sauce, uncovered, for 10 minutes.

Preheat the oven to 350°. Pour the sauce into a 9 by 13-inch glass or enamel baking dish. Arrange the stuffed chiles on their sides in the sauce. Cover the dish with foil and bake for 30 minutes. Remove the foil and bake for an additional 10 minutes. Spoon the sauce over the chiles and serve garnished with cilantro.

Quick and Easy Sautés and Stir-Fries

Sausage is so delicious that one of the best ways to serve it is sautéed or stir-fried using a bit of wine or stock to deglaze the pan to make a sauce, and adding some mushrooms, garlic, scallions, or bell peppers for flavor and texture.

Sautéing is a quick and convenient way to cook for a small group of people as only 1 to 4 portions are cooked at a time in the hot pan.

The key to successful sautés is to cut all the ingredients into bite-sized pieces and not to crowd the sauté pan. Here is a simple recipe that you can embellish with numerous variations. Sauté about 1 pound of diced or sliced sausage in a little hot oil, pour off the excess fat, deglaze the pan with 1 cup of stock or wine, add 1 cup of chopped mushrooms, onions, garlic, etc., and reduce the sauce slightly over high heat.

You can mix the sausage with some other diced meat, such as skinless chicken or veal, or use other vegetables, such as green or red bell peppers, green beans, or peas. In fact, any vegetable that requires little cooking or has been precooked will work well in a sauté. In place of wine, you can use stock, clam juice, lemon juice, cream, or a combination of cream and stock. Cream-based sautés are particularly good as pasta sauces.

To stir-fry, toss pieces of sausage or meat with cut-up vegetables in a little oil over very high heat. The trick is to keep the ingredients moving (stirring constantly) to cook them until tender, but still crunchy.

Chinese Eggplant in Black Bean Sauce

Makes 4 main-course servings or 6 servings as part of a multi-course Chinese meal

THIS IS ANOTHER RECIPE FROM EDY YOUNG, A GOOD FRIEND AND A GREAT home cook, who was raised in a Chinese-American family that loved hearty food. She grew up learning to cook a great variety of dishes in every style imaginable. She cooks Italian, Mexican, and especially Chinese, as we see in this toothsome recipe for spicy eggplant.

1 tablespoon Chinese fermented black beans

3 tablespoons chopped garlic

¼ cup vegetable oil

1 tablespoon Asian hot chili oil

¾ pound Chinese Black Bean and Shiitake Mushroom Sausage (page 98), Chinatown Crépinettes (page 96), Chinese Pork and Shrimp Sausage (page 99), or other Asian flavored sausage, in bulk or removed from casings

1 cup sliced onions

1½ pounds small Japanese eggplants, unpeeled, cut into 2-inch rounds

3 ⅛-inch-thick slices fresh ginger

¼ cup beer

2 tablespoons cider vinegar

3 tablespoons brown sugar

¼ teaspoon red pepper flakes (optional)

2 green onions or scallions, green and white parts, chopped

Float the black beans in water in a small bowl. Remove the beans with a slotted spoon, leaving any sandy sediment behind. Mash the washed beans in another bowl with the chopped garlic.

Heat the vegetable oil in a wok or large skillet over high heat. Add the black beans and garlic and chili oil, and fry until the garlic just starts to brown, about 2 minutes. Add the sausage and sliced onions and stir-fry for 5 minutes, breaking up the sausage as it cooks.

Add the eggplants and ginger along with the beer, vinegar, brown sugar, and red pepper flakes. Decrease the heat and simmer until the eggplants are quite tender, about 10 minutes.

Spoon into a serving dish, sprinkle with chopped green onions, and serve.

THIS FAMILY FAVORITE IS A GREAT HIT FOR SUNDAY DINNER WITH PLENTY OF mashed potatoes, fresh corn, and mugs of root beer. The kids do like a little ketchup in the loaf and on the side, but us older folks usually can do without it. And a sweet, amber Oktoberfest lager can replace the root beer in our mugs.

*Kids'
Favorite
Chicken
and Apple
Meat Loaf
with Cider
Gravy*

Meat Loaf

*½ pound ground turkey or
  extra-lean ground beef
1 pound Chicken and Apple
  Sausage (page 34), removed
  from casings
1 cup fresh bread crumbs
1 egg*

*¼ cup applesauce
¼ cup ketchup (optional for adults,
  kids love it!)
1 teaspoon Worcestershire sauce
½ teaspoon salt
¼ teaspoon freshly ground black
  pepper*

Cider Gravy

*1 cup apple cider
½ cup chicken stock
½ cup chopped dried apples
Pinch of ground cinnamon*

*Salt and freshly ground black
  pepper
1 tablespoon cornstarch dissolved
  in ¼ cup apple cider*

Preheat the oven to 350°.

In a large bowl, combine the ground meat, sausage, bread crumbs, egg, applesauce, ketchup, Worcestershire, salt, and pepper. Mix thoroughly, kneading with your hands, until everything is well blended. Form into a loaf on a baking sheet, and bake uncovered for 45 to 60 minutes, until the internal temperature reaches 160°.

Meanwhile, make the gravy. Combine the cider and chicken stock in a nonreactive saucepan. Boil until reduced by half. Add the dried apples, cinnamon, and salt and freshly ground black pepper. Stir in the dissolved cornstarch and simmer, stirring often, for 5 more minutes. Keep warm.

To serve, spoon some gravy over slices of meat loaf, and serve the rest on the side.

Makes 6 to 8 servings

This wonderful meat loaf is delightfully easy to prepare and is a delicious family dish. This is another recipe from Loni Kuhn, whose own family enjoyed this loaf for years. In fact, Loni's son Steven loved this dish so much that he requested it for birthday dinners. And, although Loni was a very accomplished cook with a vast repertoire of elaborate and exotic dishes, this simple preparation was the family favorite. Like all good meat loaf recipes, this makes great sandwiches cold the next day.

Use a sage-flavored sausage in this recipe. Any of the basic American farmhouse sausage recipes from this book, such as Kentucky-Style Pork Sausage or Yankee Sage Sausage, will do fine, or buy some good bulk sausage from a reliable butcher. For the ham, use a mildly smoked ham, preferably one that is not too salty. If you are feeling lazy, ask the butcher to grind it for you. It's simple to make up some bulk sausage especially for this recipe in a food processor or grinder—you'll get a leaner and more flavorful sausage than the store-bought variety.

Meat Loaf

2 pounds mildly smoked ham, ground
1½ pounds sage-flavored bulk sausage such as Kentucky-Style Pork Sausage (page 28), Yankee Sage Sausage (page 29), or Iowa Farm Sausage (page 31)

1 onion, chopped
1 cup milk
1 cup day-old bread crumbs
2 eggs, beaten

Basting Sauce

½ cup brown sugar
¼ cup cider vinegar

1½ tablespoons brown mustard such as Gulden's

Preheat the oven to 350°.

In a large bowl, combining the ham, sausage, onion, milk, bread crumbs, and eggs. Mix thoroughly, kneading the mixture until everything is well blended. Form it into a loaf on a baking sheet. Make a ¼-inch deep crosshatch pattern on top of the loaf by pressing the handle of a wooden spoon flat across the surface of the meat. This provides little gullies to hold the basting sauce on the loaf.

Meat Loaf: The Ultimate Comfort Food

Meat loaf is everybody's favorite comfort food. After a hectic day, there's nothing like sitting down to a plate of hearty meat loaf, mashed potatoes, and a savory gravy. But too often the meat loaf is bland and uninteresting, and then there's the fat and cholesterol question. Traditional recipes tend to be on the heavy side, with old-fashioned gravy loading up the fat even more.

Using chicken and turkey sausages combined with either ground turkey or lean ground beef, you can turn out a great variety of different types of meat loaf with a maximum of flavor and a minimum of fat.

Use the recipes on pages 277 to 279 as guides and improvise with various sausage, spice, and herb combinations. The basic ratio of 1 pound sausage, $1/2$ pound ground meat, 1 cup fresh bread crumbs, 1 egg, and about $1/2$ cup sauce stays the same. The type of sausage and flavorings can vary as you like.

Be sure to make plenty of meat loaf, as leftovers are never a problem. Think of cold meat loaf as "poor man's pâté," and use it for delicious snacks, appetizers, and sandwiches.

To make the basting sauce, combine the sugar, vinegar, and mustard and mix thoroughly. Divide between two bowls and set one aside. Using the sauce in the other bowl, brush the sauce generously over the meat.

Bake the loaf for $1\frac{1}{4}$ hours, until it is firm and the top is nicely browned, basting 4 or 5 times with the sauce remaining in the bowl.

Slice into $\frac{1}{2}$-inch slices and serve each slice with a generous amount of sauce from the reserved bowl on top.

Chinatown
Crépinettes
Braised
with Napa
Cabbage

Makes 6 servings

ONE OF THE MOST FRAGRANT AND DELICIOUS CHINESE DISHES IS GREENS braised with aromatic sausage. Almost any leafy vegetable is delicious cooked this way, from bitter mustard or turnip greens to the milder-flavored bok choy, or savoy or Napa cabbage. We use our Chinatown Crépinettes wrapped in caul fat, but you could easily substitute the same sausage meat stuffed into casings or in bulk. Serve this succulent dish over steamed rice with a malty Chinese beer, such as Tsingtao.

2 pounds Chinatown Crépinettes
   (8 to 10) (page 96), or
   equivalent
2 cups thinly sliced onions
2 teaspoons minced fresh ginger
1 teaspoon minced garlic
1½ pounds Napa cabbage, cut
   crosswise into ½-inch slices
½ cup Chinese rice wine or
   medium dry sherry

1 cup rich chicken stock
1 cup sliced green onions or
   scallions
2 cups coarsely chopped fresh
   cilantro
2 whole star anise
Salt and freshly ground black
   pepper

Brown the crépinettes or other sausage cut in chunks or in small patties in a heavy frying pan or Dutch oven for 5 minutes per side, turning once. Remove the sausages and add the onions, ginger, and garlic. Cook over medium heat for 10 minutes, until the onions are soft. Add the cabbage and cook for 2 to 3 minutes, stirring to coat with the pan juices. Add the wine, chicken stock, ½ cup of the green onions, 1 cup of the cilantro, and the star anise. Return the crépinettes or other sausages to the pan, decrease the heat to a simmer, and cook for 30 minutes.

Using a slotted spoon, remove the sausages and vegetables to a serving platter, and keep warm. Turn the heat to high, and reduce the liquid remaining in the skillet until it just begins to turn syrupy. Taste for salt and pepper, degrease, and pour over the sausages and cabbage. Garnish with the remaining green onions and cilantro.

Étouffée is the French Creole word for smothered, and it describes a style of slow braising in a flavorful and spicy sauce. Many of Louisiana's favorite dishes are cooked this way. Other favorite ingredients in étouffées are crawfish, shrimp, chicken, and game.

1 teaspoon freshly ground black pepper plus more to taste

2 teaspoons sweet Hungarian paprika

¾ teaspoon plus a pinch of ground cayenne pepper

2 teaspoons plus a pinch of dried thyme

1 teaspoon dried basil

2 teaspoons salt plus more to taste

6 large veal chops, ½ to ¾ pound each

1 tablespoon butter

4 tablespoons peanut oil

¼ cup all-purpose flour

Pinch of ground sage

2 cups finely chopped onion

½ cup finely chopped celery

¼ cup finely chopped red bell pepper

¼ cup finely chopped green bell pepper

¼ pound Cajun-Style Andouille (page 44) or other spicy smoked sausage, coarsely chopped

¼ pound Tasso (page 49) or smoked ham, finely diced

2 tablespoons chopped garlic

1 cup finely chopped green onions or scallions

2 cups rich chicken or veal stock

4 tablespoons tomato paste

Tabasco sauce

Hot cooked rice

Mix together 1 teaspoon black pepper, the paprika, ¾ teaspoon cayenne, 2 teaspoons thyme, the basil, and 2 teaspoons salt. Rub this spice mix all over the veal chops.

Heat the butter and 1 tablespoon of the peanut oil in a large, heavy skillet over medium-high heat. Add the veal chops and brown for 5 minutes on each side. Transfer the chops and any juices to a platter.

In the same heavy-bottomed pan, make a roux. Heat the remaining 3 tablespoons of oil over medium heat for 3 minutes. Remove from the heat and gradually stir in the flour. Return the pan to the heat and cook, continuing to stir, until the roux is a medium brown color, about 15 minutes. Add a pinch each of black pepper, cayenne, thyme, and sage, and the onion and celery. Put the pan back over medium heat. Continue stirring and scraping the pan until the vegetables are soft, about 5 minutes. The roux will continue to darken.

Add the bell peppers, Andouille, and Tasso, and cook for 2 to 3 minutes more, until the peppers are wilted. Add the garlic and green onions and cook for 2 more minutes. Add the stock and tomato paste, and stir well to make smooth. Add the veal chops and any juices. Bring to a boil, then decrease the heat to a simmer. Cover and cook over low heat for an hour, or until the veal is quite tender.

Remove the veal chops to a heated platter and reduce the sauce so it coats a spoon. Adjust the seasoning with salt, pepper, and Tabasco. Pour the sauce over the chops and serve with lots of plain rice.

Wild Rice and Pecan Salad with Grilled Venison Sausage

Makes 4 servings

WILD RICE AND ROASTED NUTS MAKE A SPLENDID COMBINATION THAT COMplements the flavor of venison beautifully. The salad also works well with our Wild Boar Sausage (page 110) or any venison sausage. Serve as a luncheon or light dinner with a hearty red wine like California Syrah or French Rhône.

1 cup raw wild rice
½ teaspoon salt
½ cup shelled pecans
1 tablespoon peanut oil
1 pound Venison Sausage (page 106) or Game Sausage with Herbs and White Wine (page 108)
2 green onions or scallions, thinly sliced

1 cup chopped fresh flat-leaf parsley
¼ cup sherry wine vinegar or red wine vinegar
½ cup walnut oil
Salt and freshly ground black pepper

To prepare wild rice, carefully wash the rice and remove any dirt or foreign material. Bring 3 cups of water to a boil in a heavy 2- to 3-quart saucepan. Add the rice and salt. When the water returns to a boil, decrease the heat, cover the pot, and simmer for 40 minutes or longer, until the rice is tender.

While the rice is cooking, roast the pecans in the peanut oil in a medium skillet over medium-low heat for 5 minutes, shaking the pan constantly. When they begin to brown, become crispy, and develop a nutty aroma, immediately remove the nuts, along with any oil remaining, to a large bowl.

To grill the sausages, prepare a medium-hot fire in a kettle-type barbecue or gas grill. Keep a spray bottle handy to dowse flare-ups and grill with the lid down, turning the sausages frequently, until the sausages are cooked through, 12 to 15 minutes. The sausages are done when an instant-read thermometer registers 155° to 160° when inserted 2 inches deep into the end of a sausage. Alternatively, pan-fry the sausages in a large heavy skillet over medium-high heat until cooked through and firm, 12 to 15 minutes, turning frequently. Transfer to a platter and let them sit while you finish the salad.

Add the cooked rice, green onions, parsley, vinegar, and walnut oil to the roasted pecans in the bowl. Toss well to combine the ingredients. The rice should be evenly coated with the oil and vinegar. Season to taste with salt and pepper. Mound the salad on a platter or in a shallow bowl. Slice the warm sausage on an angle, arrange over the rice, and serve at once.

Quick and Easy Grills

Just about every sausage discussed in this book is delicious grilled. What could be simpler or more satisfying for lunch or supper than a couple of browned and juicy grilled sausages on a plate with roasted potatoes and a green salad?

Whether you cook over charcoal or on a gas grill, you should try to keep the flames to a minimum when grilling sausages. A covered kettle-type barbecue with medium-hot charcoal is best. We find cooking with the lid on helps to control flare-ups, but a spray bottle filled with water is useful. If you grill sausages under a broiler, use the maximum heat and turn the sausages frequently. Make sure to use a broiler pan with a rack so the juices drip through and don't catch fire.

Sausages that are initially raw are best prepoached before grilling to ensure more even cooking.

The secret to grilling sausages is to turn them frequently as they cook to ensure even browning. Keep the heat as even as possible and put out any flare-ups as soon as they occur. And don't overcook the sausages. Raw fresh sausages, such as Italian sausages, will take about 12 to 15 minutes to cook. Cooked sausages, such as Smoked Bratwurst, hot dogs, or Smoked Kielbasa, will take 7 to 10 minutes to get hot all the way through. Your best bet to get the sausages exactly right is to use an instant-read thermometer. Simply slip the tip into the end of the sausage about 2 inches in so it penetrates to the center. When it registers 155° to 160°, the sausage is done.

Roasted Game Sausage with Mustard-Rosemary Glaze

Makes 8 servings

THE GAME SAUSAGE WITH ROSEMARY AND MUSTARD MAKES A GREAT PRE-SENTATION for a dinner or party buffet. Once the sausage is roasted, present it whole on a platter for your guests to admire, and then cut it into chunks at the table. This mustard-rosemary glaze is also excellent on leg of lamb, rack of lamb, or roast beef. You can also brush it on venison, elk, or boar sausages, or any full-flavored fresh sausages, and either grill or roast them.

Mustard–Rosemary Glaze

½ cup smooth Dijon mustard
1 tablespoon soy sauce
2 teaspoons minced garlic

2 teaspoons chopped fresh rosemary
2 tablespoons olive oil

Sausage

1 (4-pound) coil of Game Sausage
with Rosemary and Mustard
(page 112)

To make the glaze, mix together the mustard, soy sauce, garlic, and rosemary. Gradually whisk in the olive oil until it is absorbed into the sauce.

Preheat the oven to 375°. Place the sausage coil in a roasting pan. Brush generously with all the glaze and roast for 30 minutes, or until the glaze begins to brown and the sausage is firm and cooked through.

Sauces made by pureeing sweet red bell peppers are widely used in new American restaurants with delicate foods such as swordfish or chicken, as well as more intensely flavored meats like lamb and game. This sweet red pepper puree is particularly delicious and colorful with our Spinach, Pork, and Game Crépinettes. The tangy sauce works equally well with Seattle's Pike Place Salmon Sausage (page 117). For a truly elegant presentation, serve the dish spooned onto puff pastry cases. Otherwise, it tastes great over fresh egg noodles, home-made spaetzle, or buttered rice.

Makes 4 servings

1 large red bell pepper, fire-roasted, peeled, and seeded (page 73)
1 cup heavy cream
2 tablespoons butter
1 pound Spinach, Pork, and Game Crépinettes (page 113), sliced into 1-inch thick chunks
2 cloves garlic, minced
2 shallots, thinly sliced

2 teaspoons sweet Hungarian paprika
¼ cup chicken stock
¼ cup dry white wine
½ teaspoon dried marjoram
Salt and freshly ground black pepper
1 tablespoon chopped fresh parsley

Cut the fire-roasted bell pepper into quarters, julienne one of the quarters, and reserve. Place the other 3 quarters in a food processor and puree with ¼ cup of the heavy cream. Set aside.

In a large, heavy skillet, melt the butter over medium heat. Add the sausage and sauté for 6 to 8 minutes, or until lightly browned and cooked through. Remove the sausage with a slotted spoon and add the garlic and shallots. Sauté for 2 minutes, or until the shallots are soft but not colored. Remove from the heat and stir in the paprika so that the shallot/garlic mixture is well coated. Return to medium heat and cook for approximately 1 minute; then add the stock, wine, and mar-joram. Boil until reduced by half. Pour in the remaining ¾ cup of cream and cook for 5 minutes, or until the sauce begins to thicken. Stir in the red pepper puree and sausage and cook for 1 or 2 minutes. Season with salt and pepper. Garnish with the julienned red pepper and parsley, and serve immediately.

Chapter 15

SAUSAGE-SPIKED SIDE DISHES

Let's face it. Many side dishes—rice, potatoes, barley, even polenta, and all those veggies—can be a bit on the dull side. But sausages can give sparkle and extra flavor to bland starches and vegetables without adding a lot of fat and calories.

All you to have to do is fry up a small amount of whatever sausage you think will enhance the dish and provide a flavor profile—a signature of a cuisine—along with extra spice and interest. For example, you can transform green beans into Italian, Thai, Chinese, Mediterranean, Creole, Southwest, or down-home American dishes by lightly steaming the beans, and then quickly sautéing them with a bit of the sausage of your choice. This same technique can enliven a whole array of vegetables, including spinach, chard, cabbage, zucchini, lima beans, and many more. Experiment and have fun with vegetables, for a change.

A plus to many of our side dishes is that they can be turned into an inexpensive main course simply by adding more sausage to the recipe. Just up the amount of sausage and serve a bigger portion to turn a tasty side dish into a one-pot meal.

THIS MOIST AND CUSTARDY "BREAD" IS REALLY MORE LIKE A PUDDING. IT makes a super side dish with roast or grilled meat, poultry, or fish. Use any of our fresh or smoked farmhouse sausage recipes here or a good commercial product, but be sure to fry the sausage meat first to get rid of some of that fat.

½ pound Country Ham and Pork
   Sausage (page 30) or other
   farmhouse sausage, crumbled
   or finely chopped
2 cups milk
1 cup half-and-half

½ teaspoon salt
2 teaspoons sugar
1 cup white or yellow cornmeal
2 tablespoons butter
4 eggs, separated
1 cup fresh or frozen corn kernels

Fry the crumbled or chopped sausage in a heavy skillet over medium heat until the fat is rendered and the meat is thoroughly cooked, about 5 to 7 minutes. Remove the meat with a slotted spoon, drain on paper towels, and set aside. Save a tablespoon of the fat.

Preheat the oven to 350°.

Heat the milk, half-and-half, salt, and sugar in a heavy 3- to 4-quart saucepan over medium heat. When small bubbles form around the edge, slowly pour in the cornmeal, stirring constantly. Continue to stir as the mixture cooks and thickens. After about 5 minutes, when the cornmeal is smooth and creamy in texture, remove the pot from the heat and stir in the butter and the reserved tablespoon of sausage fat until they are completely absorbed.

Beat the egg yolks briefly, until they are a light lemon color. Gradually add them to the cornmeal mixture, beating vigorously until they are completely incorporated. Stir in the corn and the browned sausage meat.

Beat the egg whites until they form stiff, but not dry, peaks. Mix a large spoonful of the whites with the cornmeal mixture to loosen it. Then, using a rubber or wooden spatula, gently and thoroughly fold in the remaining egg whites.

Butter a 2-quart casserole or soufflé dish thoroughly. Add the spoonbread mixture, smoothing the top with a spatula. Bake for 1 hour in the middle of the oven until puffy and golden brown. Serve directly from the baking dish.

Just about every book we've ever seen on Southwest cooking includes a recipe for one of the spicy cornbreads of the region. Once you've tasted one, you'll know why—they are really delicious. This version is more of a pudding than a bread because it is quite moist and cheesy in texture. It makes a wonderful side dish to replace potatoes or rice, or it is quite satisfying eaten as a light entree or lunch with a salad of fresh young greens.

Makes 6 to 8 servings

½ pound Chorizo (page 74), removed from casing

1 cup yellow cornmeal

1 tablespoon baking powder

½ teaspoon salt

2 eggs, lightly beaten

1 cup sour cream or yogurt

1 (8-ounce) can creamed corn

4 fresh Anaheim chiles, fire-roasted, peeled, and chopped (page 73)

1 fresh jalapeño chile, seeded and finely chopped, or 1 (4-ounce) can green chiles, chopped

2 cups grated sharp Cheddar cheese

Preheat the oven to 350°.

Crumble and fry the Chorizo in a heavy skillet over medium-high heat for 5 minutes to render some of the fat. Put the sausage meat and 3 tablespoons of the fat in a large bowl. Add the cornmeal, baking powder, salt, eggs, sour cream, corn, chiles, and 1¼ cups of the cheese. Mix all the ingredients thoroughly.

Generously butter a 1½-quart casserole, 9 by 9-inch baking dish, or 10-inch heavy skillet. Spoon in the cornbread batter. Sprinkle the top with the remaining ¾ cup cheese. Bake for 45 to 55 minutes, until the cornbread turns golden and smells wonderful. Serve hot.

Grits, Sausage, and Cheese Casserole

Makes 10 to 12 side-dish or 6 to 8 main-course servings

THE SMELL OF THIS CHEESY, SMOKY CASSEROLE BAKING IN THE OVEN IS almost too much to bear. It's a great breakfast dish with poached or fried eggs, and guaranteed to get those hungry slugabeds up and to the table. It is also just fine for lunch with a fresh garden salad of young greens and marinated onions, or as a side dish to liven up the dinner table. Form any leftovers into thick patties and fry them up in a little butter—delicious for breakfast, or just about anytime.

2 tablespoons unsalted butter
½ pound smoked sausage, such as Smoked Country Sausage (page 32) or Cajun-Style Andouille (page 44), cut into ¼-inch dice
½ cup chopped onion
½ cup chopped red bell pepper
2 teaspoons minced garlic
3 cups milk
½ teaspoon salt

1 cup quick-cooking grits
2 teaspoons Tabasco sauce
2 eggs, beaten
½ cup half-and-half or heavy cream
1 cup finely sliced chives, green onions, or scallions
¼ cup chopped fresh parsley
1½ cups shredded medium or sharp Cheddar cheese

In a medium-sized skillet, melt 1 tablespoon of the butter over medium heat. Add the sausage and brown for 3 minutes. Pour off all but 2 tablespoons of the fat. Add the onion, red bell pepper, and garlic and cook them for 5 minutes more, until the onion is translucent.

Meanwhile, gradually bring the milk to a boil over medium heat in a 2- to 3-quart saucepan. Add the salt. Pour the grits slowly into the milk, stirring it constantly and keeping it boiling. Boil the milk and grits for another minute, stirring well, and then reduce the heat and simmer for 2 to 3 more minutes, until the grits have thickened and are soft. Taste to make sure. Remove the cooked grits from the heat and stir in the vegetable/sausage mixture, the Tabasco, eggs, half-and-half, chives, and parsley, along with 1¼ cups of the cheese.

Preheat the oven to 350°. Butter a 2-quart casserole with the remaining tablespoon of the butter. Spoon the grits/sausage mixture into the casserole, and sprinkle with the remaining ¼ cup cheese. Bake in the middle of the oven for 35 to 45 minutes until set. When done, the top will be beautifully puffed up and a light golden brown.

Grits Soufflé Variation

For a lighter variation, use exactly the same ingredients, but separate the eggs. After adding the vegetable/sausage mixture, egg yolks, and other ingredients to the grits, fold in the egg whites beaten to stiff peaks. Bake in a 375° oven for about 30 minutes, until puffed and browned. The texture and appearance of this dish will be more like a soufflé, more "company" than "down-home."

Smothered Cabbage with Andouille and Tomato

Makes 8 servings

THIS DISH CAN BE USED AS A SIDE DISH, BUT IF YOU ADD ANOTHER HALF POUND of andouille, it is substantial enough to serve as a main course.

4 tablespoons (½ stick) butter or bacon fat
½ pound Cajun-Style Andouille (page 44) or other spicy smoked sausage, cut into ¼-inch dice
2 onions, thinly sliced
½ cup diced carrots
1 tablespoon minced garlic
1 head cabbage, quartered, cored, and shredded

2 bay leaves
¾ cup rich chicken or beef stock
¼ cup dry sherry
1 teaspoon dried thyme
½ teaspoon ground cayenne pepper
4 tomatoes, peeled and coarsely chopped
Tabasco sauce
Salt and freshly ground black pepper

Heat the butter or bacon fat in a 4- to 6-quart pot over medium heat. Add the sausage and brown for 2 to 3 minutes. Add the onions and carrots, and cook, covered, for 10 minutes, or until the onions begin to color lightly. Add the garlic, cabbage, and bay leaves. Cover, and cook, stirring occasionally, until the cabbage is well coated and begins to wilt, about 10 minutes. Pour in the stock and sherry and stir well to deglaze the bottom of the pot. Add the thyme and cayenne along with the tomatoes, cover, and cook at a low heat for 10 more minutes, until the cabbage is quite tender. Season to taste with Tabasco, salt, and pepper. Serve warm.

"The Spinach"

Makes 4 to 6 servings

THIS IS ANOTHER SIMPLE AND WONDERFUL RECIPE FROM LONI KUHN, A good friend and gifted cook. This way of preparing spinach became so popular in the Kuhn household over the years that it was simply referred to as "The Spinach." Any smoked country-style sausage will work well in this dish. Good-quality smoky bacon is a fine substitute for the sausage.

2 tablespoons butter
¾ pound smoked sausage, such as
    Smoked Kielbasa (page 64),
    Linguiça (page 89), Smoked
    Country Sausage (page 32),
    or Smoked Bratwurst (page 54),
    diced
1 large onion, chopped
1 tablespoon all-purpose flour
⅛ teaspoon freshly grated nutmeg

1 teaspoon minced fresh rosemary
    or ½ teaspoon dried
¾ cup milk
1 chicken bouillon cube, crumbled
2 bunches fresh spinach (about
    2 pounds), washed and roughly
    chopped
Salt and freshly ground black
    pepper

In a large heavy, skillet or Dutch oven, melt the butter over medium heat. Add the sausage and cook for 5 minutes to render some fat, but do not brown the sausage. Add the onion and continue to cook until pale gold in color. Drain off the excess fat. Add the flour and stir until the onion is well coated. Add the nutmeg and rosemary, and fry briefly for 1 minute, stirring constantly. Add the milk and cook, stirring constantly, until the sauce thickens. Add the bouillon cube and spinach. Simmer for 2 to 3 minutes, until the spinach has wilted and is just barely cooked. Taste for salt and pepper. This dish can be made ahead, refrigerated overnight, and rewarmed on top of the stove or in the oven the next day.

Potato, Sausage, and Leek Gratin

Makes 4 to 6 servings

The EARTHY FLAVORS OF POTATO, SAUSAGE, AND LEEKS SEEM TO GO perfectly with each other and are combined in a wide variety of traditional casseroles, soups, and stews. This recipe can be served as a side dish or a main course, depending on how much sausage you include. To convert the recipe below into a main dish, just double the amount of sausage. Use a mild-flavored sausage here.

4 tablespoons (½ stick) butter
4 cups diced unpeeled red potatoes
1 cup finely chopped leeks, white part only
½ cup finely chopped green onions or scallions
Salt and freshly ground black pepper
2 to 3 tablespoons all-purpose flour

½ pound Smoked Kielbasa (page 64), Smoked Bratwurst (page 54) or Linguiça (page 89), or other smoked sausage, chopped
Milk
½ cup fresh bread crumbs

Garnish
Chopped chives

Preheat oven to 375°. Butter a 2- to 3-quart casserole or baking dish. Spread half the potatoes, leeks, and green onions in the bottom and sprinkle with salt, pepper, and half the flour. Add all the sausage, and then spread the remaining potatoes, leeks, and green onions on top. Sprinkle with salt, pepper, and the remaining flour. Pour over enough milk to just cover the mixture in the pan, and sprinkle the bread crumbs over the top. Dot with the remaining butter.

Bake, covered, for 1 hour, until the potatoes are tender. Remove the cover, and bake for 15 to 20 minutes more until the top is brown. Sprinkle with chopped chives just before serving.

Hot Potato and Sausage Salad

Makes 6 to 8 servings

THIS DELICIOUS POTATO SALAD IS BEST EATEN WARM. IF YOU HAVE ANY LEFT-overs, fry the salad in a heavy pan until lightly brown, rather than eat it cold. This results in delectably tangy home fries.

2 pounds small red boiling potatoes, unpeeled
1 tablespoon salt plus more to taste
6 tablespoons cider vinegar
½ cup finely chopped red onion
½ cup finely chopped green onions or scallions
¼ cup finely chopped fresh parsley
6 tablespoons olive oil
¾ pound Garlic, Pork, and Ham Cervelat (page 60), Smoked Bratwurst (page 54), Smoked Kielbasa (page 64), or other smoked sausage, cut into ¼-inch dice

1 clove garlic, minced
¾ teaspoon ground cayenne pepper
1 tablespoon Dijon mustard
½ teaspoon cracked black pepper
6 drops Tabasco sauce

In a large pot, cover the potatoes with water, add 1 tablespoon salt, and bring to a boil. Cover and cook for 20 to 30 minutes, or until a knife inserted into a potato meets no resistance. Drain the potatoes, and when cool enough, cut each in half. Cut each half into ¼-inch slices and put in a large bowl. Sprinkle them with 3 tablespoons of the cider vinegar. Add the red onion, green onions, and parsley.

In a heavy pan, heat the olive oil over medium-high heat. Add the sausage pieces and fry until they begin to brown, about 5 minutes. Remove with a slotted spoon and add to the potatoes. To the fat remaining in the pan, add the garlic, cayenne, mustard, remaining 3 tablespoons cider vinegar, black pepper, and Tabasco. Bring to a boil while whisking continuously. This should loosen any sausage bits and produce a smooth creamy dressing. Salt to taste.

Pour the dressing over the sausages and potatoes, and mix lightly. Serve immediately.

Down in Louisiana they would probably use this stuffing in mirliton (chayote) squash, but it is equally good in zucchini, pattypan, or yellow crookneck squash. You could adapt it to sweeter winter squash, such as acorn or butternut, by adding a tablespoon or two of brown sugar or sweet sherry to the stuffing. Winter squash will take about one-third longer to cook. This stuffing is also excellent in bell peppers, artichokes, and eggplant.

4 medium-sized zucchini or
    8 pattypan squash (2 to
    3 inches in diameter) or other
    small squash
1 tablespoon olive oil, plus more
    for baking
1 pound Spicy Louisiana Poultry
    Sausage (page 39)
1 red bell pepper, seeded, deveined,
    and finely chopped

2 cups fresh bread crumbs
½ cup chopped ripe tomatoes
½ cup chopped green onions or
    scallions, white and green parts
1 egg, lightly beaten
2 teaspoons Worcestershire sauce
½ teaspoon salt
¼ teaspoon freshly ground black
    pepper

Preheat the oven to 350°. Slice the squash in half lengthwise (slice the pattypan through the scalloped edge), score the center deeply with a sharp knife, and scoop out most of the pulp with a teaspoon or melon baller. Leave enough so that the squash will keep their shape. Remove and discard any seeds. Chop pulp and reserve.

Heat the olive oil in a skillet over medium-high heat. Add the sausage and brown, breaking it up as it cooks, for 2 to 3 minutes. Add the squash pulp and bell pepper and cook for 5 minutes more.

In a large bowl, mix together the bread crumbs, tomatoes, green onions, egg, Worcestershire, salt, and pepper. Add the cooked sausage mixture and any juices in the pan and mix thoroughly.

Stuff the squash liberally with the bread crumb mixture. Mound the stuffing, packing it in fairly tightly. (Any leftover stuffing can be baked in a small pan alongside the squash or used to make meatballs.)

Oil a large baking dish and arrange the squash in it, drizzle the tops with oil, and bake, uncovered, until the tops are lightly browned, 20 to 25 minutes. Serve warm.

Quick and Easy Stuffed Vegetables

Stuffing vegetables, such as tomatoes, peppers, artichokes, and squash, with a savory mixture of sausage, bread crumbs, and flavorings is a delicious way to take advantage of the harvest's bounty. Most vegetables are at their best (and cheapest) in late summer, and stuffed vegetables make wonderful summer meals. They are light, but flavorful, and are easy and quick to prepare. With a salad and a crusty loaf of bread, stuffed vegetables make a lovely light dinner, which is inexpensive, nourishing, and low in calories.

For a tasty and unusual appetizer, stuff baby zucchini, pattypan squash, or small tomatoes, and serve warm or at room temperature. Small vegetables will take about one-third less time to cook. Artichokes and eggplant both are delicious stuffed: Use our Creole stuffing (page 295) for them.

Use the recipes as guidelines. The basic mixture of 1 pound of sausage to 2 cups of fresh bread crumbs or rice plus 1 egg and seasonings can be varied depending on what vegetables you are stuffing and what flavor accents you desire.

Makes 6 side-dish or 4
main-course servings

THESE LITTLE SAUSAGE–SPIKED PANCAKES ARE A GREAT WAY TO SPICE UP VEG-
etables and get the family to clean their plates while getting rid of all
those raw or cooked veggies that are cluttering up the fridge. The
basic technique is simple: Shred 'em, spice 'em, and fry 'em up in a
zesty pancake. If you use raw zucchini, crookneck, or pattypan squash,
sprinkle the shredded vegetables with salt, let them sit, and drain to
remove some of the excess water, and then chop. With cooked vegetables, simply chop them. In addition to summer squash, some of our
favorite veggies for this dish are raw onions, chard, and bitter or mild
greens, or cooked carrots, turnips, cauliflower, and cabbage.

1 tablespoon olive oil
¼ pound Chicken and Turkey
  Merguez (page 93) or other
  spicy fresh sausage, removed
  from casings
¼ cup finely chopped onion
2 cups shredded raw or cooked
  vegetables

1 tablespoon all-purpose flour
3 eggs, lightly beaten
Pinch of salt
Pinch of freshly ground black
  pepper
¼ cup vegetable oil

Garnish

Cucumber and Yogurt Sauce
  (page 181) (optional)

In a small skillet, heat the olive oil over medium-high heat. Add the
sausage and onion and fry, stirring often, for 5 minutes, breaking the
sausage apart as it cooks. Transfer to a mixing bowl and stir in the vegetables, flour, eggs, salt, and pepper.

Heat the vegetable oil in a large skillet over medium heat. Spoon
in the vegetable-egg mixture to make several 3- to 4-inch pancakes.
Fry until golden on one side, about 5 minutes, and flip. Fry for
another 2 to 3 minutes until golden. Serve 2 to 3 pancakes per person, and garnish with Cucumber and Yogurt Sauce.

Savory Bread Pudding

Makes 10 to 12 servings

LIGHTER THAN STUFFING AND EASY TO PREPARE AHEAD OF TIME, THIS RICH and cheesy bread pudding is a welcome side dish for a large holiday meal or any special dinner. Chef Nancy Oakes serves it at her San Francisco restaurant, Boulevard, along with pork chops, veal, or roast chicken. Leftovers are no problem, as this savory pudding is even more delicious rewarmed.

½ stick (4 tablespoons) unsalted
   butter
4 large leeks, cleaned and sliced,
   white parts only (about
   2 pounds)
1½ pounds Italian Turkey and
   Sundried Tomato Sausage
   (page 85) or any other Italian
   sausage

½ pound fresh mushrooms, sliced
8 to 10 cups cubed day-old bread
3 cups half-and-half
6 eggs, beaten
1 teaspoon kosher salt
1 teaspoon freshly ground black
   pepper
½ cup freshly grated Asiago or
   Romano cheese

Preheat the oven to 350°.

In a large skillet, melt the butter over medium-high heat. Add the leeks and sauté until soft, about 5 minutes. Add the sausage and cook for 5 minutes, breaking it up as it browns. Add the mushrooms and cook for 2 minutes more, stirring well.

In a large bowl, toss together the bread cubes and the sausage-vegetable mixture. In another bowl, whisk together the half-and-half, eggs, salt, pepper, and cheese and stir into the bread mixture. Pour into a greased 9 by 13-inch baking dish and press down firmly. Allow the pudding to set for 30 minutes before baking. Bake for 1 hour, until nicely brown on top.

Not only is this stuffing great for turkey, but it makes an enjoyable side dish for ham, chicken, or duck. For a lighter version, bake the stuffing separately in a casserole. That way, it doesn't pick up juice and fat from the roasting bird. Our Chicken and Apple Sausage makes a delicious, albeit mild, stuffing. For something a bit spicier, use half Chicken and Apple Sausage and half spicy sage sausage, such as Spicy Fresh Country Sausage.

Makes 8 to 10 servings

2 tablespoons olive oil
2 pounds Chicken and Apple
  Sausage (page 34), Spicy Fresh
  Country Sausage (page 27),
  or a combination of both, in
  bulk or removed from casings
2 cups chopped onions
1 cup chopped celery
1 tablespoon dried sage
¼ cup dry white wine or apple
  cider

8 to 10 cups dried bread cubes
4 cups peeled, cored, and diced
  green apples (such as Granny
  Smith)
2 to 3 cups or more chicken stock,
  preferably homemade
Salt and freshly ground black
  pepper to taste

Preheat the oven to 350°, if baking the stuffing in a casserole.

Heat the oil in a large, heavy skillet or Dutch oven over medium heat. Add the sausage and fry for 3 minutes, breaking it up as it cooks. Add the onions, celery, sage, and wine or cider. Cover and cook until the vegetables are soft, stirring occasionally, about 10 minutes.

In a large bowl, mix the sausage-vegetable mixture, bread cubes, and apples. Moisten with the stock until the mixture is moist enough to hold together when molded in a large spoon, but not sopping wet. Use more stock if needed. Taste for salt and pepper.

At this point, you can stuff the dressing lightly into a turkey or large chicken and roast it, following your favorite recipe. This recipe yields enough stuffing for 1 medium turkey (14 pounds), 2 large roasting chickens (5 to 6 pounds each), 3 frying chickens (3 to 4 pounds each), or 6 to 8 squabs or quail.

Or you can bake the stuffing separately in an oiled 3- to 4-quart casserole. If you bake it in a casserole, stir in a bit more stock to make up for the liquid the stuffing would absorb from the bird. Cover the casserole and bake for 45 minutes. Serve warm.

Sausage and Cornbread Stuffing

Makes 8 to 10 servings

USE ANY PREMIUM FRESH BULK SAUSAGE COMBINED WITH A GOOD-QUALITY smoked sausage in this recipe, such as our Kentucky-Style Pork Sausage and Cajun-Style Andouille. The recipe below will make enough stuffing for a 14- to 16-pound turkey, so scale down as necessary (or up, if you are thinking of stuffing a wild boar or a great bustard). This stuffing is not only good with turkey and chicken, but delicious with roast pork or ham.

4 tablespoons (½ stick) butter
1 pound Kentucky-Style Pork
    Sausage (page 28) or other
    sage-flavored fresh sausage, in
    bulk or removed from casings
1 pound Cajun-Style Andouille
    (page 44), or other smoked
    sausage, cut into ¼-inch dice
4 ribs celery, chopped
3 cups chopped onions

1 medium green bell pepper,
    chopped
1 medium red bell pepper, chopped
8 to 10 cups cornbread cut into
    coarse crumbs and dried
1 teaspoon dried thyme
1 teaspoon ground sage
2 to 3 cups turkey or chicken stock
Salt and freshly ground black
    pepper

Preheat the oven to 350°, if baking the stuffing in a casserole.

Melt the butter in a large skillet over medium heat. Add the fresh sausage and brown for 5 minutes. Break it apart with a fork as it cooks. Put in the smoked sausage and fry for 3 minutes more. Add the celery and onions, cover, and cook for about 10 minutes, until the vegetables are soft. Add the peppers and cook, covered, for 5 minutes.

In a large bowl, mix the cornbread, sausage, and vegetables (including pan juices) with the thyme and sage. Add 2 cups of stock and mix well. The stuffing should stick together when mounded on a spoon. Add more stock, if necessary. Add salt and pepper to taste.

At this point, you can stuff the dressing lightly into a turkey or large chicken and roast it, following your favorite recipe. This recipe yields enough stuffing for 1 medium turkey (14 pounds), 2 large roasting chickens (5 to 6 pounds each), 3 frying chickens (3 to 4 pounds each), or 6 to 8 squabs or quail.

Or you can bake the stuffing separately in a buttered 3- to 4-quart casserole. If you bake it in a casserole, stir in a bit more stock to make up for the liquid the stuffing would absorb from the bird. Cover the casserole and bake for 45 minutes. Serve warm.

Italian Sausage and Fresh Fennel Stuffing

Makes 8 to 10 servings

Fresh fennel, or finocchio, is a delicious and unusual vegetable that is available during the winter months. It adds a subtle anise flavor and a delightful crunchy texture to this flavorful dressing. Use it to stuff a turkey, or scale the recipe down for chicken, veal or pork roasts, or extra-thick pork chops.

4 tablespoons (½ stick) butter
1½ pounds Italian Sweet Fennel Sausage (page 84), removed from casings
1 large bulb fennel, coarsely chopped
2 ribs celery, coarsely chopped

1 onion, coarsely chopped
1 tablespoon minced garlic
1 teaspoon ground sage
8 to 10 cups dried bread cubes
2 to 3 cups turkey or chicken stock
Salt and freshly ground black pepper

Preheat the oven to 350° if baking the stuffing in a casserole.

Melt the butter in a large heavy skillet over medium heat. Add the sausage and fry for about 5 minutes, breaking up the meat into small pieces. Add the fennel, celery, onion, garlic, and sage to the sausage and cook for 10 minutes, until the vegetables are soft.

Transfer the sausage and vegetable mixture to a large bowl along with the bread cubes. Add 2 cups of the stock, season with salt and pepper, and mix well. The stuffing should be moist enough to hold together when mounded on a spoon. Add more stock if necessary.

At this point, you can stuff the dressing lightly into a turkey or large chicken and roast it, following your favorite recipe. This recipe yields enough stuffing for 1 medium turkey (14 to 16 pounds), 2 large roasting chickens (5 to 6 pounds each), 3 frying chickens (3 to 4 pounds each), or 6 to 8 squabs or quail.

Or you can bake the stuffing separately in a buttered 3- to 4-quart casserole. If you bake it in a casserole, stir in a bit more stock to make up for the liquid the stuffing would absorb from the bird. Dot the surface of the stuffing with butter. Cover the casserole and bake for 45 minutes. Serve warm.

Sausage, Spinach, and Mushroom Stuffing

Makes 8 to 10 servings

THIS STUFFING TASTES DECIDEDLY MEDITERRANEAN AND IS NOT ONLY GREAT in turkey, but also as a side dish with roast pork or veal. To give it more of an Italian taste, use Italian Sweet Fennel Sausage (page 84) or Italian Turkey and Sundried Tomato Sausage (page 85).

2 tablespoons (¼ stick) unsalted butter
1 pound Loukanika (page 88), Spinach, Pork, and Game Crépinettes (page 113), or other mild, flavorful fresh sausage, in bulk or removed from casings
1 cup chopped onion
½ cup chopped celery

½ pound mushrooms, sliced
2 bunches spinach, coarsely chopped (about 2 pounds)
½ teaspoon dried thyme
8 to 10 cups dried bread cubes
½ cup grated Parmesan cheese
1 to 2 cups chicken stock
Salt and freshly ground black pepper

Preheat the oven to 350°.

Melt the butter in a large heavy frying pan or Dutch oven over medium heat. Add the sausage and fry until no longer pink, about 5 minutes, breaking up the meat into small pieces. Add the onion and celery and sauté for 10 minutes, or until soft. Add the mushrooms, spinach, and thyme and cook for 1 to 2 minutes, until the spinach is wilted.

In a large bowl, mix together the bread cubes, vegetable-sausage mixture, and Parmesan cheese. The stuffing should be moist but not wet. If needed, add some of the chicken stock. Taste for salt and pepper.

At this point, you can stuff the dressing lightly into a turkey or large chicken and roast it, following your favorite recipe. This recipe yields enough stuffing for 1 medium turkey (14 to 16 pounds), 2 large roasting chickens (5 to 6 pounds each), 3 frying chickens (3 to 4 pounds each), or 6 to 8 squabs or quail.

Or you can bake the stuffing separately in a buttered 3- to 4-quart casserole. If you bake it in a casserole, stir in a bit more stock to make up for the liquid the stuffing would absorb from the bird. Dot the surface of the stuffing with butter. Cover the casserole and bake for 45 minutes. Serve warm.

THIS RICH AND SPICY STUFFING MIGHT BE A BIT TOO POTENT FOR THE Thanksgiving turkey, but it will certainly enliven chicken, game hens, or other small poultry. There is enough here (8 cups) for 8 game birds, two 3-pound chickens, or a 6- to 8-pound capon or roaster. We used El Paso Beef, Pork, and Chile Sausage, but any lean, spicy chorizo would do as well.

Makes 6 to 8 servings

2 tablespoons olive oil
2 cups finely diced onions
2 teaspoons finely chopped garlic
2½ pounds El Paso Beef, Pork, and Chile Sausage (page 75) or Chorizo (page 74), removed from casings
4 Anaheim chiles, fire-roasted, peeled, seeded, and coarsely chopped (page 73)

4 cups cooked rice
Salt and freshly ground black pepper
2 eggs, beaten lightly
1 bunch (4 to 6 ounces) cilantro, coarsely chopped (1 cup) (optional)

Preheat the oven to 350°.

Heat the olive oil in a large heavy skillet over medium heat. Add the onions and sauté until soft, about 10 minutes. Add the garlic, sausage, and chiles, and cook for 10 minutes, breaking up the meat with a fork. In a large bowl, combine the rice with the sausage-vegetable mixture. Taste for salt and pepper, then add the eggs and cilantro. Mix well.

At this point you can stuff the dressing lightly into a large chicken or game birds and roast, following your favorite recipe. Or you can bake the stuffing separately in a buttered 3- to 4-quart casserole. Cover the casserole and bake for 40 minutes. Serve warm.

Sausage and Chestnut Stuffing

Makes 8 to 10 servings

THE RECIPE WILL STUFF 2 LARGE ROASTING CHICKENS. FOUR TIMES THIS recipe will make more than can be stuffed into a medium-sized turkey, so you should have plenty left over for hungry guests.

1 cup fresh chestnuts (about
    ¾ pound)
1 cup chicken or turkey stock
1 tablespoon unsalted butter
½ pound Yankee Sage Sausage
    (page 29), Iowa Farm
    Sausage patties (page 31),
    mild Italian, or other fresh
    sausage, in bulk or removed
    from casings

½ cup chopped onion
¼ cup chopped celery
½ teaspoon dried oregano
¼ cup dry white wine
2 cups dried bread cubes
Salt and freshly ground black
    pepper
Butter (optional)

To prepare the chestnuts, preheat the oven to 450°. Cut a deep cross on one side of each chestnut. Roast for 15 minutes, or until the shells begin to open. Remove the shells and inner skin. Bring the stock to a boil in a medium pot. Add the chestnuts, reduce the heat to low, and simmer until tender, about 20 minutes. Drain the chestnuts and reserve the stock. Chop the cooked chestnuts coarsely.

Reduce the oven temperature to 350°.

Melt the butter in a large heavy skillet over medium heat. Add the sausage and fry for 5 minutes, breaking up the meat into small pieces. Add the onion, celery, and oregano. Cook until the onion is soft, about 10 minutes. Pour in the white wine and cook for 5 minutes more.

In a large bowl, mix together the chestnuts, sausage-vegetable mixture, and bread cubes. Mix well and add some of the reserved stock to moisten. The dressing should be moist but not wet. Taste for salt and pepper.

Loosely stuff the birds and roast at 350° until done, about 1½ to 2 hours for a 5- to 6-pound roasting chicken (meat thermometer should read 170°).

To bake the stuffing outside the birds, add a little more stock. Butter a 3- to 4-quart casserole, fill with stuffing, dot with butter, cover, and bake, covered, for 45 minutes. Serve warm.

Oyster
Stuffing
with Fresh
and
Smoked
Country
Sausage

Oyster stuffing is not only an excellent complement to turkey, but it goes well with roast chicken or pork as well. The recipe below calls for baking the dressing by itself in a casserole next to the bird. If you are going to stuff a turkey or chicken, use a little less liquid, since the dressing will absorb liquid as the bird cooks. We've given amounts for a 5- to 6-pound roasting chicken or small turkey. Use any good-quality country-style smoked sausage such as andouille and fresh bulk country sausage. For hard-core stuffing addicts: Try stuffing a turkey with this oyster stuffing in the neck cavity and the Sausage and Cornbread Stuffing (page 300) in the body of the bird.

Makes 6 to 8 servings

2 tablespoons butter
½ pound Smoked Country Sausage
(page 32), Cajun-Style
Andouille (page 44), or other
smoked sausage, finely chopped
½ pound Spicy Fresh Country
Sausage (page 27) or other
sage-flavored fresh bulk sausage
1 cup finely chopped onion
¼ cup finely chopped celery
¼ cup finely chopped green bell
pepper
½ cup finely chopped red bell
pepper
½ cup finely chopped green onions
or scallions
1 teaspoon minced garlic

1 (12-ounce) jar oysters, or
18 medium shucked oysters
½ teaspoon dried thyme
½ teaspoon ground sage
¼ teaspoon dried savory
½ teaspoon ground cayenne
pepper
½ teaspoon freshly ground black
pepper
3 to 4 cups dried bread cubes,
preferably homemade from
French bread
1 to 2 cups chicken stock blended
with oyster liquid
Salt
Tabasco sauce

Preheat the oven to 350°.

Melt the butter over medium-high heat in a large heavy skillet. Add the sausage and brown for 5 minutes, breaking up the meat into small pieces. Decrease the heat to medium and add the onion and celery. Cover the pan and cook for about 10 minutes, or until the vegetables begin to color. Add the green and red bell peppers, the green onions, and the garlic, and cook for 5 minutes more.

Meanwhile, drain the oysters, saving the liquid. If they are large, coarsely chop them into ¾-inch pieces; otherwise leave them whole.

Mail-Order Sources

Asian Ingredients

House of Rice
4112 University Way NE
Seattle, WA 98105
(206) 545-6956

Kim Man Food
200 Canal Street
New York, NY 10013
(212) 571-0330

Oriental Pantry
423 Great Road
Acton, MA 01720
(800) 828-0368

Tokyo Fish Market
122 San Pablo Avenue
Berkeley, CA 94706
(510) 524-7243

Creole and Cajun Seasonings

Catahoula
1457 Lincoln Avenue
Calistoga, CA 94515
(707) 942-2275
New Orleans red gravy

Catfish Wholesale
PO Box 759
Abbeville, LA 70510
(318) 643-6700

Louisiana Fish Fry Products
5267 Plank Road
Baton Rouge, LA 70805
(504) 356-2905

Country Hams

Smithfield Collection
PO Box 497
Smithfield, VA 23430
(800) 628-2242

Wallace Edwards & Sons
PO Box 25
Surry, VA 23883
(800) 222-4267

Mexican/Southwest Ingredients

Carmen's of New Mexico
PO Box 7310
Albuquerque, NM 87194
(800) 851-4852

The Chile Shop
109 East Water Street
Santa Fe, NM 87501
(505) 983-6080

El Nopalito #1
560 Santa Fe Drive
Encinitas, CA 92024
(760) 436-5775

The Kitchen Food Shop
218 Eighth Avenue
New York, NY 10011
(212) 243-4433

Texas Spice Company
PO Box 3769
Austin, TX 78764-3769
(800) 880-8007
(512) 444-2223

Sausages and Specialty Meats

Aidells Sausage Company
1625 Alvarado Street
San Leandro, CA 94577
(800) 546-5795
www.aidells.com

Balducci's
424 Avenue of the Americas
New York, NY 10011
(800) 822-1444

Summerfield Farm
10044 James Monroe Highway
Culpeper, VA 22701
(540) 547-9600

Sausage-Making Supplies and Equipment

Carlson Butcher Supply
50 Mendell #12
San Francisco, CA 94124
(415) 648-2601

The Sausage Maker
1500 Clinton Street
Buffalo, NY 14206
(716) 824-6510

Specialty Products, Herbs, and Spices

Adriana's Caravan
409 Vanderbilt Street
Brooklyn, NY 11218
(800) 316-0820

Bette's Diner Products
4240 Hollis Street, Suite 120
Emeryville, CA 94608
(510) 601-6980
Pancake mixes, baking supplies

Dean & DeLuca
560 Broadway
New York, NY 10012
(800) 221-7714
(212) 431-1691

Kalustyan's
123 Lexington Avenue
New York, NY 10016
(212) 685-3451

Penzey's, Ltd.
PO Box 933
Muskego, WI 53150
(414) 574-0277

Zingermans
422 Detroit Street
Ann Arbor, MI 48104
(313) 663-3354
(888) 636-8162

Index

Ham
  buying, 30
  country, 31
  Étouffée, of veal chop, Andouille
    and, 281
  grilled shrimp wrapped in, 141
  hash, 125
  and sausage loaf, 278-279
  sausage recipes with, 30, 60
  squid stuffed with chorizo, and, 222-
    223
Hash, Andouille, 125
Herbs
  how to add to homemade sausage, 27
  in sausage, 6
Homemade sausage
  advantages over commercial, 3
  equipment for making, 3-5, 15, 16-17
  fat content of, 3, 5-6, 23
  handling, 8-10
  method for making, 10-13
  safety tips for handling, 8-10, 20-21
  smoking, 13-17
  storing, 8-9, 12, 27
  telling when done, 6
Hominy and crispy onions, chicken or
  rabbit stew with sausage and, 230-
  231
Hot Boudin, 40-42
Hot Dogs, 66-68
  regional variations, 177
Hot Links, 43
  recipes that use, 172, 210
Hot peppers, sausage recipes with, 74, 85
Hot Sausage, 46
Hot Sausage Po' Boy, 178
Hungarian dishes, 261, 266
Hungarian Paprika Sausage, 65
  recipes that use, 244, 261, 266
Hunter's Sausage, 58
  in beer-braised sandwiches, 185

Iowa Farm Sausage, 28
  recipes that use, 278, 304
Italian dishes, 180, 186, 189-197, 213,
  222, 258
Italian sausages, 81, 83-87
Italian Sweet Fennel Sausage, 84-85
  appetizers and side dish recipes that use,
    146, 301
  main course recipes that use, 195, 198,
    236, 258, 260
  soup and sandwich recipes that use, 166,
    180

Italian Turkey and Sundried Tomato
  Sausage, 85
  recipes that use, 190, 193, 206, 236, 298

Kentucky-Style Pork Sausage, 28
  recipes that use, 264, 278, 300
Kielbasa, 63, 64
Kosher sausage, 59

Lamb
  sausage recipes with, 92, 103, 113
  shanks, braised, 262
  shoulder, in pastitsio, 198
  shoulder, sausage recipe with, 88
Lasagna, 196, 258
Lebanese sausages, 81
Leek, potato, and sausage gratin, 293
Leeks, sausage recipes with, 57
Lemon, basil capellini with sausage, 190
Lentils and Cotechino, 204-205
Lettuce, soup with braised, stuffed, 174
Lettuce, Thai sausage salad with, 158
Lime pickled onions, 183
Linguiça, 89
  breakfast and side dishes that use, 129,
    208, 292, 293
  main course recipes that use, 218, 222,
    242-245, 262
Linking sausage, 11-12
Lobster, sausage recipe with, 116
Lobster tails stuffed with sausage, 140
Lop Chong, 97
Louisiana Hot Sausage, 46
Louisiana sausages, 36-50, 114-115
Loukanika, 88
  recipes that use, 182, 198, 302

Macaroni dishes, 196-198
Main course dishes, 161-285
  appetizers that can be, 141, 146
  turning side dishes into, 287
Meat dishes, 207, 251-285
Meat for sausage, choosing, 5
Meat grinders, 4, 10
Meat loaf, 277-279
Mediterranean sausage recipes, 81-93
Mexican dishes, 128, 170, 183, 240, 272
Mexican sausages, 74-75
Michigan Dutch Farmer's Sausage, 70
Middle Eastern Vegetable Pancakes, 296
Midwestern sausages, 31, 51-70
Mild sausage recipes, 34, 57, 63, 70, 84
Minnesota Potato Sausage, 69
Mixed grill, Asian, 254